Nāgārjuna's Middle Way

Classics of Indian Buddhism

The flourishing of Buddhism in South Asia during the first millennium of the Common Era produced many texts that deserve a place among the classics of world literature. Exploring the full extent of the human condition and the limits of language and reason, these texts have the power to edify and entertain a wide variety of readers. The *Classics of Indian Buddhism* series aims to publish widely accessible translations of important texts from the Buddhist traditions of South Asia, with special consideration given to works foundational for the Mahāyāna.

The Mūlamadhyamakakārikā

This is a translation of Nāgārjuna's *Mūlamadhyamakakārikā*, the foundational text of the Madhyamaka, or "middle path," school of South Asian Buddhism. In it Nāgārjuna sought to philosophically articulate and defend the Mahāyāna teaching that all things are *empty*, or devoid of intrinsic nature. To achieve this end, he developed a variety of arguments on many topics. Once the background assumptions and the underlying logic are spelled out, these arguments are not as difficult to understand and evaluate as they might initially seem. This new translation also includes a running commentary on the verses, distilling information from the four extant classical Indian commentaries in order to make clear the background context and reasoning of each argument.

CLASSICS OF INDIAN BUDDHISM

Nāgārjuna's Middle Way

Mūlamadhyamakakārikā

Mark Siderits and Shōryū Katsura

Wisdom

Wisdom Publications
199 Elm Street
Somerville, MA 02144 USA
wisdompubs.org

Library of Congress Cataloging-in-Publication Data
Nāgārjuna, 2nd century.
[Madhyamakakārikā. English]
Nāgārjuna's Middle way : the Mūlamadhyamakakārikā / Mark Siderits and Shōryū Katsura.
pages cm. — (Classics of Indian Buddhism)
Includes bibliographical references and index.
ISBN 1-61429-050-4 (pbk. : alk. paper)
1. Mādhyamika (Buddhism)—Early works to 1800. I. Siderits, Mark, 1946– translator, writer of added commentary. II. Katsura, Shōryū, 1944– translator, writer of added commentary. III. Title.
BQ2792.E5S53 2013
294.3'85—dc23

2012047730

ISBN 978-1-61429-050-6 ebook ISBN 978-1-61429-061-2

21 20 19 18
6 5 4 3

Cover and interior design by Gopa&Ted2. Set in Diacritical Garamond Pro 11.75/15.75.
Cover image © The Trustees of the British Museum (Detail of a stone slab image depicting a five-headed nāga guarding the entryway to a stūpa. From the Great Stūpa of Amarātī).

Wisdom Publications' books are printed on acid-free paper and meet the guidelines for permanence and durability of the Production Guidelines for Book Longevity of the Council on Library Resources.

This book was produced with environmental mindfulness.
For more information, please visit wisdompubs.org/wisdom-environment.

Printed in the United States of America.

FSC www.fsc.org MIX Paper from responsible sources FSC® C011935

Please visit fscus.org.

Publisher's Acknowledgment

THE PUBLISHER gratefully acknowledges the generous help of the Hershey Family Foundation in sponsoring the publication of this book.

Contents

Preface

OUR COLLABORATION had its inception in a cottage on the island of Miyajima in 1999. We had both worked independently on the *Mūlamadhyamakakārikā* for some years, having each arrived at our own tentative translations of the bulk of the work. Pooling our resources seemed like a natural step to take at the time, though we were no doubt overly optimistic about how long it would take us to complete the project. We each feel we have profited enormously from our joint enterprise, and we hope the reader will concur in our judgment.

Many individuals and institutions contributed to our project. Mark Siderits was greatly helped by the generous research support he received from BK Foundation, and research support from the Numata Foundation facilitated his stay in Kyoto in 2006. Shōryū Katsura wishes to thank the Japan Society for the Promotion of Science, which supported his visit to Korea in 2011 as well as Siderits' short stay in Kyoto in 2012, by providing a Grant-in-Aid for Scientific Research.

We thank Paul Harrison for his comments on an early draft and for urging us to consider publishing our work with Wisdom. Graham Priest made very useful comments on a later draft. David Kittelstrom has proven an extraordinarily able editor whose sage advice and encouragement have been greatly appreciated. And we wish to thank Megan Anderson for her assiduous proofing, Laura

Cunningham for her competence in guiding the book through production, and the rest of the Wisdom staff for their help in bringing our work to fruition.

Introduction

THE *Mūlamadhyamakakārikā* (MMK) by Nāgārjuna (ca. 150 C.E.) is the foundational text of the Madhyamaka school of Indian Buddhist philosophy. It consists of verses constituting twenty-seven chapters. In it, Nāgārjuna seeks to establish the chief tenet of Madhyamaka, that all things are empty (*śūnya*) or devoid of intrinsic nature (*svabhāva*). The claim that all things are empty first appears in the Buddhist tradition in the early Mahāyāna sūtras known collectively as Prajñāparamitā, beginning roughly in the first century B.C.E. Earlier Buddhist thought was built around the more specific claim that the person is empty: that there is no separately existing, enduring self, and that the person is a conceptual construction. Realization of the emptiness of the person was thought to be crucial to liberation from saṃsāra. The earliest Mahāyāna texts go considerably beyond this claim, asserting that not just the person (and other aggregate entities like the chariot) but everything is devoid of intrinsic nature. While they assert that all things are empty, however, they do not defend the assertion. Nāgārjuna's task in MMK is to supply its philosophical defense.

As is usual in texts of this nature, the arguments are presented in highly compressed form and so are extremely difficult to comprehend without a commentary. This is due to the nature and purpose of such texts. A *kārikā* is a work in verse form that contains a concise formulation of some (often philosophical) doctrine; the *kārikā*s are the individual verses making up the work. Texts of this sort were originally used because it is easier to memorize information when it is put in verse form. The regular cadence that results when a verse is constructed out of its four feet (referred to as *a*, *b*, *c*, and *d*), each consisting of eight syllables, serves as an important mnemonic aid. On the other hand, it would be difficult to clearly formulate and fully defend a sophisticated philosophical thesis within the form's constraints. But texts of this genre were not composed with that end in mind. The original expectation seems to have been that the student would commit the verses to memory, recite them to the teacher to demonstrate mastery, and then receive an account from the teacher that fully explained the content of each verse. In time these explanations of individual teachers came to be written down in the form of prose commentaries. It is text plus commentary that together are meant to do the work of formulating and defending the philosophical thesis in question. Memorizing the verses would have given students the outline they need in order to remember the full details of the system spelled out in the commentary.

We know of four Indian commentaries on MMK: the *Akutobhayā* (author unknown), the *Madhyamakavṛtti* by Buddhapālita, the *Prajñāpradīpa* by Bhāviveka, and the *Prasannapadā* by Candrakīrti. They do not all agree on the interpretation of every verse, and some provide more detailed explanations of particular points than others. But they generally agree on such things as what the argument of a particular verse is and which specific views are the subject of refutation in a chapter. And without this information one would be free to read any number of different interpretations into the verses. Of course we cannot be certain that any of the classical Indian commentaries reflect Nāgārjuna's original intentions. But it would be presumptuous on our part to suppose that we knew better than they what Nāgārjuna really meant.

Our translation of the verses has been guided by the commentaries. This applies to more than just the question of which English term to choose where the Sanskrit is ambiguous. In many cases a translated verse will contain some material in square brackets. These are words the Sanskrit equivalents of which are not in the original verse itself but without which the verse simply does not make sense. When we supply such bracketed material, it is because the commentaries make clear just what has been omitted. That there will be such omissions in the verses proper is understandable given the constraints imposed by the verse form discussed above. We should add that we have tried quite hard to keep the number of square brackets to a minimum; we have, in other words, been fairly liberal in our interpretation of what is "in the original verse itself." Where the context seems to make abundantly clear that a certain term has been omitted just for the sake of brevity, we supply its English equivalent without the use of square brackets. But those who wish to check our translation's fidelity to the Sanskrit original might wish to consult an earlier version that was published in *The Journal of Indian and Tibetan Studies*, where square brackets are used in a more rigorously scholarly fashion.

Rather than translating any one of the commentaries, we have provided our own running commentary to our translation of the verses of MMK based on the four classical Indian commentaries. We have tried to keep our interpretive remarks to a minimum. Seldom do our elucidations go beyond anything stated by at least one of these authors. It is our hope that the arguments will speak for themselves once the larger context has been properly spelled out. We do each have our own preferred ways of understanding Nāgārjuna's overall stance and how his arguments are meant to function. But we have tried to avoid using this translation as a vehicle to promote our own views on these matters.

Each chapter of MMK contains an analysis of a particular doctrine or concept, usually one held by some rival Buddhist school. The text as we have it does not tell us whether Nāgārjuna supplied titles for each chapter, and if so what they were. We have generally used the chapter titles supplied by Candrakīrti. But in a few cases where we thought it would be more informative, we employed the title supplied by another commentator.

At this point some general introductory remarks concerning Nāgārjuna's goals and strategies might not be amiss. In MMK Nāgārjuna is addressing an audience of fellow Buddhists. (In the other work generally accepted as by Nāgārjuna, the *Vigrahavyāvartanī*, his interlocutors also include members of the non-Buddhist Nyāya school.) Of particular importance is the fact that his audience holds views that are based on the fundamental presuppositions behind the Abhidharma enterprise. Abhidharma is that part of the Buddhist philosophical tradition that aims at filling out the metaphysical details behind the Buddha's core teachings of nonself, impermanence, and suffering. A number of different Abhidharma schools arose out of significant controversies concerning these details. They held in common, however, a core set of presuppositions, which may be roughly sketched as follows:

1. There are two ways in which a statement may be true, conventionally and ultimately.
    a. To say of a statement that it is conventionally true is to say that action based on its acceptance reliably leads to successful practice. Our commonsense convictions concerning ourselves and the world are for the most part conventionally true, since they reflect conventions that have been found to be useful in everyday practice.
    b. To say of a statement that it is ultimately true is to say that it corresponds to the nature of reality and neither asserts nor presupposes the existence of any mere conceptual fiction. A conceptual fiction is something that is thought to exist only because of facts about us concept-users and the concepts that we happen to employ. For instance, a chariot is a conceptual fiction. When a set of parts is assembled in the right way, we only believe there is a chariot in addition to the parts because of facts about our interests and our cognitive limitations: We have an interest in assemblages that facilitate transportation, and we would have

trouble listing all the parts and all their connections. The ultimate truth is absolutely objective; it reflects the way the world is independently of what happens to be useful for us. No statement about a chariot could be ultimately true (or ultimately false).

2. Only *dharma*s are ultimately real.
   a. To say of something that it is ultimately real is to say that it is the sort of thing about which ultimately true (or false) statements may be made. An ultimately real entity is unlike a mere conceptual fiction in that it may be said to exist independently of facts about us.
   b. The ultimately real dharmas are simple or impartite. They are not products of the mind's tendency to aggregate for purposes of conceptual economy. They are what remain when all products of such activity have been analytically resolved into their basic constituents. They may include such things as indivisible material particles, spatio-temporally discrete occurrences of color and shape, pain sensations, particular occurrences of basic desires such as hunger and thirst, and individual moments of consciousness. (Different Abhidharma schools give somewhat different accounts of what dharmas there are.)
   c. All the facts about our commonsense world of people, towns, forests, chariots, and the like can be explained entirely in terms of facts about the dharmas and their relations with one another. The conventional truth can be explained entirely in terms of the ultimate truth.
3. Dharmas originate in dependence on causes and conditions.
   While not all Abhidharma schools hold that all dharmas are subject to dependent origination (*pratītyasamutpāda*), all agree that most dharmas are. And since anything subject to origination is also subject to cessation, most (or all) dharmas are also impermanent.
4. Dharmas have intrinsic nature (*svabhāva*).
   a. An intrinsic nature is a property that is intrinsic to its bearer—

that is, the fact that the property characterizes that entity is independent of facts about anything else.

b. Only dharmas have intrinsic nature. The size and shape of a chariot are not intrinsic natures of the chariot, since the chariot's having its size and shape depends on the size, shape, and arrangement of its parts. The size and shape of the chariot are instead extrinsic natures (*parabhāva*) since they are not the "its own" of the chariot but are rather borrowed.

c. Dharmas have only intrinsic natures. A characteristic that a thing can have only by virtue of its relation to another thing (such as the characteristic of being taller than Mont Blanc) is not intrinsic to the thing that has it. To suppose that the thing nonetheless has that characteristic is to allow mental construction to play a role in our conception of that which is real. For it requires us to suppose that a thing can have a complex nature: an intrinsic nature—what it itself is like apart from everything else—plus those properties it gets by virtue of its relations to other things. To the extent that this nature is complex, it is conceptually constructed by the mind's aggregative tendencies.

d. A given dharma has only one intrinsic nature. Since dharmas are what remain at the end of analysis, and analysis dissolves the aggregating that is contributed by mental construction, a given dharma can have only one intrinsic nature.

5. Suffering is overcome by coming to realize the ultimate truth about ourselves and the world.

   a. Suffering results from the false belief that there is an enduring "I," the subject of experience and agent of actions, for which events in a life can have meaning.

   b. This false belief results from failure to see that the person is a mere conceptual fiction, something lacking intrinsic nature. What is ultimately real is just a causal series of dharmas. Suffering is overcome by coming to see reality in a genuinely objective way, a way that does not project any conceptual fictions onto the world.

Nāgārjuna does not deny that this is what dharmas would be like. Instead he rejects the further implication that there actually are dharmas. His position is that if there were ultimately real things, they would be dharmas, things with intrinsic nature; but there cannot be such things. Not only are the person and other partite things devoid of intrinsic nature and so mere conceptual fictions, the same holds for dharmas as well. This is what it means to say that all things are empty.

Given the nature of this claim, there can be no single argument that could establish it. Such a "master argument" would have to be based on claims about the ultimate natures of things, and given what would be required to establish that such claims are ultimately true, this would involve commitment to intrinsic natures of some sort or other. Nāgārjuna's strategy is instead to examine a variety of claims made by those who take there to be ultimately real entities and seek to show of each such claim that it cannot be true. Indeed the commentators introduce each chapter as addressing the objection of an opponent to the conclusion of the preceding chapter. The expectation is that once opponents have seen sufficiently many of their central theses refuted, they will acknowledge that further attempts at finding the ultimate truth are likely to prove fruitless.

This expectation is based in part on the fact that Nāgārjuna employs a number of common patterns of reasoning in his refutations. Once one has seen how a particular reasoning strategy may be used to refute several quite distinct hypotheses, it becomes easier to see how it might apply as well to one's own preferred view concerning some metaphysical issue. Some patterns that occur particularly often in MMK are the following. It is important to note that in each case the hypothesis that is being refuted is meant by the opponent to be ultimately true.

Infinite Regress: This is meant to show that hypothesis H cannot be true, since the same reasoning that leads to H would, when applied to H itself, lead to a further hypothesis H', a similar process would lead to hypothesis H", and so on. But H was introduced in order to explain some phenomenon P. And a good explanation must end somewhere. So H cannot be the correct explanation of P. For examples of this style of reasoning see 2.6, 5.3, 7.1, 7.3, 7.6, 7.19, 10.13, 12.7, 21.13.

Neither Identical Nor Distinct: This is meant to refute a hypothesis to the effect that *x* and *y* are related in some way R. If they were, then *x* and *y* would have to be either two distinct things or else really just one and the same thing (under two different descriptions). But if *x* and *y* were distinct, then *x* exists apart from *y*. And if *x* exists apart from *y*, *x* is not characterized by R. So it cannot be ultimately true that *x* bears R to *y*. If, on the other hand, *x* and *y* were identical, then *x* would bear relation R to itself, which is absurd. Where R is the relation "being the cause of," for instance, it would be absurd to suppose that some event could be the cause of itself. For examples of this style of reasoning see 2.18, 6.3, 10.1–2, 18.1, 21.10, 22.2–4, 27.15–16.

The Three Times: This is meant to refute a hypothesis to the effect that *x* has some property P. For the hypothesis to be true, *x* must have P at one of the three times: past, future, or present. But, it is argued, for various reasons it cannot be true that *x* has P at any of the three times. Quite often the third possibility—that of the present moment—is eliminated on the grounds that there is no such thing as a present moment distinct from past and future. The present is, in other words, a mere point without duration; what we think of as an extended present is conceptually constructed out of past and future. But in some cases the third possibility is ruled out on the grounds that the ultimately real dharmas must be impartite simples. For examples of this style of reasoning see 1.5–6, 2.1, 2.12, 2.25, 3.3, 7.14, 10.13, 16.7–8, 20.5–8, 21.18–21, 23.17–18.

Irreflexivity: This is usually deployed when the opponent seeks to head off an infinite regress by claiming that an entity *x* bears relation R to itself. The principle of irreflexivity says that an entity cannot operate on itself. Commonly cited supportive instances include the knife that cannot cut itself and the finger that cannot point at itself. Nāgārjuna utilizes and supports this principle at 3.2, 7.1, 7.8, 7.28.

Nonreciprocity: This is meant to refute a hypothesis to the effect that *x* and *y* are in a relation of mutual reciprocal dependence—that *x* is dependent on *y* in a certain way and *y* is dependent in the same way on *x*. Instances of this may be found at 7.6, 10.10, 11.5, 20.7.

We have used the La Vallée Poussin edition (LVP) of MMK as the basis of our translation of the verses, though where Ye's more recent edition (Y) differs substantially from the former, we have generally followed the latter. All references to Candrakīrti's commentary are given with the pagination of the *Prasannapadā* in the former edition (LVP). Citations from the other three commentaries are from the Pandeya edition (P). Since the Sanskrit of these commentaries is Pandeya's reconstruction, in all doubtful cases we checked the Tibetan version. References to MMK are always by chapter and verse; thus "See 1.7" refers the reader to verse 7 of chapter 1. Abbreviations for the titles of other texts we regularly refer to are given at the beginning of the bibliography. Those with an interest in the text-critical study of MMK might wish to consult the following:

MacDonald, Anne. 2007. "Revisiting the *Mūlamadhyamakakārikā*: Text-Critical Proposals and Problems." *Studies in Indian Philosophy and Buddhism* (Tokyo University) 14: 25–55.

Saitō, Akira. 1985. "Textcritical Remarks on the *Mūlamadhyamakakārikā* as Cited in the *Prasannapadā*." *Journal of Indian and Buddhist Studies* 33(2): 24–28.

———. 1986. "A Note on the *Prajñā-nāma-mūlamadhyamakakārikā* of Nāgārjuna." *Journal of Indian and Buddhist Studies* 35(1): 484–87.

———. 1995. "Problems in Translating the *Mūlamadhyamakakārikā* as Cited in Its Commentaries." In *Buddhist Translations: Problems and Perspectives,* edited by Doboom Tulku, pp. 87–96. Delhi: Manohar.

Mūlamadhyamakakārikā

BY NĀGĀRJUNA

Dedicatory Verse

anirodham anutpādam anucchedam aśāśvatam |
anekārtham anānārtham anāgamam anirgamam ||
yaḥ pratītyasamutpādaṃ prapañcopaśamaṃ śivam |
deśayāmāsa saṃbuddhas taṃ vande vadatāṃ varam ||

I salute the Fully Enlightened One, the best of orators, who taught the doctrine of dependent origination, according to which there is neither cessation nor origination, neither annihilation nor the eternal, neither singularity nor plurality, neither the coming nor the going [of any dharma, for the purpose of nirvāṇa characterized by] the auspicious cessation of hypostatization.

THIS VERSE serves not only as a dedication of the work to the Buddha but also as an announcement of purpose. One often finds at the beginning of an Indian treatise a statement indicating why one should read it: how one will benefit from its contents. Nāgārjuna does not explicitly claim here that this work will help one achieve liberation from saṃsāra (it is Candrakīrti who says this is the purpose of the text), but what he does say suggests that is the intention behind his work.

The verse begins with the famous eight negations: "neither cessation nor origination" and so on. (Our English translation reverses the word order of the Sanskrit original in order to make the meaning more easily intelligible.) These negations are said to describe the content of the Buddha's central teaching of dependent origination (*pratītyasamutpāda*). The verse thus claims that when we say everything is subject to dependent origination, what this actually means is that nothing really ceases or arises, nothing is ever annihilated nor is there anything eternal, that things are neither really one nor are they many distinct things, and that nothing really ever comes here from elsewhere or goes away from here.

Some of this would come as no surprise to Nāgārjuna's fellow Buddhists. For instance, the claim that nothing ever really moves (discussed in chapter 2) was widely accepted by Buddhist philosophers as one consequence of the impermanence of existents; the idea that dependently originated entities form a causal series was thought to explain why it appears to us that there is motion. Likewise "Neither annihilation nor the eternal" echoes the Buddha's claim that dependent origination represents the correct middle path between the extremes of eternalism and annihilationism. This is discussed in chapters 15, 17, 18, 21, 22, and 27, though in ways that go considerably beyond what had been the orthodox understanding. But the claim that there is neither cessation nor origination (discussed in chapters 1, 7, 20, 21, and 25) would have come as a shock to many, since dependent origination was thought to involve (and explain) the origination and cessation of ultimately real entities. And while "neither one nor many" will have a familiar ring to many Buddhists (the Buddha did say that the person in one life and the reborn person in another are "neither identical nor distinct," e.g., at S II.62, S II.76, S II.113), the standard Abhidharma account of dependent origination relies on the notion that there are many ultimately real dharmas that are mutually distinct. So when (as in chapters 6, 14, and 27) Nāgārjuna claims that what are thought of as two distinct things can ultimately be neither one nor many, this will surprise quite a few.

The purpose is not to shock, though. Instead, the commentators tell us, the point of understanding dependent origination through these eight negations is to bring about nirvāṇa by bringing an end to hypostatizing (*prapañca*). By *hypostatization* is meant the process of reification or "thing-ifying": taking what is actually just a useful form of speech to refer to some real entity. Because the doctrine of dependent origination plays so central a role in the Buddha's teachings, Abhidharma scholars developed a complex web of concepts designed to explicate it. The suggestion is that the eight negations are meant to remind us that conceptual proliferation can distract us from the real goal—liberation—and perhaps even serve as a barrier to the achievement of the cessation of suffering. (See 18.6, as well as chapters 24 and 27.) But these negations (as well as other allied negations) are not to be accepted because some wise person has told us so. MMK consists of philosophical arguments meant to refute such things as cessation and origination. This work would then be designed to help foster liberation by enlisting the tool of philosophical rationality in the task of putting in their proper place the sorts of conceptual distinctions developed by other Buddhist philosophers. The "proper place" of these concepts is in the toolkit carried by every skillful Buddhist teacher, to be used when appropriate given the circumstances of a particular suffering being. (See 18.5–12.)

1. An Analysis of Conditions

THIS IS THE first of several chapters investigating the concept of causation. It is important to note at the outset that in classical Indian philosophy causation is usually understood as a relation between entities ("the seed, together with warm moist soil, is the cause of the sprout") and not, as in modern science, between events ("the collision caused the motion of the ball"). It begins with a statement of the thesis: that existing things do not arise in any of the four logically possible ways that causation might be thought to involve. The Ābhidharmika opponent (i.e., a member of one of the Abhidharma schools) then introduces a conditions-based analysis of causation, which is a version of the second of the four possible views concerning causation. The remainder of the chapter consists of arguments against the details of this theory that entities arise in dependence on distinct conditions. In outline the chapter proceeds as follows:

1.1 Assertion: No entity arises in any of the four possible ways: (a) from itself, (b) from a distinct cause, (c) from both itself and something distinct, or (d) without cause.
1.2 General refutation of arising on possibilities a–d
1.3 Opponent: Entities arise (b) in dependence on distinct conditions of four kinds.
1.4 Refutation of relation between conditions and causal activity

1.5–6 Definition of "condition" and argument for the impossibility of anything meeting the definition
1.7–10 Refutations of each of the four conditions
1.11–14 Refutation of thesis that effect arises from conditions

na svato nāpi parato na dvābhyāṃ nāpy ahetutaḥ |
utpannā jātu vidyante bhāvāḥ kvacana kecana ||1||

1. Not from itself, not from another, not from both, nor without cause:
Never in any way is there any existing thing that has arisen.

This is the overall conclusion for which Nāgārjuna will argue in this chapter: that existents do not come into existence as the result of causes and conditions. There are four possible ways in which this might be thought to happen, and he rejects all of them. According to the first, when an effect seems to arise, it does so because it was already in some sense present in its cause; its appearance is really just the manifestation of something that already existed. The second view claims instead that cause and effect are distinct entities. The third has it that cause and effect may be said to be both identical and distinct. The fourth claims that things originate without any cause; since there are thus no causes, an originating thing could not be said to originate either from itself or from something distinct—it does not originate *from* anything.

We follow Ye 2011 and accordingly diverge from translations that follow the La Vallée Poussin edition, in reversing the order of the second and third verses of this chapter. (This ordering is clearly attested to by the *Akutobhayā* and the commentaries of Buddhapālita and Bhāviveka.) On this reading, general arguments against all four views are given in the next verse. But in his comments on this verse Bhāviveka anticipates by giving arguments against the four views. He says, for instance, that the fourth view would mean that anything could be produced from anything at any time, something we know is false.

na hi svabhāvo bhāvānāṃ pratyayādiṣu vidyate |
avidyamāne svabhāve parabhāvo na vidyate ||2||

2. The intrinsic nature of existents does not exist in the conditions, etc.
The intrinsic nature not occurring, neither is extrinsic nature found.

According to the *Akutobhayā*, 2ab gives the argument against the first possibility mentioned in verse 1, that an existent arises from itself (the view known as *satkāryavāda*). The argument is that if that out of which the existent arose were really that existent itself, then it should have the intrinsic nature (*svabhāva*) of the existent. But this is simply not the case. Indeed as all the other commentators point out, if this were the case, then arising would be pointless. For instance we want to know the cause of fire because we want to produce something with its intrinsic nature, heat. If that nature were already present in its cause, then it would be pointless to produce fire. For then in order to feel heat we would only need to touch unignited fuel.

Again according to the *Akutobhayā*, 2cd gives the argument against the second possibility mentioned in verse 1, that an existent arises from something distinct from itself (*asatkāryavāda*). This would mean that the existent must borrow its nature from its cause, thus making its nature something that is extrinsic (*parabhāva*). The argument is that in the absence of the intrinsic nature of the existent in question, its extrinsic nature is likewise not to be found. This is because in order for something to exist, its intrinsic nature must occur: There is, for instance, no fire without the occurrence of heat. And something cannot be in the position of borrowing a nature from something else unless it exists. So an existent cannot arise from something distinct. (For more on *satkāryavāda* and *asatkāryavāda* see chapters 10 and 20.)

The third possibility is to be rejected on the grounds that it inherits all the faults of the first and second. And according to the *Akutobhayā*, the fourth is false because it is one of the extreme views rejected by the Buddha. (Other commentators give more philosophically respectable reasons to reject this view.)

catvāraḥ pratyayā hetur ārambaṇam anantaram /
tathaivādhipateyaṃ ca pratyayo nāsti pañcamaḥ //3//

3. [The opponent:] There are four conditions: the primary cause, the objective support, the proximate condition,
and of course the dominant condition; there is no fifth condition.

The commentators represent this as the view of a Buddhist opponent, someone who holds the second of the four possible views about the relation between cause and effect mentioned in verse 1. Candrakīrti has this opponent begin by rehearsing the reasons for rejecting the first, third, and fourth views. On the first, origination would be pointless, since the desired effect would already exist. We seek knowledge of causes because we find ourselves wanting to produce something that does not currently exist. The third view is to be rejected because it is the conjunction of the first and second, and we already know that the first is false. The fourth view, that of causelessness, is one of the absurd extremes said to be false by the Buddha (M I.408, A I.173). But, the opponent claims, the second view was taught by the Buddha and so should not be rejected.

The classification of four kinds of condition is the Abhidharma elaboration of the Buddha's teaching of origination. (See AKB 2.64a.) (1) The primary cause is that from which the effect is thought to have been produced—for example, the seed in the case of a sprout. (2) Only a cognition has an objective support, namely its intentional object, that of which it is conscious. A visual cognition has a color-and-shape dharma as its objective support, an auditory cognition has a sound, etc. (3) The proximate condition is that entity or event that immediately precedes the effect and that cedes its place to the effect. (4) The dominant condition is that without which the effect would not arise. After criticizing the basic notion of causation, Nāgārjuna will take up each of these four types in turn: primary cause in verse 7, objective support in verse 8, proximate condition in verse 9, and dominant condition in verse 10.

Candrakīrti sets the stage for verse 4 by having the opponent answer the question raised by 2cd as follows: "Then, given such a refutation of the view that origination is by means of conditions, the view will be entertained that origination is by means of an action (*kriyā*). The conditions such as vision and color-and-shape do not directly cause consciousness [as effect]. But conditions are so called because they result in a consciousness-producing action. And this action produces consciousness. Thus consciousness is produced by a condition-possessing, consciousness-producing action, not by conditions, as porridge [is produced] by the action of cooking" (LVP p. 79).

kriyā na pratyayavatī nāpratyayavatī kriyā /
pratyayā nākriyāvantaḥ kriyāvantaś ca santy uta //4//

4. An action does not possess conditions; nor is it devoid of conditions.
Conditions are not devoid of an action; neither are they provided with an action.

This "action" is supposed to be the causal activity that makes the cause and conditions produce the right kind of effect. It is supposed to explain why only when a seed is planted in warm moist soil does a sprout appear (and why a sprout doesn't arise from a stone). But if this action is the product of the co-occurrence of the conditions, and thus may be said to possess the conditions, then presumably it occurs when these conditions are assembled. But is this before or after the effect has arisen? If before, then it does not perform the producing activity that makes an event an action. If after, then since the effect has already been produced, the producing activity is no longer to be found. And, adds Candrakīrti, there is no third time when the effect is undergoing production, since that would require that the effect be simultaneously existent and nonexistent, which is a contradictory state.

If, on the other hand, one were to say that the action occurs independently of the conditions, then we would be unable to explain why the productive action takes place at one time and not at others. The action, being free of dependence on conditions, would be forever occurring, and all such undertakings as trying to make a fire would be pointless.

Given that one cannot specify a time when this action occurs, it follows that it does not ultimately exist. And from this it follows that it cannot be ultimately true that conditions either possess an action or do not possess an action.

utpadyate pratītyemān itīme pratyayāḥ kila /
yāvan notpadyata ime tāvan nāpratyayāḥ katham //5//

5. They are said to be conditions when something arises dependent on them.
When something has not arisen, why then are they not nonconditions?

naivāsato naiva sataḥ pratyayo 'rthasya yujyate /
asataḥ pratyayaḥ kasya sataś ca pratyayena kim //6//

6. Something cannot be called a condition whether the object [that is the supposed effect] is not yet existent or already existent.

If nonexistent, what is it the condition of? And if existent,
what is the point of the condition?

These two verses explain in greater detail the argument of verse 4. The supposed conditions for the arising of a visual cognition—functioning eyes, presence of an object, light, and so on—cannot be said to be conditions at the time when the visual cognition does not yet exist, since they have not yet performed the productive activity required to make them be what are properly called "conditions." But when the visual cognition does exist, no productive activity is to be found. We might think there must be a third time between these two, a time when the visual cognition is undergoing production. But while we could say this about a chariot, it could not hold of something ultimately real such as a cognition. A chariot might be thought of as something that gradually comes into existence when its parts are being assembled. But precisely because we would then have to say that during that process the chariot both exists and does not exist, we must admit that the chariot is not ultimately real. That we can say this about a chariot shows that it is a mere useful fiction.

This pattern of argumentation, which we might call the "argument of the three times," will figure prominently in chapter 2. The point of the argument as applied to the present case of origination is that for those who hold that cause and effect are distinct (proponents of the view known as *asatkāryavāda*), the producing relation can only be a conceptual construction. According to *asatkāryavāda*, cause and conditions occur before the effect arises. To claim that the effect originates in dependence on the cause and conditions, we must take there to be a real relation between the two items. But that relation is not to be found in either of the two available times. As for the third time, it holds only with respect to conceptually constructed entities such as the chariot. It follows that the relation of production or causation must be conceptually constructed. It is something that we impute upon observing a regular succession of events, but it is not to be found in reality.

na san nāsan na sadasan dharmo nirvartate yadā /
kathaṃ nirvartako hetur evaṃ sati hi yujyate //7//

7. Since a dharma does not operate whether existent,
   nonexistent, or both existent and nonexistent,
   how in that case can something be called an operative cause?

Candrakīrti explains that by "operative cause" (*nirvartakahetu*) is meant primary cause, the first of the four kinds of conditions identified in verse 2. A dharma is an ultimately real entity, something with intrinsic nature. The argument is that in order for an entity to perform the operation of producing an effect, it must undergo change, going from the state of not yet having produced the effect to the state of having produced the effect. But an ultimately real entity, a dharma, cannot undergo change when it exists, since its existence just consists in the manifestation of its intrinsic nature. Nor can it undergo change when it does not exist, since at that time there is no "it" to serve as the subject of change. As for the third option, that the dharma is both existent and nonexistent, the commentators explain that this thesis inherits the defects of the first and second theses and that moreover the properties of being existent and being nonexistent are mutually incompatible.

anārambaṇa evāyaṃ san dharma upadiśyate /
athānārambaṇe dharme kuta ārambaṇaṃ punaḥ //8//

8. A dharma, being existent, is said to indeed be without objective support.
   Then why again posit an objective support in the case of a dharma without an objective support?

The object of a mental state such as a visual cognition is said to be the objective support (*ālambana-pratyaya*) of that cognition. To call this a kind of condition is to say that the cognition cannot arise without its object. The argument against there being such a condition is once again like that of verses 6–7. At the time when a cognition exists, its supposed objective support cannot be said to produce it. Only something that does not yet exist can be produced.

Note that this argument differs from the time-lag argument that Sautrāntikas use to support a representationalist theory of perception. Both arguments rely on the fact that the objective support exists before the cognition. But the Sautrāntika argument uses this fact to argue that the cognition cannot be directly aware of what is called its objective support. The argument here, by contrast, uses this fact to prove that what is called the objective support cannot be said to be a causal condition of the cognition.

anutpanneṣu dharmeṣu nirodho nopapadyate /
nānantaram ato yuktaṃ niruddhe pratyayaś ca kaḥ //9//

9. Destruction does not hold when dharmas have not yet originated.
Thus nothing can be called a proximate condition; if it is destroyed, how can it be a condition?

The argument here is also similar to that of verses 4–7, only this time directed against the idea of a proximate condition (*samanantara-pratyaya*), the third of the four types of condition. The proximate condition can perform its function neither before nor after the arising of the effect. A proximate condition must undergo destruction in order to bring about its effect: It would not be the immediately preceding condition unless it went out of existence before the effect arose. But before the effect has arisen, it has not yet undergone destruction. And once it has undergone destruction, since it no longer exists, it cannot be said to be productive of an effect.

bhāvānāṃ niḥsvabhāvānāṃ na sattā vidyate yataḥ /
satīdam asmin bhavatīty etan naivopapadyate //10//

10. Since things devoid of intrinsic nature are not existent,
"This existing, that comes to be" can never hold.

"This existing, that comes to be" is one standard formulation of dependent origination, the Buddha's doctrine of causation. The "this" in the formula is identified by the Ābhidharmika as the dominant condition (*adhipati-pratyaya*), the fourth type of condition mentioned in verse 2. The claim here is that there can be no such dominant condition for things that are ultimately real. The argument is that anything that did originate in accordance with the formula would lack intrinsic nature. We saw it claimed in verses 4–7 that there is no third time when an ultimately real effect is undergoing production. This is because for something to be ultimately real, it must bear its own intrinsic nature and not borrow that nature from other things, in the way in which a chariot borrows its nature (e.g., its size, shape, and weight) from the natures of its parts. And this in turn means that something that is ultimately real must be simple in nature. Something simple in nature either does exist or does not exist; there is no third intermediate state when it is coming into existence. Only things that are not ultimately real, such as a chariot, could be said to undergo production. Hence the formula "This existing, that comes to be" cannot apply to things that are ultimately existent.

na ca vyastasamasteṣu pratyayeṣv asti tat phalam /
pratyayebhyaḥ kathaṃ tac ca bhaven na pratyayeṣu yat //11//

11. That product does not exist in the conditions whether they are taken separately or together.
What does not exist in the conditions, how can that come from the conditions?

athāsad api tat tebhyaḥ pratyayebhyaḥ pravartate |
phalam apratyayebhyo 'pi kasmān nābhipravartate ||12||

12. If that which does not exist [in them] is produced from those conditions,
how is it that the product does not also come forth from nonconditions?

The argument so far has focused on the conditions. Now it turns to the effect but makes similar points. Here the view in question is that the effect is distinct from its cause and conditions. In verse 11 the difficulty is raised that there is then no explanation as to why this particular effect arises from these conditions. Candrakīrti gives the example of the cloth that is said to arise from the threads, loom, shuttle, pick, and so on. The cloth is not in these conditions taken separately, for the cloth is not found in the separate threads, the loom, etc., and if it were in each of them, then it would be many cloths, not one. Nor is the cloth in the conditions taken collectively or in the assembled state. For when the threads are assembled, the cloth as a whole is not found in each of the many threads that are its individual parts. Consequently the cloth and its conditions must be said to be utterly distinct. In verse 12 it is pointed out that it would then be equally sensible to expect the effect to arise from anything at all—that is, from what would ordinarily be identified as nonconditions with respect to that effect. (Cf. verse 3cd.) For as Bhāviveka points out, threads are just as distinct from curd as they would then be from cloth, so we should expect to be able to get curd from threads.

phalaṃ ca pratyayamayaṃ pratyayāś cāsvayaṃmayāḥ |
phalam asvamayebhyo yat tat pratyayamayaṃ katham ||13||

13. The product consists of the conditions, but the conditions do not consist of themselves.

How can that which is the product of things that do not consist of themselves consist of conditions?

Here the view in question is that the product or effect, while distinct from the cause and conditions, arises from them in that it consists in them or is composed of them. (The Nyāya school held this view.) It differs from the view in question in verses 11–12 in that it restricts the term "condition" to just those things that the effect can be said to be made of. The example used by the commentators is that of the threads and a piece of cloth. Now we can say that the cloth is made up of the threads. But it is not true that a thread is made up of itself. The thread is in turn made up of its parts, such as its two tips and the intermediate parts. But if something is composed of something else, the intrinsic nature of that thing should be found in what it is composed of. For instance the color of the cloth should be found in the threads. And the property of being composed of threads, while found in the cloth, is not to be found in the threads. A thread does not consist of itself; it consists of its tips and the other parts. So the view in question cannot be correct.

tasmān na pratyayamayaṃ nāpratyayamayaṃ phalam /
saṃvidyate phalābhāvāt pratyayāpratyayāḥ kutaḥ //14//

14. Therefore neither a product consisting of conditions nor one consisting of nonconditions
exists; if the product does not exist, how can there be a condition or noncondition?

As verse 13 showed, the effect cannot be said to be made up of its conditions, since the effect could derive its nature only from things that do not in turn derive their nature from yet other things. The alternative would be to say that the effect is made up of nonconditions. If the cloth is not made up of threads, then perhaps it is made up of straw, which is the condition with respect to a mat but a noncondition with respect to cloth. But this is obviously absurd. So there is no plausible account of the origination of a real effect. And in the absence of a real effect, nothing can be said to be either a condition or a noncondition.

2. An Analysis of the Traversed, the Not Yet Traversed, and the Presently Being Traversed

THE TOPIC of this chapter is motion. It begins with the assertion that there is no going in any of the three times—past, present, and future. The opponent objects that motion does occur in the present; this is followed by a detailed rebuttal. The remainder of the chapter investigates the question of whether anything could be the entity that is involved in going, commencing to go, and ceasing to go. In outline the chapter proceeds as follows:

2.1	Assertion: There is no going in any of the three times.
2.2	Opponent: There is going in the present time.
2.3–7	Refutation of going occurring in the present
2.8	Assertion: There is no entity that goes.
2.9–11	Reason for the thesis "A goer does not go"
2.12	Assertion: A goer cannot commence motion in the three times.
2.13–14	Reason for this assertion
2.15	Assertion: There is no entity that stops moving (*trilemma*).
2.16–17ab	Reason for the thesis "A goer does not stop"
2.17cd	Summary: There is no act of going, nor the commencing or ceasing of going.
2.18–21	A goer is neither identical with nor distinct from the act of going.
2.22–23	Refutation of the thesis that a goer is characterized by the property of going

2.24–25ab Summary: No entity, whether a goer, a nongoer, or a goer-nongoer, goes in any of the three locations.

2.25cd Ultimate conclusion: There is no going, no goer, and no destination.

gataṃ na gamyate tāvad agataṃ naiva gamyate |
gatāgatavinirmuktaṃ gamyamānaṃ na gamyate ||1||

1. Just as the path traversed is not being traversed, neither is the path not yet traversed being traversed.
The path presently being traversed that is distinct from the portions of path traversed and not yet traversed is not being traversed.

If motion is possible, then it should be possible to say where the activity of going is taking place. It is not taking place in that portion of the path already traversed, since the activity of going has already occurred there. Nor is it taking place in the portion not yet traversed, since such activity still lies in the future. And there is no third place, the presently being traversed, where it could take place. As the *Akutobhayā* explains, there is no present going distinct from the already traversed and the not yet traversed, just like the flame of a lamp. Chapter 9 of the *Abhidharmakośabhāṣya* (AKB p. 472) explains the example of the moving lamp as follows. When we say that a lamp moves, it is actually a continuous series of flames we are referring to, each flame lasting just an instant (that amount of time of which there can be no shorter). Since each flame only occurs in one particular spot, none of them actually moves. But because each flame arises in a different place from where its predecessor was, it appears as if one enduring thing is moving. Since only the momentary flames are real, strictly speaking there is no motion. Only when we run together past, present, and future flames is there the illusion of motion. It is important to keep this example in mind throughout the rest of the chapter. Many of the arguments depend on the assumption that nothing lasts longer than an instant.

This is an instance of the argument of the three times, in this case to the effect that going cannot take place in past, future, or present. Similar reasoning was also used in 1.5–6. The argument here is the same as that of Zeno's paradox of the arrow. Like that paradox, it relies on the assumption that space and time are both infinitely divisible.

ceṣṭā yatra gatis tatra gamyamāne ca sā yataḥ /
na gate nāgate ceṣṭā gamyamāne gatis tataḥ //2//

2. [The opponent:] Where there is movement, there is the act of going. And since movement occurs in the path presently being traversed,
not in the traversed nor the not yet traversed, the act of going occurs in the path presently being traversed.

gamyamānasya gamanaṃ kathaṃ nāmopapatsyate /
gamyamānaṃ vigamanaṃ yadā naivopapadyate //3//

3. [Response:] How will it hold that the act of going is in the path being traversed
when it does not hold that there is a presently being traversed without the act of going?

For something to be the locus of present going, there has to be an act of going. And something x can't be the locus of something else y unless x and y are distinct things. In the ensuing verses 4–6, Nāgārjuna will use this point to show that it cannot be correct to locate going in the present.

gamyamānasya gamanaṃ yasya tasya prasajyate |
ṛte gater gamyamānaṃ gamyamānaṃ hi gamyate ||4||

4. If you say the act of going is in the path presently being traversed, it would follow
that the path being traversed is without the act of going,
since [for you] the path presently being traversed is being traversed.

Since the locus of present going and the going are distinct (verse 3), the locus itself must be devoid of any activity of going.

gamyamānasya gamane prasaktaṃ gamanadvayam |
yena tad gamyamānaṃ ca yac cātra gamanaṃ punaḥ ||5||

5. If the act of going is in the path presently being traversed,
then two acts of going would follow:
that by which the path presently being traversed [is said to be such], and moreover that which supposedly exists in the act of going.

For the locus to serve as locus of the act, it must itself be something whose nature is to be presently being traversed. But this requires an act of going, since something can't be being traversed without there being an act of going. So we now have two acts of going: the one for which we are seeking a locus, and the one that makes this the right locus for the first.

dvau gantārau prasajyete prasakte gamanadvaye |
gantāraṃ hi tiraskṛtya gamanaṃ nopapadyate ||6||

6. If two acts of going are supplied, then it would follow that
there are two goers,

for it does not hold that there is an act of going without a
goer.

Since this is an absurd consequence, the opponent's hypothesis of verse 2 that led to it must be rejected. Note that there is no reason to stop at two goers; the logic of the argument leads to an infinite regress of goers. (See 5.3 for another example of this.)

gantāraṃ cet tiraskṛtya gamanaṃ nopapadyate |
gamane 'sati gantātha kuta eva bhaviṣyati ||7||

7. If it does not hold that there is an act of going without a goer,
how will there be a goer when the act of going does not exist?

It having been refuted that there is an act of going in the path being traversed, it follows that there can be no goer there. Notice, though, that for this to follow, what is required is that there be no goer without an act of going and not (as is said here) that there can be no act of going without a goer.

gantā na gacchati tāvad agantā naiva gacchati |
anyo gantur agantuś ca kas tṛtīyo 'tha gacchati ||8||

8. Just as a goer does not go, neither does a nongoer go,
and what third person is there, apart from the goer and the
nongoer, who goes?

The argument so far has concerned what the locus of going might be—the path traversed, not traversed, and so on. Attention now shifts to the question whether there is anything that might be the agent of the act of moving. Three possibilities come to mind: that the agent is a goer, something characterized by movement; that the agent is a nongoer, something not characterized by movement; and that the agent is both a goer and a nongoer, something that is qualified both by movement and by nonmovement. The claim is that none of these can be the agent of going. The next three verses give arguments against the first possibility. No explicit argument is given against the second, for obvious reasons. As for the third, it should be clear that nothing can be characterized by contradictory properties.

gantā tāvad gacchatīti katham evopapatsyate |
gamanena vinā gantā yadā naivopapadyate ||9||

9. How, first of all, will it hold that a goer goes
when it does not hold that there is a goer in the absence of the act of going?

pakṣo gantā gacchatīti yasya tasya prasajyate |
gamanena vinā gantā gantur gamanam icchataḥ ||10||

10. If you hold the thesis that a goer goes, it would follow that
the goer is without the act of going, for you wish to ascribe the act of going to the goer.

Candrakīrti sees the reasoning here as parallel to that of verse 5. He comments, "As for the thesis that someone is a goer precisely because he or she is provided with an act of going, since such a theorist wishes to say that the goer goes, it would have to be said that the goer goes without the going, because the theorist designated the goer by means of going. For there is no second act of going. Hence it would not be correct to say that the goer goes" (LVP p. 99).

gamane dve prasajyete gantā yady uta gacchati |
ganteti cājyate yena gantā san yac ca gacchati ||11||

11. If a goer does indeed go, then it would follow that there are two acts of going:
that by which the goer is said to be a goer and that by which the goer really goes.

gate nārabhyate gantuṃ gantuṃ nārabhyate 'gate /
nārabhyate gamyamāne gantum ārabhyate kuha //12//

12. Going is not begun in the path traversed, going is not begun in the path not yet traversed,
and going is not begun in the path presently being traversed. Then where is going begun?

A new problem is raised for those who think there is such a thing as a goer: When does that going whereby someone comes to be a goer commence? The reasoning is spelled out in the next two verses.

prāg asti gamanārambhād gamyamānaṃ na no gatam /
yatrārabhyeta gamanam agate gamanaṃ kutaḥ //13//

13. Before the act of going begins, there is neither a path presently being traversed nor one already traversed
where the act of going could begin. And how could the act of going begin in the path not yet traversed?

gataṃ kiṃ gamyamānaṃ kim agataṃ kiṃ vikalpyate /
adṛśyamāna ārambhe gamanasyaiva sarvathā //14//

14. How can the path already traversed, presently being traversed, or not yet traversed be imagined
when the beginning of the act of going is not in any way to be found?

At this point we can imagine an opponent objecting that since there is such a thing as standing still, there must be such a thing as going. For, the opponent would claim, standing still happens when going stops, so there must first be going for there to be standing still. Nāgārjuna replies in verses 15–17.

gantā na tiṣṭhati tāvad agantā naiva tiṣṭhati /
anyo gantur agantuś ca kas tṛtīyo 'tha tiṣṭhati //15//

15. It is not, first, a goer who stops, nor indeed is it a nongoer who stops.
And who could be the third person distinct from goer and nongoer who stops?

gantā tāvat tiṣṭhatīti katham evopapatsyate /
gamanena vinā gantā yadā naivopapadyate //16//

16. How will it ever hold, in the first place, that a goer stops when it never holds that there is a goer without an act of going?

It could not be the goer who stops, since the goer is defined as the agent of the act of going, and that act is incompatible with stopping, which is its cessation. But neither can it be the nongoer who stops. Since the nongoer is not characterized by the act of going, the nongoer cannot be characterized by its cessation. And there is no third possibility, since something could not be both a goer and a nongoer.

na tiṣṭhati gamyamānān na gatān nāgatād api /
gamanaṃ saṃpravṛttiś ca nivṛttiś ca gateḥ samā //17//

17. The goer is not said to stop when on the path presently being traversed, the already traversed, or the not yet traversed.

The same [analysis] that applies to the case of the act of going
also applies to the commencing and ceasing of the act of going.

Nāgārjuna points out that the same reasoning that refuted the act of going (vv. 3–6) also refutes the beginning (vv. 12–14) and the ending (vv. 15–17) of going.

yad eva gamanaṃ gantā sa eveti na yujyate |
anya eva punar gantā gater iti na yujyate ||18||

18. It is not right to say that the goer is identical with the act of going;
nor, again, is it right to say that goer and act of going are distinct.

A new question for the opponent is now brought up: Is the goer identical with the act of going, or are these two distinct things? Nāgārjuna will give arguments against each possibility in the next two verses.

yad eva gamanaṃ gantā sa eva hi bhaved yadi |
ekībhāvaḥ prasajyeta kartuḥ karmaṇa eva ca ||19||

19. If act of going and the goer were identical,
then it would also follow that agent and action are one.

The commentators use the example of a cutter and the action of cutting: It is considered obvious to all that an agent such as a cutter cannot be identical with the action of cutting that he or she performs. By the same token, then, the goer and the act of going cannot be identical.

anya eva punar gantā gater yadi vikalpyate |
gamanaṃ syād ṛte gantur gantā syād gamanād ṛte ||20||

20. If, on the other hand, the goer were thought to be distinct from the act of going,
then there would be the act of going without a goer, and a goer without an act of going.

If they are not identical, must they not then be distinct? Not according to Nāgārjuna. For to say that they are distinct is to say that each has its nature independently of the other. And then the act of going would exist without its being the act of any goer, and the goer would be a goer without an act of going. The underlying logic of this argument is spelled out more carefully in 5.1–4.

ekībhāvena vā siddhir nānābhāvena vā yayoḥ |
na vidyate tayoḥ siddhiḥ kathaṃ nu khalu vidyate ||21||

21. If two things are not established as either identical or distinct,
then how will they be established at all?

To say something is not established is to say there is no reason to believe it exists. The claim here is that if goer and going were real then they would have to be either identical or distinct. Since they can be neither, there is no reason to think they are real.

gatyā yayājyate gantā gatiṃ tāṃ sa na gacchati |
yasmān na gatipūrvo 'sti kaścit kiṃcid dhi gacchati ||22||

22. A goer does not obtain that going through which it is called a goer,
since the goer does not exist before the going; indeed someone goes somewhere.

The argument here is similar to that of verse 10. It spells out in more detail the reasoning behind the denial in verse 20 that goer and going are distinct. The idea is that in order to obtain going as an attribute, and thereby become a goer, the goer must exist distinct from the going. But something that existed distinct from going would not be a goer; to be a goer is to go somewhere, which requires the act of going.

gatyā yayājyate gantā tato 'nyāṃ sa na gacchati |
gatī dve nopapadyete yasmād ekatra gantari ||23||

23. A goer does not obtain going by means of something other than that going through which it is called a goer,
since it cannot be held that there are two goings when just one goes.

The second going is the one that would be needed to make the goer be a goer before it obtains the act of going. Once again there is an infinite regress threatening.

sadbhūto gamanaṃ gantā triprakāraṃ na gacchati |
nāsadbhūto 'pi gamanaṃ triprakāraṃ sa gacchati ||24||

24. One who is a real goer does not perform a going of any of the three kinds.
Neither does one who is not a real goer perform a going of any of the three kinds.

gamanaṃ sadasadbhūtaḥ triprakāraṃ na gacchati |
tasmād gatiś ca gantā ca gantavyaṃ ca na vidyate ||25||

25. One who is a both-real-and-unreal goer does not perform a going of any of the three kinds.
Thus there is no going, no goer, and no destination.

Going of "the three kinds" are going in the path traversed, in the path not yet traversed, and the path presently being traversed. The claim in 24ab is thus a summary of what has been argued for in most of this chapter. The "one who is not a real goer" discussed in 24cd is the "non-goer" of verse 8. No separate argument has been given for the claim made in 24cd, but perhaps none is needed: Something that is not characterized by motion is not a good candidate to be the thing that goes. And the same can be said for the claim of 25ab. The final conclusion, stated in 25cd, is that there can ultimately be no such thing as going, a goer, and a destination. No separate argument has been given for there being no such thing as a destination, but here too the point seems obvious: A destination is the place that is the objective of the goer's going, so without an ultimately real goer and going there could be no such thing as a destination.

3. An Analysis of the Āyatanas

THE *āyatana* classification is one of three systems for classifying existing things that the Buddha employed in presenting his teachings about the nature of reality. This doctrine divides all existents up into twelve basic kinds consisting of six sense faculties and their respective objects: vision and the visible (color-and-shape), hearing and the audible, and so on. (The sixth sense is the inner sense known as "mind" [*manas*], which has mental objects.) The aim of this chapter is to refute the view that these things are ultimately real. It begins with a rehearsal of the Abhidharma doctrine of the twelve āyatanas. The argument begins with a defense of the claim that the faculty of vision cannot be ultimately real. From this it then follows that there is no seer and no field of visible entities. The argument is then generalized to the other sense faculties and their fields. In outline the chapter proceeds as follows:

- 3.1 Statement of the Abhidharma doctrine that there exist sense faculties and sense fields
- 3.2 Argument for the claim that the faculty of vision does not see visible things
- 3.3 Reply to an objection to this argument
- 3.4–5ab Refutation of the existence of the faculty of vision
- 3.5cd–6 Refutation of the existence of the seer and the field of the visible

3.7 Consequences of the nonexistence of the faculty of vision and the field of the visible
3.8 Generalization of the argument to the other sense faculties and fields

darśanaṃ śravaṇaṃ ghrāṇaṃ rasanaṃ sparśanaṃ manaḥ /
indriyāṇi ṣaḍ eteṣāṃ draṣṭavyādīni gocaraḥ //1//

1. Vision, hearing, taste, smell, touch, and the inner sense (*manas*)
are the six faculties; the visible and so on are their fields.

This is the doctrine of the twelve āyatanas, which divides reality up into six sense faculties and their respective fields. Abhidharma takes these to be ultimately real. Nāgārjuna will examine the sense faculty of vision and try to show that it cannot be ultimately real. In verse 8 he will claim that the same argument can be used to refute the rest of the āyatanas.

svam ātmānaṃ darśanaṃ hi tat tam eva na paśyati /
na paśyati yad ātmānaṃ kathaṃ drakṣyati tat parān //2//

2. In no way does vision see itself.
If vision does not see itself, how will it see what is other?

It is generally acknowledged that an entity cannot operate on itself: A knife cannot cut itself, a finger cannot point at itself, and so on. Hence vision does not see itself. The argument here is that because this is true, it follows that vision does not see things other than itself either (i.e., vision does not see anything at all). This argument seems puzzling. Why should it follow from the fact that vision does not see itself that it sees nothing else? There are two possible ways of interpreting the argument. The first represents how Bhāviveka and Candrakīrti understand it. The second is not advanced by any commentator but seems plausible nonetheless.

(1) The scent of jasmine first pervades the flower and then pervades what comes in contact with the flower. The general principle to be inferred from this is that a property of something can come to pervade something else only if that property first pervades the thing itself. For an object to be seen is for it to be pervaded by the property of being seen. By the general principle just mentioned, this can be so only if vision itself is first pervaded by the property of being seen. But since vision does not see itself, this is not so. It follows that no distinct object can be seen by vision either.*

(2) If seeing is the intrinsic nature of vision, then vision must manifest this intrinsic nature independently of other things. This means that vision should be able to see even in the absence of any visible object. For otherwise its manifesting vision would be dependent on the existence of the visible object. But seeing requires that there be something that is seen, and in the absence of any visible object, only vision itself could be what vision sees. But vision does not see itself. Hence seeing could not be the intrinsic nature of vision, so it could not be ultimately true that vision sees visible objects.

To this argument we are to imagine the opponent raises an objection: The principle of irreflexivity (that an entity cannot operate on itself) does not hold, since there are counterexamples. A fire, while burning its fuel, also burns itself. Hence it has not been proven that vision does not see itself.

* The view that one must perceive the sense organ in order to perceive an external object by means of that sense organ was held by the Stoics. See George Boys-Stones, "Physiognomy and Ancient Psychological Theory," in *Seeing the Face, Seeing the Soul: Polemon's Physiognomy from Classical Antiquity to Medieval Islam*, ed. Simon Swain (Oxford: Oxford University Press, 2007), pp. 84–85.

na paryāpto 'gnidṛṣṭānto darśanasya prasiddhaye /
sadarśanaḥ sa pratyukto gamyamānagatāgataiḥ //3//

3. [Reply to implicit objection:] The example of fire is not adequate for the establishment of vision.
Indeed that, together with vision, is refuted by the analysis [in chapter 2] of "the presently being traversed, the traversed, and the not yet traversed."

The *Akutobhayā* commentary explains, "Just as the act of going is not found in the traversed, the not yet traversed, or in what is presently being traversed, so the act of burning is not to be found in the burnt, the not yet burnt, or the presently burning." The reply is thus that since no account may be given of how an ultimately real fire could burn anything, fire cannot be said to burn itself. Consequently it does not work as a counterexample to the irreflexivity principle. The relation between fire and fuel is examined systematically in chapter 10.

This commentary also suggests that this might be the missing argument for the conclusion in verse 2. If vision cannot be said to see anything in any of the three times, then it cannot be said to see. The difficulty with this interpretation is that it is unclear what work is then left for the premise—that vision does not see itself—to do. If the argument of the three times shows that vision never sees anything, then one does not need to point out that vision does not see itself in order to prove that vision does not see.

nāpaśyamānaṃ bhavati yadā kiṃ cana darśanam /
darśanaṃ paśyatīty evaṃ katham etat tu yujyate //4//

4. When there is no vision whatsoever in the absence of seeing, how can it be right to say "vision sees"?

This is the idea behind interpretation (2) of the argument in verse 2. If vision were ultimately real, its intrinsic nature would be seeing. So it makes no sense to suppose that vision might exist in the absence of any seeing. Note that to attribute the *capacity* for seeing to a vision that is not actually seeing is to make vision's nature of seeing dependent on something else. In that case seeing would not be its *intrinsic* nature.

paśyati darśanaṃ naiva naiva paśyaty adarśanam |
vyākhyāto darśanenaiva draṣṭā cāpy avagamyatām ||5||

5. Vision does not see, nor does nonvision see.
One should understand that the seer is explained in the same way as vision.

draṣṭā nāsty atiraskṛtya tiraskṛtya ca darśanam |
draṣṭavyaṃ darśanaṃ caiva draṣṭary asati te kutaḥ ||6||

6. There is no seer with vision or without.
If the seer is nonexistent, how will there be what is to be seen and vision?

Something is a seer through possessing vision. But vision can make something a seer only if vision sees. Since (by the result of verses 1–4) vision does not see, and nonvision obviously does not see, there appears to be no acceptable analysis of how something could be a seer. If we then define the visible as what can be seen by a seer, it is unclear how the visible could be ultimately real. The same reasoning applies to vision.

At this point Candrakīrti quotes the following verse (4.55) from Nāgārjuna's *Ratnāvalī*:

Just as the production of the son is said to depend on the mother and father,

just so the production of consciousness is said to depend on
vision and *rūpa*.

Rūpa here refers to what is visible (color-and-shape) and not to the category of the physical in the doctrine of the five skandhas. According to the doctrine of dependent origination, consciousness arises in dependence on sense faculty and sense object (see S II.95–97). Given this doctrine, the consequences of the denial of vision can now be spelled out.

draṣṭavyadarśanābhāvād vijñānādicatuṣṭayam |
nāstīty upādānādīni bhaviṣyanti punaḥ katham ||7||

7. Due to the nonexistence of vision and what is to be seen, the
four, consisting of consciousness and so on,
do not exist. How then will appropriation and so on come
to be?

"The four" are consciousness, contact, feeling, and desire. In the formula of dependent origination, these are identified as successive steps leading to appropriation (*upādāna*), which is the affective stance of taking the elements of the causal series as one's own. So the argument is that in the absence of vision there cannot be, with respect to all visual experience, the sense of ownership that is relevant to the origination of suffering.

vyākhyātaṃ śravaṇaṃ ghrāṇaṃ rasanaṃ sparśanaṃ manaḥ |
darśanenaiva jānīyāc chrotṛśrotavyakādi ca ||8||

8. One should know that hearing, smelling, tasting, touch, and
the inner sense are explained
by means of vision, as well as indeed the hearer and what is
heard, etc.

The same reasoning may be applied to the other five sense faculties. The result will be that the conclusion of verse 8 extends to all possible experience. Nāgārjuna will follow the same strategy elsewhere: focusing on one example and then claiming that the argument generalizes to an entire class. See, for example, chapters 4, 5, and 19.

4. An Analysis of the Skandhas

THE *skandha* classification is the second of three major systems for classifying existing things that the Buddha employed in presenting his teachings about the nature of reality. This doctrine divides all existents up into five basic kinds: rūpa (the corporeal or physical),* feeling, perception, volition, and consciousness. Since the Buddha used this classificatory scheme (along with those of the āyatanas and dhātus) in his instructions for more advanced disciples, Abhidharma thinkers took the skandhas to be ultimately real. In this chapter Nāgārjuna argues that the skandhas cannot be ultimately real entities. The argument uses the example of rūpa and then in verse 7 generalizes the conclusion. One argument is that rūpa and its cause (the *mahābhūta*s) cannot exist separately from one another (such mutual dependence being incompatible with the asymmetrical dependence relation of causation). A second argument is that of the three times introduced in 1.5–6. A third argument is that a causal relation cannot hold between two things whether they resemble one another or not. The thread of the argument is as follows:

4.1 Assertion: (a) Rūpa is not distinct from its cause; (b) its cause is not distinct from rūpa.

* *Rūpa* is often translated as "form," but here that would be misleading, since the rūpa skandha consists of the objects of the five external senses; smells and tastes, for instance, do not have a "form" or shape.

4.2 Argument for (a)
4.3 Argument for (b)
4.4 Whether rūpa does or does not exist, there is no cause of rūpa.
4.5 Rūpa cannot be said to be uncaused.
4.6 Effect can neither resemble cause nor not resemble cause.
4.7 Generalization of argument to the other four skandhas
4.8–9 Defense of the generalization in reply to an implicit objection

rūpakāraṇanirmuktaṃ na rūpam upalabhyate /
rūpeṇāpi na nirmuktaṃ dṛśyate rūpakāraṇam //1//

1. Rūpa is not found separate from the cause of rūpa.
Nor is the cause of rūpa seen without rūpa.

According to Abhidharma doctrine, rūpa skandha is made up of the five external sense-field āyatanas: the visible (rūpa in the narrow sense, color-and-shape), the audible, the tangible, tastes, and smells. These are said to have as their cause the four elements of earth, water, fire, and air (the *mahābhūta*). The four elements occur in the form of atoms, and an atom of one sort is always accompanied by an atom of each of the other three sorts. They are said to be the cause of rūpa in the sense that the visible and so on never occur apart from occurrences of the four elements. The four elements thus serve as the support of the occurrence of the sensible phenomena that make up rūpa; their causal role is to be a kind of material cause. As Candrakīrti explains the claim of 1ab, if rūpa is distinct from the four elements, it is no more their effect than a piece of cloth is the effect of a pot. On the other hand, 1cd asserts, if there is no rūpa, then nothing can be said to be the cause of rūpa. The two claims of this verse are defended in the next five verses.

rūpakāraṇanirmukte rūpe rūpaṃ prasajyate |
āhetukaṃ na cāsty arthaḥ kaścid āhetukaḥ kvacit ||2||

2. If rūpa were separate from the cause of rūpa, then it would follow that rūpa is
uncaused; but no object whatsoever is without any cause.

If rūpa were distinct from its cause, the four elements, then it would be possible for rūpa to exist separately from them. But then it would exist independently of the four elements, just as the cloth exists separately from the pot. But the fact that the pot and the cloth exist separately is what makes it true that the cloth is not the effect of the pot. So rūpa would be without cause. Buddhapālita explains that this would have two absurd consequences: (1) It would be possible for anything to come into existence at any time, and (2) all effort at producing something would be futile.

rūpeṇa tu vinirmuktaṃ yadi syād rūpakāraṇam |
akāryakaṃ kāraṇaṃ syād nāsty akāryaṃ ca kāraṇam ||3||

3. Moreover, if the cause of rūpa were separate from rūpa,
the cause would be without effect; but there is no cause that is without effect.

There are likewise absurd consequences if the cause, the four elements, were distinct from rūpa. To say they are separate is to say they exist independently of one another, as a bowl exists independently of a pot. But if they exist independently, then the elements do not cause rūpa as effect. And an effectless cause is absurd, because by definition a cause must have an effect.

rūpe saty eva rūpasya kāraṇaṃ nopapadyate |
rūpe 'saty eva rūpasya kāraṇaṃ nopapadyate ||4||

4. If rūpa exists, it does not hold that there is a cause of rūpa.
If rūpa does not exist, it does not hold that there is a cause of rūpa.

If the four elements are the cause of rūpa, they must be its cause either when rūpa already exists or else when it does not yet exist. But something *x* cannot be a cause of something else *y* when *y* already exists. As Buddhapālita asks, what would be the point of a cause in that case? If, on the other hand, the effect does not exist, how can something be said to be its cause? An existing thing cannot bear any sort of real relation, including the relation of being a cause, to something unreal. The reasoning here is just like that of 1.5–6.

niṣkāraṇaṃ punā rūpaṃ naiva naivopapadyate /
tasmād rūpagatān kāṃścin na vikalpān vikalpayet //5//

5. But it also does not at all hold that rūpa exists without a cause—not at all.
Thus one should not impose any concepts on rūpa.

Given what was said in verse 4, it would be natural to think Nāgārjuna wants us to conclude that rūpa is without cause. But that would be incorrect. We have good reason to deny that rūpa is uncaused. If it were, then as the *Akutobhayā* points out, all undertakings would be pointless. Here Nāgārjuna points out that one can deny that rūpa has a cause without affirming that rūpa is causeless. If there are good reasons to deny both that rūpa has a cause and that rūpa is causeless, then perhaps we should affirm neither ("not impose any concepts on rūpa") and instead look for some hidden assumption that leads to the paradoxical situation. One possibility is the assumption that rūpa is ultimately real, something with intrinsic nature.

na kāraṇasya sadṛśaṃ kāryam ity upapadyate |
na kāraṇasyāsadṛśaṃ kāryam ity upapadyate ||6||

6. It does not hold that the effect resembles the cause.
   It does not hold that the effect does not resemble the cause.

The question of whether effect resembles cause was widely discussed among Indian philosophers. For those who maintained that the effect is something new, existing distinct from the cause, there is the difficulty of explaining why we can only produce pots from clay and not from milk (which is just as distinct from a pot as is a lump of clay). If they could claim the effect always resembles the cause, this might help them answer the question. But there are cases where effect does not resemble cause, as when we produce solid curds from liquid milk. Suppose we were to ask this question concerning rūpa and its cause. Nāgārjuna would call this a case of "imposing concepts on rūpa," something he has just said we should not do. Rūpa and the four elements do not resemble one another. For instance, as Candrakīrti points out, rūpa is cognized by vision, hearing, smell, and taste, while the four elements are cognized by touch. So one could not say this is a case where the effect resembles the cause. But even if they did resemble one another, this would not be sufficient to establish causality. There is no reciprocal cause-effect relation between similar grains of rice. On the other hand, the cause-effect relation is not the relation of dissimilarity. A grain of rice and nirvāṇa are dissimilar, but neither is the cause of the other.

vedanācittasaṃjñānāṃ saṃskārāṇāṃ ca sarvaśaḥ |
sarveṣām eva bhāvānāṃ rūpeṇaiva samaḥ kramaḥ ||7||

7. Feeling, consciousness, perceptions, and the volitions, collectively—
   indeed all existents should be considered in the same way as rūpa.

The argument of the chapter so far generalizes to all the skandhas. As Candrakīrti puts it, "Indeed, when the Mādhyamika seeks to prove the emptiness of one dharma, that of all dharmas [is proven]" (LVP p. 127). The argument against rūpa has depended on there being something that is held to be the cause of rūpa. But as the commentators point out, it is generally agreed that the other four skandhas originate in dependence on rūpa. If rūpa is not ultimately real, then the other four skandhas cannot be either.

vigrahe yaḥ parīhāraṃ kṛte śūnyatayā vadet /
sarvaṃ tasyāparihṛtaṃ samaṃ sādhyena jāyate //8//

8. There being a refutation based on emptiness, were someone to utter a confutation,
for that person all becomes a question-begging nonconfutation.

vyākhyāne ya upālambhaṃ kṛte śūnyatayā vadet /
sarvaṃ tasyānupālabdhaṃ samaṃ sādhyena jāyate //9//

9. There being an explanation based on emptiness, were someone to utter a criticism,
for that person all becomes a question-begging noncriticism.

According to Candrakīrti, the opponent here is someone who thinks the refutation of rūpa skandha can be answered or confuted by asserting the ultimate reality of feeling skandha, etc. The difficulty in this opponent's strategy is precisely that he ignores the lesson of verse 7, that the same reasoning that undermines the ultimate reality of rūpa applies equally well to the other four skandhas. Since the reasoning that undermines the ultimate reality of rūpa applies equally to the other skandhas, it is up to the opponent to show how they might be real; this cannot merely be assumed. To do so is to commit the logical fallacy known as begging the question—merely assuming the point that is in question and so needs to be proven.

This point is important to Madhyamaka methodology. Nowhere does Nāgārjuna give an argument that can be taken as a conclusive proof of emptiness. Instead he refutes specific views of specific opponents who hold that there are non-empty things, things with intrinsic nature. His strategy thus depends on the opponent seeing that the strategy of a particular refutation may be applied to other cases. The opponent who, in the face of a refutation of the existence of rūpa, simply pounds the table, insisting that the reality of feeling and so on shows that there are real skandhas, is failing to meet his obligation as a participant in a philosophical discussion.

5. An Analysis of the Dhātus

THE *dhātu* classification is the last of the three major ways of analyzing reality accepted in Abhidharma. It is commonly given as a list of eighteen kinds: the twelve āyatanas plus the six resulting forms of consciousness. But here it is the variant list of six that is investigated: earth, water, fire, air, space, and consciousness. (See, e.g., M III.237.) The dhātu space is the target of the chapter, but the argument is said to generalize to the other dhātus as well. The argument focuses on the relation between space as an entity and the defining characteristic that makes it be the sort of entity that it is. In outline it proceeds as follows:

- 5.1ab Assertion: Space does not exist prior to its defining characteristic.
- 5.1cd–2 Argument for assertion
- 5.3 Refutation of defining characteristic
- 5.4–5 Consequent refutation of bearer, defining characteristic, and existent entities
- 5.6 Consequent refutation of nonexistent and both-existent-and-nonexistent entities
- 5.7 Summary and generalization to the other dhātus
- 5.8 Soteriological significance of refutation

nākāśaṃ vidyate kiṃcit pūrvam ākāśalakṣaṇāt /
alakṣaṇaṃ prasajyeta syāt pūrvaṃ yadi lakṣaṇāt //1//

1. Space does not at all exist prior to the defining characteristic of space.
If it existed prior to its defining characteristic, it would follow that something exists without defining characteristic.

As a dhātu, space is held by the Ābhidharmika to be ultimately real. This means it must have its own intrinsic nature, which is here called a "defining characteristic" (*lakṣaṇa*). The defining characteristic of space is said to be nonresistance: If there is space between the desk and the wall, then one may put something there without the space resisting. The subject of Nāgārjuna's examination will be the relation between space and its defining characteristic. Since these are said to be related (through the characterizing relation), the question arises how these two things come to be so related. Is it that space, as the bearer of the defining characteristic, is in itself a bare something that is devoid of defining characteristic? On this view the bearer would in itself be a characterless substrate, something that comes to be *space* (that which is nonresistant) through being characterized by the defining characteristic of nonresistance. Nāgārjuna rejects this view on the grounds that it would require there to be something that is devoid of defining characteristic.

alakṣaṇo na kaścic ca bhāvaḥ saṃvidyate kvacit /
asaty alakṣaṇe bhāve kramatāṃ kuha lakṣaṇam //2//

2. Nowhere does there exist any such thing as an existent without defining characteristic.
An existent devoid of defining characteristic being unreal, where would a defining characteristic function?

None of the commentators provides an argument for the claim that there could be no existent devoid of defining characteristic. This is no doubt because it seemed to the Abhidharma opponent perfectly obvious that real things must have their own distinctive natures. But it might seem to us that we can, after all, make sense of the idea of a bare stuff that then takes on the nature it is given by its defining characteristic. When we think this, though, we are covertly attributing a defining characteristic to this bearer: the defining characteristic of "bare-stuffness." This would suggest that the idea of a character-less bearer is actually incoherent.

nālakṣaṇe lakṣaṇasya pravṛttir na salakṣaṇe |
salakṣaṇālakṣaṇābhyāṃ nāpy anyatra pravartate ||3||

3. There is no functioning of the defining characteristic whether the bearer is without defining characteristic or with defining characteristic.
And it does not function anywhere other than where there is or is not a defining characteristic.

The function of a defining characteristic is to characterize its bearer. In the case of space this would mean making it something whose nature is to be nonresistant. Now this function requires that there be a bearer, and that bearer is (prior to the functioning of the defining characteristic) itself either without defining characteristic or with defining characteristic. Since there is no such thing as space that is devoid of defining characteristic, the first possibility is ruled out. Candrakīrti sees two problems with the second:

(1) A defining characteristic would then be superfluous. Since space would already have a nature, why would it need something else to make it be the sort of thing it already is?

(2) An infinite regress results. To explain how nonresistance$_1$ functions to characterize space, we suppose that space already has a defining

characteristic, nonresistance$_2$. But now we can ask the same question about nonresistance$_2$ that we asked about nonresistance$_1$: Does it characterize a bearer that is without defining characteristic or a bearer already with its own defining characteristic? The former has been ruled out. The latter answer means we must supply a nonresistance$_3$. And the regress shows no sign of stopping here.

lakṣaṇāsaṃpravṛttau ca na lakṣyam upapadyate /
lakṣyasyānupapattau ca lakṣaṇasyāpy asaṃbhavaḥ //4//

4. And if there is no function of the defining characteristic, it does not hold that there is a bearer of defining characteristic.
   And if a bearer of defining characteristic does not hold, a defining characteristic is likewise impossible.

tasmān na vidyate lakṣyaṃ lakṣaṇaṃ naiva vidyate /
lakṣyalakṣaṇanirmukto naiva bhāvo 'pi vidyate //5//

5. Therefore neither a bearer of defining characteristic nor a defining characteristic exists.
   And certainly no existent whatsoever occurs devoid of both a bearer of defining characteristic and a defining characteristic.

Space cannot be an ultimately real existent, since we can make sense neither of space as bearer nor of nonresistance as defining characteristic.

avidyamāne bhāve ca kasyābhāvo bhaviṣyati /
bhāvābhāvavidharmā ca bhāvābhāvāv avaiti kaḥ //6//

6. When the existent is not real, with respect to what will there come to be nonexistence?

And existent and nonexistent are contradictory properties;
who cognizes something, whether existent or nonexistent?

To deny that space is an existent is not to affirm that it is nonexistent. To affirm the nonexistence of space, one would need to be able to say what space is. As Buddhapālita puts it, "It would be the nonexistence of what existent?" (P p. 93). And the argument so far has been to the effect that we cannot say what an ultimately real space would be. Moreover, there is no third possibility apart from saying that space is existent and saying that space is nonexistent. So apparently no statement about space could be ultimately true.

Although the commentaries do not mention it, one implication of this is worth pointing out. Opponents of Madhyamaka often claim that its doctrine of emptiness leads to the absurd result that nothing whatsoever exists—"metaphysical nihilism." The argument of the present chapter has been that space is not ultimately real. If this argument can be generalized, then it would seem to lead to the conclusion that no supposed existent can be said to be ultimately real. The objection of metaphysical nihilism seems to be sustained. But metaphysical nihilism is the doctrine that all supposedly existing things are ultimately nonexistent. If the argument of verse 6 is correct, can this be true?

tasmān na bhāvo nābhāvo na lakṣyaṃ nāpi lakṣaṇam /
ākāśam ākāśasamā dhātavaḥ pañca ye 'pare //7//

7. Therefore space is not an existent, not a nonexistent, not a bearer of defining characteristic, nor indeed a defining characteristic.
The other five dhātus are the same as space.

The argument generalizes to the other dhātus—earth, water, fire, air, and consciousness—as well.

astitvaṃ ye tu paśyanti nāstitvaṃ cālpabuddhayaḥ |
bhāvānāṃ te na paśyanti draṣṭavyopaśamaṃ śivam ||8||

8. But those of little intellect who take there to be existence and nonexistence with respect to things,
they do not see the auspicious cessation of what is to be seen.

The *Akutobhayā* explains that by "auspicious cessation" is meant nirvāṇa, which is the cessation of hypostatization. Apparently the conclusion to be drawn from this is that those who seek nirvāṇa should cease hankering after ultimate reality. Note that this is not because our deluded intellects are incapable of grasping the ultimate nature of reality. It seems instead to be because the very idea of an ultimate nature of reality is incoherent.

6. An Analysis of Desire and the One Who Desires

THE SUBJECT of this chapter is the relation between a state, such as desire, and the possessor of that state, its subject, such as the one who desires. It is widely thought that a state cannot exist unless there also exists something that has that state—that there cannot, for instance, be desire unless there is a subject that is the locus of the desire. The question examined here is whether there is any coherent account of the relation between state and subject. By "the one who desires" we ordinarily understand a person. But for the Ābhidharmika, persons are not ultimately real. In verse 10 Nāgārjuna will generalize the argument concerning desire and the one who desires to all dharmas or ultimately real things. So we should understand this as an argument concerning the relation between state and subject in general, with desire and the one who desires serving as mere illustrative examples.

The argument proceeds by looking at all possible temporal relations between subject and state: that subject exists prior to state, that state exists prior to subject, and that subject and state arise simultaneously. The last of these being the commonly accepted view, it receives the greatest attention. The argument against it is based on the assumption that co-occurring entities must be either identical or distinct. The thread of the argument is as follows:

6.1–2ab Refutation of desire on the assumption that desirer exists before the desire and that it exists after the desire

6.2cd Refutation of desirer on the assumption that desire exists before the desirer and that it exists after the desirer

6.3 Assertion: Desirer and desire cannot arise together or co-occur.

6.4–9 Argument for the assertion based on fact that co-occurring entities must be either identical or distinct

6.10 Summary and generalization of argument

rāgād yadi bhavet pūrvaṃ rakto rāgatiraskṛtaḥ |
taṃ pratītya bhaved rāgo rakte rāgo bhavet sati ||1||

1. If the one who desires existed prior to and without desire,
then desire would be dependent on that; there being the one
who desires, desire would then exist.

Either state and subject arise together or one precedes the other. If the subject preceded the state, then they would be distinct, and the state would be dependent on the subject. But it is absurd to suppose that desire could be dependent on something that is itself free of desire, for their natures are contradictory. (Candrakīrti provides the example of an *arhat*, someone who is by nature free of craving.) To suppose there is a subject who goes from being without desire to being with desire, we must conceptually construct an enduring thing with distinct parts, for instance the part that exists before the occurrence of desire and the part that exists when the desire has arisen. So we would no longer be considering something that is ultimately real by Abhidharma standards.

rakte 'sati punā rāgaḥ kuta eva bhaviṣyati |
sati vāsati vā rāge rakte 'py eṣa samaḥ kramaḥ ||2||

2. But how will desire itself come to be if there is none who desires?
Whether the desire exists or not, the analysis with respect to
the one who desires will also go the same way.

To suppose, on the other hand, that desire, something whose occurrence is dependent on a locus of desire, could exist in the absence of a desiring subject is likewise absurd. So says 2ab. In 2cd, according to Candrakīrti, Nāgārjuna is replying to an opponent who points out that so far we've only had an argument against the existence of desire, not against the possessor of desire. The argument was that whether or not the subject exists, desire cannot arise. This does not show that the subject does not exist. And if we can say there is a possessor of desire, we will have to say there is desire as well, so the difficulty will be resolved. Nāgārjuna replies that the same kind of analysis he used against desire in 1–2ab can be turned on the subject; it can be shown that the subject cannot exist whether desire exists or not. For if desire existed prior to the possessor of desire, then desire would occur without a locus, which is absurd. And if there were no desire, how could there come to be one who desires?

sahaiva punar udbhūtir na yuktā rāgaraktayoḥ /
bhavetāṃ rāgaraktau hi nirapekṣau parasparam //3//

3. But moreover it cannot be that desire and the one who desires
arise together;
desire and the one who desires would then be mutually
independent.

So far we have considered the possibility that desire and the one who desires arise successively. Suppose on the other hand it were said that state and subject arise together. This might be thought to ground a relation of mutual or reciprocal causation, wherein each supports the other. But this will turn out to be problematic. The problems begin with the fact that if they are said to arise together, then they must be thought of as two distinct, independently existing things. The reason for this is spelled out in 4ab.

naikatve sahabhāvo 'sti na tenaiva hi tat saha /
pṛthaktve sahabhāvo 'tha kuta eva bhaviṣyati //4//

4. If there is unity [of state and subject] there is no co-occurrence;
   there is not that with which the thing comes together.
   If there is distinctness, how indeed will there be
   co-occurrence?

Co-occurrence (*sahabhāva*) is the existing simultaneously of two things. (It is an important constituent of the causal relation.) But now state and subject must be either identical or distinct. Suppose state and subject were really just one thing (perhaps one that was presented in two different ways). Then we could not say there is co-occurrence between them: It takes two to be concomitant. Nāgārjuna then asserts that co-occurrence is likewise incompatible with there being two distinct things. The reason for this will emerge in verses 5–9.

ekatve sahabhāvaś cet syāt sahāyaṃ vināpi saḥ /
pṛthaktve sahabhāvaś cet syāt sahāyaṃ vināpi saḥ //5//

5. If there were co-occurrence in the case of unity, then that
   would be possible without one of the relata.
   If there were co-occurrence in the case of distinctness, then
   that too would be possible without one of the relata.

Suppose there is the relation of co-occurrence between *x* and *y*. Then either *x* and *y* are really just one thing ("the case of unity") or they are distinct things. If they were one thing, then the co-occurrence of *x* and *y* would really be just the co-occurrence of the one thing *x*. But co-occurrence is a binary relation, a relation between two things. It would be absurd to say that this relation holds between a thing and itself. If on the other hand *x* and *y* were distinct, then it would be possible for each of them to occur separately from the other. And if co-occurrence-with-*y* is really a state of *x*, then when *x* occurs separate from *y*, it should be in the state of co-occurrence-with-*y*, which is absurd.

pṛthaktve sahabhāvaś ca yadi kiṃ rāgaraktayoḥ |
siddhaḥ pṛthakpṛthagbhāvaḥ sahabhāvo yatas tayoḥ ||6||

6. And in the case of distinctness, if there were co-occurrence,
   how would desire and the one who desires
be established as mutually distinct, on the basis of which
   there could be co-occurrence of the two?

Candrakīrti cites the case of a cow and a horse as an example of two things that may co-occur. But these are two distinct things precisely because each may occur independently of the other. Desire and the one who desires do not, he says, occur separately, so they may not be said to co-occur.

siddhaḥ pṛthakpṛthagbhāvo yadi vā rāgaraktayoḥ |
sahabhāvaṃ kim artham tu parikalpayase tayoḥ ||7||

7. Alternatively if the distinctness of desire and the one who
   desires is established,
what would be the point of this co-occurrence that you
   suppose between them?

pṛthag na sidhyatīty evaṃ sahabhāvaṃ vikāṅkṣasi |
sahabhāvaprasiddhyarthaṃ pṛthaktvaṃ bhūya icchasi ||8||

8. Saying that one is not established distinct from the other, you aim at co-occurrence,
 [yet] you posit distinctness for the sake of establishing co-occurrence.

To say that the two are co-occurrent, one must first establish that they are separate, distinct existents. Having done so, however, one has thereby undermined their co-occurrence.

pṛthagbhāvāprasiddheś ca sahabhāvo na sidhyati |
katamasmin pṛthagbhāve sahabhāvaṃ satīcchasi ||9||

9. And if distinctness is not established, co-occurrence is not established.
 If there is distinctness of the two, in which do you posit co-occurrence?

evaṃ raktena rāgasya siddhir na saha nāsaha |
rāgavat sarvadharmāṇāṃ siddhir na saha nāsaha ||10||

10. Thus there is establishing of desire neither together with the one who desires nor apart from the one who desires.
 As with desire, so for all dharmas, there is establishing neither together nor apart.

That is, no coherent account can be given of those features of reality that depend for their occurrence on the occurrence of something else in the way in which desire is thought to depend on the locus in which it occurs. Notice that this does not mean that state and the locus that is its subject are really one. It means instead that wherever we find this relation of dependence, neither of the relata can be thought of as ultimately real.

7. An Analysis of the Conditioned*

All dharmas are said to be conditioned—that is, dependent for their existence on factors other than themselves. As such they are characterized by origination, duration, and cessation. (See AKB 2.46, where it is discussed whether there is a fourth characteristic of aging.) Moreover, their being conditioned is said to itself be an observable phenomenon and as such to also be conditioned (cf. A I.152, S III.37). It was disputed among Ābhidharmikas how to interpret this, but some took it to mean that for each conditioned dharma, there are three more dharmas representing the conditioned dharma's origination, duration, and cessation. The question then arose whether for each of those dharmas there are three additional dharmas. This is the question with which Nāgārjuna will begin his examination. But this leads to the larger question of how we should take the claim that existing things are subject to dependent origination (*pratītya-samutpāda*). Since the doctrine of dependent origination is central to the Buddha's teachings, it might seem problematic for a Buddhist to maintain anything that calls into question the reality of dependent arising.

The greater part of the chapter is taken up with arguments against

*We follow our usual practice of giving the chapter the title found in the LVP edition of *Prasannapadā* (here found also in the *Akutobhayā*), but Ye (2011, 107) corrects this to "An Analysis of Origination, Duration, and Cessation," the title given also by Buddhapālita and Bhāviveka.

the ultimate existence of origination; in the remainder parallel arguments are given against duration and cessation. The examination of origination begins with the point that if it is ultimately real, it must either itself be a conditioned entity or else be unconditioned. Since the first option is the more plausible, a variety of ways of making it work are explored, among them the view that there is the origination of origination and the view that origination is reflexive (originates itself as well as other things). The argument in outline is as follows:

7.1–3 Introduction to the problem
- 7.1: Difficulty 1: Origination is either itself conditioned or not.
- 7.2: Difficulty 2: Origination, duration, and cessation either occur simultaneously or not.
- 7.3: Difficulty 3: Origination is either characterized by origination, duration, and cessation or not; if so then there is an infinite regress; if not then origination will not originate, etc.

7.4–21 Refutation of origination
- 7.4: Opponent: Origination_2 originates origination_1, which in turn originates origination_2.
- 7.5–7: Refutation of opponent's thesis
- 7.8: Opponent: Origination is reflexive, like light that illuminates itself.
- 7.9–12: Refutation of example of light
- 7.13: Refutation of thesis that origination is reflexive
- 7.14–21: Further arguments against origination

7.22–25 Parallel refutations of duration

7.26–32 Parallel refutations of cessation

7.33–34 Conclusion: Absent origination and so on, there can be neither the conditioned nor the unconditioned; origination and so on are illusory appearances.

yadi saṃskṛta utpādas tatra yuktā trilakṣaṇī /
athāsaṃskṛta utpādaḥ kathaṃ saṃskṛtalakṣaṇam //1//

1. If origination is conditioned, then the three characteristics [of origination, duration, and cessation] apply to it.
But if origination is not conditioned, how can it be a characteristic of the conditioned?

Suppose that origination is something that is conditioned. If everything conditioned is characterized by the three characteristics, then origination must itself be subject to origination, duration, and cessation. According to the *Akutobhayā*, this must be rejected since it leads to an infinite regress: The origination of origination will likewise be subject to its own origination, duration, and succession, and so on. Candrakīrti thinks the problem is instead that then what is supposed to be a characteristic of dharmas becomes itself another dharma that is among the things to be characterized by the characteristics of origination and so on. And how can a characteristic characterize itself? (In Candrakīrti's interpretation, the problem of infinite regress will come later, as a result of the opponent's attempts to escape this difficulty.)

If, on the other hand, we suppose that origination is not conditioned, then it would have to be permanent. In that case it would be difficult to also claim that it characterizes those dharmas that are themselves conditioned and thus impermanent.

utpādādyās trayo vyastā nālaṃ lakṣaṇakarmaṇi /
saṃskṛtasya samastāḥ syur ekatra katham ekadā //2//

2. If the three consisting of origination, etc., occurred separately, they would not be able to function as characterizing the conditioned.
If they occurred together, how could they exist in the same place at the same time?

Do the three characteristics occur separately or together when they characterize a conditioned entity? If separately, then origination would occur apart from duration and cessation. So origination would not endure, and neither would it cease and thus make way for duration and cessation. Likewise duration would never originate, etc. Hence the three characteristics would not perform their function of making a conditioned thing impermanent. But if they occurred together, then origination and cessation would exist simultaneously, which is absurd since they have contradictory natures.

utpādasthitibhaṅgānām anyat saṃskṛtalakṣaṇam /
asti ced anavasthaivaṃ nāsti cet te na saṃskṛtāḥ //3//

3. If origination, duration, and cessation possessed another set of characteristics of the conditioned [i.e., origination, etc.], there would be an infinite regress; if not, then they would not be conditioned.

In order to avoid the problem of verse 2, the opponent might introduce the idea that the origination of a conditioned thing itself has an origination (as well as a duration and a cessation). Suppose the origination of a conditioned thing were itself conditioned. As a conditioned thing it would require its own origination, duration, and cessation. But the same would apply to these, etc. So there would be an infinite regress. Suppose on the other hand they were not conditioned. Then they should be eternal. It is precisely because space is unconditioned that it is thought (by some Ābhidharmikas) to be eternal. So the origination of a conditioned thing would go on forever, and likewise its duration and its cessation. And it is difficult to see how something unconditioned and eternal could characterize things that are conditioned and impermanent.

utpādotpāda utpādo mūlotpādasya kevalam /
utpādotpādam utpādo maulo janayate punaḥ //4//

4. [Opponent:] The origination of origination is only the origination of the primary origination;
that primary origination in turn brings about the origination of origination.

The opponent introduces a distinction between the primary (*maula*) origination, which is the origination of a dharma, and the origination of origination, which is what originates the primary origination. In order to avoid the infinite regress that arises when we ask (as in verse 3) what originates the origination of the origination, the opponent claims this is originated by the primary origination.

utpādotpāda utpādo mūlotpādasya te yadi /
maulenājanitas taṃ te sa kathaṃ janayiṣyati //5//

5. [Reply:] If, according to you, origination is what originates the primary origination,
then how, on your account, will this, which is not produced by the primary origination, produce that [primary origination]?

How, in other words, does the origination of origination itself originate? If it is what originates the primary origination, then as a conditioned thing it must also originate. How does that come about? Suppose the opponent answers that the origination of origination is originated by the primary origination. Nāgārjuna responds:

sa te maulena janito maulaṃ janayate yadi /
maulaḥ sa tenājanitas tam utpādayate katham //6//

6. If, as you say, that which is produced by the primary origination produces the primary,
the primary is not produced by that [origination of origination]; how will it originate that?

The question here is how the origination of origination, which supposedly originates the primary origination, itself originates. Since the origination of origination originates the primary, it cannot be that the primary originates the origination of origination; that would be circular. Candrakīrti explains, "If the origination known as the origination of origination, which is produced by the primary origination, produces the primary origination, how will that primary origination produced by the origination of origination, being [as yet] unreal, produce the origination of origination? It is thus incorrect to say that an existing origination of origination produced by the primary origination produces the primary. And thus because there is no mutual reciprocal causation, there is indeed the absurd consequence of infinite regress; there is no origination" (LVP p. 150).

ayam utpadyamānas te kāmam utpādayed imam /
yadīmam utpādayitum ajātaḥ śaknuyād ayam //7//

7. Granted you may say that this [primary origination] while
 undergoing origination would bring about the origination
 of that [origination of origination] on its own,
if you said that this, though unproduced, was capable of
 bringing about the origination of that.

Here the difficulty in mutual reciprocal causation is spelled out. If the primary origination originated the origination of origination while the origination of origination was originating the primary origination, then the primary origination would have to be able to originate something before it came into existence. And that is clearly impossible. The opponent will thus proceed to try a new tack.

pradīpaḥ svaparātmānau saṃprakāśayate yathā /
utpādaḥ svaparātmānāv ubhāv utpādayet tathā //8//

8. [Opponent:] As a light illuminates both itself and what is other,
so origination brings about the origination of both itself and
what is other.

The opponent now abandons the idea that there is an origination of origination in addition to the primary origination. In its place the opponent introduces the hypothesis that just as light illuminates itself as well as other things, so origination originates both itself and the distinct dharma that is undergoing origination. Like the example of fire that supposedly burns itself, the example of the light is another alleged counterexample to the irreflexivity principle. The ensuing discussion of the hypothesis will be more thorough than the discussion in chapter 3, verse 3, of the example of fire. Nāgārjuna gives a similar treatment of the claim that light illuminates itself at *Vigrahavyāvartanī*, vv. 34–39.

pradīpe nāndhakāro 'sti yatra cāsau pratiṣṭhitaḥ |
kiṃ prakāśayate dīpaḥ prakāśo hi tamovadhaḥ ||9||

9. [Reply:] There is no darkness either in the light or where it is
placed.
What does the light illuminate? Illumination is in fact the
destruction of darkness.

To illuminate is to destroy darkness. There is no darkness in the light itself or in the place it occupies. So a light cannot be said to be illuminated.

katham utpadyamānena pradīpena tamo hatam |
notpadyamāno hi tamaḥ pradīpaḥ prāpnute yadā ||10||

10. How is darkness destroyed by a light that is originating,
when an originating light does not come in contact with
darkness?

Perhaps it will be said that light destroys darkness when it originates. And when it originates there is darkness where the light is. So the problem pointed out in verse 9 is overcome. Nāgārjuna responds that there is likewise no darkness when a light is originating. As Buddhapālita, Bhāviveka, and Candrakīrti all explain, light and darkness are mutually contradictory qualities, so one cannot occur where the other is. But for one thing to destroy another, the two things must come in contact. And contact requires that the two occur in the same place.

aprāpyaiva pradīpena yadi vā nihataṃ tamaḥ /
ihasthaḥ sarvalokasthaṃ sa tamo nihaniṣyati //11//

11. Or if darkness is destroyed by a light that has not yet come in contact with it,
then [the light] that is here will destroy darkness located throughout the world.

The only remaining option is that light need not come in contact with darkness to destroy it. This would explain how light could destroy darkness while it is originating. But it has the absurd consequence that a single light would illuminate the entire world. The *Akutobhayā*: "For the noncontact is the same. What difference is there between destroying darkness situated where the light is and destroying darkness situated throughout the world?" (P p. 120).

pradīpaḥ svaparātmānau saṃprakāśayate yadi /
tamo 'pi svaparātmānau chādayiṣyaty asaṃśayam //12//

12. If light illuminates both itself and what is other,
then darkness as well will certainly conceal both itself and what is other.

Does darkness conceal itself as well as other things? Then darkness could never be perceived. But if we say that light illuminates itself, we seem committed to saying this as well.

anutpanno 'yam utpādaḥ svātmānaṃ janayet katham /
athotpanno janayate jāte kiṃ janyate punaḥ //13//

13. How could this origination that is not yet originated produce itself?
If you say it produces [itself] having already been originated, how can it be produced for the second time?

In order for something to produce, it must already exist. But to exist it must already have been originated. So in order to originate itself, it would have to bring itself into existence after it has already been brought into existence. Hence "be produced for the second time."

The focus now shifts to the claim that origination brings about the arising of what is distinct from itself. The question is raised whether origination does this to something already originated, something not yet originated, or something undergoing origination:

notpadyamānaṃ notpannaṃ nānutpannaṃ kathaṃcana /
utpadyate tad vyākhyātaṃ gamyamānagatāgataiḥ //14//

14. In no way whatsoever is the presently originating, the already originated, or the not yet originated
originated, just as was expounded [in chapter 2] about the presently being traversed, the traversed, and the not yet traversed.

The argument of the three times, as developed in chapter 2, will apply here as well. Origination cannot happen to what is already originated nor to what is not yet originated, and there is no third state of presently originating.

According to Candrakīrti, the opponent's next move is to introduce an act of origination. (Cf. 2.2, where the opponent made a similar move.) "It is indeed the presently originating that is originated, not the originated and not the not yet originated. What you believe, that the presently originating is not originated because it is not possible for there to be a presently originating distinct from the originated and the not yet originated, that is wrong. Since the presently originating is designated in connection with the act of originating, where there is the act of origination, because the establishment of presently originating is dependent on the act of origination, it is the presently originating that is originated, and origination originates that presently originating" (LVP p. 158). Nāgārjuna replies:

utpadyamānam utpattāv idaṃ na kramate yadā |
katham utpadyamānaṃ tu pratītyotpattim ucyate ||15||

15. As the presently originating does not succeed an act of origination,
why is presently originating nonetheless said to depend on an act of origination?

As Buddhapālita understands it, the argument is that for this strategy to work, it must be said how presently originating—for example, of a cloth—is to be individuated when it is dependent on an act of origination. The difficulty is that there is no distinction to be drawn between the presently originating of the cloth and the act of origination. The one is never found without the other. So the presently originating of the cloth cannot be said to depend on the act of origination. And in that case we are back to the difficulty of verse 14: The presently originating of the cloth cannot be found, so it cannot be said to be what is originated.

At this point, the commentators agree, the opponent raises a pointed objection: If you deny origination, you must deny dependent origination, the doctrine at the heart of the Buddha's teachings: "When this exists, that exists; when this arises, that arises. When this does not exist, that does not exist; when this ceases, that ceases" (M III.63). The Mādhyamika is, in short, a nihilist. Nāgārjuna then replies:

pratītya yad yad bhavati tat tac chāntaṃ svabhāvataḥ /
tasmād utpadyamānaṃ ca śāntam utpattir eva ca //16//

16. Whatever exists in dependence, that is free of intrinsic nature.
Hence the presently originating is free [of intrinsic nature], as
is the act of origination itself as well.

Candrakīrti takes Nāgārjuna to be turning the tables on the opponent—showing that it is the opponent, not the Mādhyamika, whose views are at odds with the Buddha's teaching of dependent origination. For it is agreed that what is ultimately real must have intrinsic nature: "A real entity has intrinsic nature, it invariably possesses its own intrinsic nature by means of its own essence. Because it is real, it depends on nothing else, nor is it originated" (LVP p. 160). But this means that what is ultimately real cannot be dependently originated. And presently originating and an act of origination would have to originate in dependence on other things. So it is incompatible with the Buddha's teaching of dependent origination to claim that presently originating and the act of origination are ultimately real.

The Mādhyamika holds that the teaching of dependent origination should be understood in two ways. Understood as a conventional truth, it applies to such things as the pot and the cloth, which arise in dependence on causes and conditions. Understood as an ultimate truth, however, it is the teaching that no ultimately real things ever arise. (See 1.1; also 24.18, where it is asserted that anything dependently originated must be empty.) The opponent has grasped only the conventional meaning of dependent origination and has failed to appreciate the deeper truth of emptiness, the truth that all things are "free of intrinsic nature."

yadi kaścid anutpanno bhāvaḥ saṃvidyate kvacit /
utpadyeta sa kiṃ tasmin bhāva utpadyate sati //17//

17. If some sort of unoriginated entity existed somewhere,
then it could be originated; but what is originated when that entity already exists?

For some action to be done to some object, the object must already exist. So for the action of origination to be done to something like a pot, the pot must already exist. The hypothesis under consideration here is that the object has a kind of being: It exists as an as-yet-unoriginated entity. (Although the commentaries do not mention a particular school here, the Sarvāstivādins did hold such a view.) But if the pot had this peculiar sort of shadowy future being, then it could not be said to undergo origination, for origination is the coming into existence of something that did not exist before.

utpadyamānam utpādo yadi cotpādayaty ayam /
utpādayet tam utpādam utpādaḥ katamaḥ punaḥ //18//

18. And if this origination originated the presently originating,
then which origination would in turn originate that origination?

anya utpādayaty enaṃ yady utpādo 'navasthitiḥ /
athānutpāda utpannaḥ sarvam utpadyatāṃ tathā //19//

19. If another origination is what originates that [presently originating], there is an infinite regress.
If on the other hand what is originated were without another origination, then everything should likewise be originated.

If the presently originating requires another origination to explain it, then an infinite regress ensues. If on the other hand another origination is not required, then the presently occurring origination is without cause. This means that absolutely anything could be originated at any time.

satas ca tāvad utpattir asataś ca na yujyate |
na sataś cāsataś ceti pūrvam evopapāditam ||20||

20. It is not right to say that there is the act of origination,
    whether of the existent, of the nonexistent,
    or of what both exists and does not exist; this was shown
    earlier.

See the argument of 1.6–7.

nirudhyamānasyotpattir na bhāvasyopapadyate |
yaś cānirudhyamānas tu sa bhāvo nopapadyate ||21||

21. It cannot hold that an entity that is undergoing cessation is
    originating.
    But it also does not hold that there is an entity that does not
    undergo cessation.

The act of origination cannot occur when the entity is undergoing cessation. Undergoing origination and undergoing cessation are, as the *Akutobhayā* says, contradictory properties, so they cannot be properties of one and the same thing. Hence the act of origination would have to take place at a time when cessation is not occurring—that is, a time when the entity is exempt from impermanence. And, says Candrakīrti, there is no such present time distinct from past and future.

The argument now shifts to the second of the three characteristics of conditioned things, duration. Then in verses 26–32, cessation will be the subject of attack.

na sthitabhāvas tiṣṭhaty asthitabhāvo na tiṣṭhati /
na tiṣṭhate tiṣṭhamānaḥ ko 'nutpannaś ca tiṣṭhati //22//

22. An entity that has already endured is not enduring, an entity that has not yet endured is not enduring,
that which is presently enduring is not enduring, and what unoriginated entity is there that is enduring?

An existing thing that, by virtue of existing, has endured is not what the characteristic of duration characterizes, for what role could the characteristic play in something that is already enduring? As Buddhapālita says, to claim that it is through contact with duration that the existing thing endures is to supply a second duration (which threatens to lead to an infinite regress). Something that has not yet endured is likewise not what duration characterizes, since enduring and not yet enduring are contradictory properties. As for the third possibility, there is no such thing as presently enduring: At any given moment either something has endured or it has not. And since every existing thing is impermanent, everything must originate at some time or other. Thus there could not be real things that are unoriginated, and so the unoriginated could not be what endures.

sthitir nirudhyamānasya na bhāvasyopapadyate /
yaś cānirudhyamānas tu sa bhāvo nopapadyate //23//

23. It does not hold that an entity that is presently undergoing cessation is enduring,
but it also does not hold that there is an entity that does not undergo cessation.

jarāmaraṇadharmeṣu sarvabhāveṣu sarvadā /
tiṣṭhanti katame bhāvā ye jarāmaraṇaṃ vinā //24//

24. It being the case that all entities are always characterized by aging and death,
which entities are they that endure without aging and death?

The argument of verses 23–24 parallels that of verse 21. Aging and death may be interpreted as just special cases of cessation.

sthityānyayā sthiteḥ sthānaṃ tayaiva ca na yujyate |
utpādasya yathotpādo nātmanā na parātmanā ||25||

25. It is not right to say that the enduring of duration is by means of another duration or by itself,
just as the origination of origination is not by means of itself or by means of another origination.

See verses 4–13 for the argument against the origination of origination.

nirudhyate nāniruddhaṃ na niruddhaṃ nirudhyate |
tathā nirudhyamānaṃ ca kim ajātaṃ nirudhyate ||26||

26. What is not yet ceased is not undergoing cessation, what has already ceased is not undergoing cessation;
likewise for what is currently undergoing cessation, and what unarisen thing is there that is undergoing cessation?

The argument here is exactly as in verse 22.

sthitasya tāvad bhāvasya nirodho nopapadyate |
nāsthitasyāpi bhāvasya nirodha upapadyate ||27||

27. Just as it does not hold that an entity that is enduring is undergoing cessation,

so it does not hold that an entity that is not enduring [i.e., is nonexistent] is undergoing cessation.

The argument here parallels that of verse 23. Cessation must characterize something that exists and so endures. But duration and destruction are contradictory characteristics.

tayaivāvasthayāvasthā na hi saiva nirudhyate /
anyayāvasthayāvasthā na cānyaiva nirudhyate //28//

28. A given state is not itself made to cease by means of that very state;
nor is it the case that a given state is made to cease by some distinct state.

The first possibility is ruled out by the irreflexivity principle. It can also be seen to be impossible from the fact that it would require the entity in question both to exist (in order to bring something about) and to not exist (since the effect of cessation is nonexistence). The second requires us to suppose that when milk ceases to exist through turning into buttermilk, it is the buttermilk that brings about the cessation of the milk. The difficulty here is that since the milk no longer exists when the buttermilk exists, the latter cannot bring about the cessation of the former.

yadaiva sarvadharmāṇām utpādo nopapadyate /
tadaivaṃ sarvadharmāṇāṃ nirodho nopapadyate //29//

29. Just as it does not hold that there is the origination of any dharma,
so it does not hold that there is the cessation of any dharma either.

Since it was shown earlier that there can be no origination of an ultimately real thing, and it is also true that a real thing would have to be originated, it follows that there can be no ultimately real thing for cessation to characterize.

sataś ca tāvad bhāvasya nirodho nopapadyate |
ekatve na hi bhāvaś ca nābhāvaś copapadyate ||30||

30. On the one hand it does not hold that an entity that exists is undergoing cessation,
for one thing cannot be both existent and nonexistent.

asato 'pi na bhāvasya nirodha upapadyate |
na dvitīyasya śirasaś chedanaṃ vidyate yathā ||31|

31. On the other hand it does not hold that an entity that does not exist is undergoing cessation,
just as there is no cutting off of a second head.

To say that an existent undergoes cessation is to say that an existing entity is nonexistent. What is the entity that both exists and is nonexistent? But it likewise cannot be the nonexistent that ceases. Cessation renders something nonexistent, and it would be superfluous to render nonexistent something that is already nonexistent. To this it could be added that cessation cannot characterize something that is both existent and nonexistent, nor something that is neither existent nor nonexistent.

na svātmanā nirodhasya nirodho na parātmanā |
utpādasya yathotpādo nātmanā na parātmanā ||32||

32. The cessation of cessation does not take place by means of itself, nor does it take place by means of another cessation,

just as the origination of origination is not by means of itself
or by means of another origination.

Cessation must itself cease, lest it continue on forever. What makes it cease? The cessation of the milk cannot be what makes that very cessation cease. But if there is a distinct cessation that makes this cessation cease, we have the start of an infinite regress.

utpādasthitibhaṅgānām asiddher nāsti saṃskṛtam /
saṃskṛtasyāprasiddhau ca kathaṃ setsyaty asaṃskṛtam //33//

33. Since origination, duration, and cessation are not established,
there is nothing that is conditioned.
And in the absence of the establishment of the conditioned,
what unconditioned thing will be established?

The conditioned would have to undergo origination, duration, and cessation. Since none of these three characteristics can be made sense of, we must conclude that the conditioned does not exist. But according to Nāgārjuna, we should not conclude from this argument that what is ultimately real must be unconditioned. For we could say that something is unconditioned only if we could explain how something could be conditioned. And it has been the gist of this chapter that we cannot do that. The reasoning here parallels that of 5.6.

yathā māyā yathā svapno gandharvanagaraṃ yathā /
tathotpādas tathā sthānaṃ tathā bhaṅga udāhṛtam //34//

34. Like an illusion, like a dream, like the city of the gandharvas,
so origination, duration, and cessation are declared to be.

The gandharvas are a class of mythical beings that supposedly live in the sky. "The city of the gandharvas" is a stock example of a mirage or illusion.

8. An Analysis of Object and Agent

By "agent" (*kartṛ/kāraka*) is here meant anything that engages in an activity aimed at some goal. And by "object" (*karman*) is meant the goal of the agent, the entity or state that its activity is intended to bring about. This terminology derives from the theory of *kāraka*s, or grammatical cases, developed by the school of Grammarians. This semantic analysis of the categories expressed by six different case-endings of nouns in a Sanskrit sentence was widely accepted and employed by Indian philosophers. The present use of "agent" is not confined to the instance of persons. Since anything that can be the subject of a verb in the active voice can play the role, it includes all that may be thought of as causally efficacious. (Cf. chapter 6, where the concept of "the one who desires" was likewise not restricted to persons.) So a rock would count as an agent if it performed the action of falling with the object of hitting the ground. The investigation will concern the relation between the agent and the object that it is thought to produce.

The two entities involved in this relation may both have the same ontological status at a given time—both real, both unreal, both real-and-unreal—or they may have different ontological statuses—agent real and object unreal, agent real and object real-and-unreal, and so on. For instance it might be thought that the agent currently exists while the object does not yet exist; this would be a case of real agent and unreal object. All together there are then nine possible ways in which the relation between agent and object might hold. (For another case of this ninefold analysis, see Candrakīrti's *Prasannapadā* comments on 2.24 [LVP p. 108], where goer and going may each have any of the three ontological statuses at a given time.) Nāgārjuna gives arguments against each of these nine possible combinations with respect to agent and object. It is clearly crucial to Nāgārjuna's goal that the nine possibilities he considers are really all the possibilities there might be.

In the following table a number is assigned to each of the nine possible cases, with these numbers used in the outline of the chapter's line of argumentation given below.

AGENT	OBJECT	#
real	real	1
unreal	unreal	2
real-and-unreal	real-and-unreal	3
real	unreal	4
real	real-and-unreal	5
unreal	real	6
unreal	real-and-unreal	7
real-and-unreal	real	8
real-and-unreal	unreal	9

8.1 Assertion: Agent and object cannot (1) both be real, nor can they (2) both be unreal.
8.2 Refutation of (1)
8.3 Refutation of (2)
8.4–6 Unwanted consequences of the result of both being unreal
8.7 Refutation of possibility (3) that agent and object are both real-and-unreal
8.8 Refutation of possibility (4) that agent is real and object unreal and (6) that agent is unreal while object is real

8.9 Refutation of possibility (4) that real agent produces object that is unreal or (5) that is both real and unreal
8.10 Refutation of possibility (6) that unreal agent produces object that is real or (7) that is both real and unreal
8.11 Refutation of possibility (8) that a both-real-and-unreal agent produces an object that is real or (9) that is unreal
8.12 Reply to implicit objection that Mādhyamika is a nihilist: conventional reality of agent and action
8.13 Soteriological significance of refuting agent and object: applying the refutation to the case of appropriation

sadbhūtaḥ kārakaḥ karma sadbhūtaṃ na karoty ayam /
kārako nāpy asadbhūtaḥ karmāsadbhūtam īhate //1//

1. A real agent does not bring about a real object;
nor does an unreal agent aim at an unreal object.

Nāgārjuna's strategy will be to first show that agent and object cannot have the same ontological status (both are real, both are unreal, etc.). In this verse he asserts the conclusion he will argue for in verses 2–6: that if both are real or both are unreal, the agent cannot be said to bring about the object.

sadbhūtasya kriyā nāsti karma ca syād akartṛkam /
sadbhūtasya kriyā nāsti kartā ca syād akarmakaḥ //2//

2. There is no activity (*kriyā*) with respect to an agent that is real, [so] the object would be without an agent.
There is no activity with respect to an object that is real, so too the agent would be without an object.

According to Candrakīrti, the arguments for both claims involve denying that there is a second activity (*kriyā*). So the arguments parallel those of 2.3–6. The argument for the first claim is that something that is a really existing agent may be called such only by virtue of there being an activity associated with it, namely the activity of bringing about some object. If it is already an agent, this activity must already have occurred. But if the object also truly exists, there should be an activity that explains how the agent brought it about. This would require a second activity, and it would be unwarranted to supply one in order to make up this deficiency. So the object cannot truly exist.

The argument for the second claim is that a truly existing object may be designated as such only if it is associated with an activity, namely the activity consisting of the production of that object. So if it is already an existing object, that activity must already have occurred. There would then need to be a second activity that explains how the agent (which we are supposing is also presently existing) comes to be an agent. And no such second activity can be supplied. So the agent cannot truly exist.

karoti yady asadbhūto 'sadbhūtaṃ karma kārakaḥ /
ahetukaṃ bhavet karma kartā cāhetuko bhavet //3//

3. If an unreal agent brought about an unreal object,
the object would be without cause and the agent would be
without cause.

Suppose neither the agent nor the object were presently existent. The cause of the object is the productive activity of the agent. And a productive activity cannot exist in something unreal. So the object would then be without cause. And the agent would likewise be uncaused.

hetāv asati kāryaṃ ca karaṇaṃ ca na vidyate /
tadabhāve kriyā kartā kāraṇaṃ ca na vidyate //4//

4. If there is no cause, then the effect and the causal condition do not exist.
In their absence, productive activity, agent, and instrument do not exist.

dharmādharmau na vidyete kriyādīnām asaṃbhave /
dharme cāsaty adharme ca phalaṃ tajjaṃ na vidyate //5//

5. Virtue and vice do not exist if productive activity and so on are not possible.
Virtue and vice not existing, the fruit produced by them does not exist.

phale 'sati na mokṣāya na svargāyopapadyate /
mārgaḥ sarvakriyāṇāṃ ca nairarthakyaṃ prasajyate //6//

6. The fruit not existing, it cannot hold that there are paths to liberation and to heaven.
And there follows the pointlessness of all productive activity.

The results of the argument of verse 3 are applied to the case of karmic causation. According to the doctrine of karma, every action produces a fruit: Morally good actions produce pleasurable fruits, and morally bad actions produce painful fruits. But actions are not possible if there are no agents and productive activity. So if we accept the initial hypothesis, we must conclude that there is no karma. Notice, however, that Nāgārjuna does not accept this conclusion. Here, as in 24.33–37, he is treating the denial of karma as an unacceptable consequence of the opponent's theory.

kārakaḥ sadasadbhūtaḥ sadasat kurute na tat /
parasparaviruddhaṃ hi sac cāsac caikataḥ kutaḥ //7//

7. An agent that is both real and unreal does not bring about an object that is both real and unreal,
for how can the real and the unreal, which are mutually contradictory, be one?

To complete the consideration of the hypothesis that object and agent have the same ontological status, it is necessary to consider the possibility that each of them is both real and unreal. This can be taken to mean that agent and object are no longer nonexistent (i.e., merely future), but not yet fully existent (i.e., presently existing) either. It is easy to rule out this hypothesis. There can be no such thing as what is both existent and nonexistent; the two states are incompatible. So this possibility can be rejected.

satā ca kriyate nāsan nāsatā kriyate ca sat /
kartrā sarve prasajyante doṣās tatra ta eva hi //8//

8. An unreal object is not brought about by a real agent, and neither is a real object brought about by an unreal agent.
In that case all the same difficulties follow that were already indicated.

If it were said that some existing thing is the agent of an object that does not yet exist, there would be the difficulty pointed out in 2ab. If it were said that an existing object is produced by an agent that does not now exist, there would be the problem pointed out in 4ab.

nāsadbhūtaṃ na sadbhūtaḥ sadasadbhūtam eva vā /
karoti kārakaḥ karma pūrvoktair eva hetubhiḥ //9//

9. A real agent does not bring about an unreal object, and neither does it bring about an object that is both real and unreal, for the reasons given earlier.

When the agent exists but the object does not, the agent cannot be said to be acting. And the object cannot be said to be both existent and nonexistent, since there is no third possibility besides existent and nonexistent.

nāsadbhūto 'pi sadbhūtaṃ sadasadbhūtam eva vā /
karoti kārakaḥ karma pūrvoktair eva hetubhiḥ //10//

10. An unreal agent does not bring about a real object, and neither does it bring about an object that is both real and unreal, for the reasons given earlier.

karoti sadasadbhūto na san nāsac ca kārakaḥ /
karma tat tu vijānīyāt pūrvoktair eva hetubhiḥ //11//

11. An agent that is both real and unreal does not bring about an object that is real or one that is unreal; that should be understood for the reasons given earlier.

As was pointed out in verse 3, an unreal agent can do nothing. Likewise, as we saw in verse 2, a real object cannot be produced. And as was argued in verse 7, there can be no such thing as an agent that is both real and unreal. And so on for the rest of the possibilities under consideration here. This completes the treatment of the hypothesis that agent and action have different ontological status. All the logical possibilities have now been examined, and on none of them can it be said that an agent brings about an object. Candrakīrti summarizes the situation as follows:

> There is no productive activity with respect to what is real, and the doer would be without object—this is why a real object is not brought about. Also an unreal object would be causeless; it would not be brought about for the reason

> given earlier, "If there is no cause, then the effect . . ." Thus the establishment of agent and object through all possible theses of sameness being incorrect, what was said [by the opponent]—that compounded dharmas with compounded natures, such as consciousness and the like, are found due to the real relation of agent and object—is incorrect.

He then introduces the next verse by having the opponent accuse the Mādhyamika of nihilism.

> Here it is said [by the opponent], "Is it believed by you that things do not exist?" [We reply:] Not at all. But for you who believe that existents have intrinsic nature, the refutation of all existents is possible, due to the absence of intrinsic nature with respect to existents. As for us, on the other hand, since all existents are dependently arisen, we do not perceive intrinsic nature, so what is there to be refuted? . . . How can it be established that all existents are, as you say, devoid of intrinsic nature? The worldly delusion being accepted, the establishment of conventionally real entities, which are imagined like the water of a mirage, is through agreement on the basis merely of dependence of this on that and not in any other way. (LVP p. 188)

pratītya kārakaḥ karma taṃ pratītya ca kārakam /
karma pravartate nānyat paśyāmaḥ siddhikāraṇam //12//

12. The agent occurs in dependence on the object, and the object occurs in dependence on the agent; we see no other way to establish them.

It is the opponent who is the (unwitting) nihilist. For the Mādhyamika, on the other hand, agent and object are merely conventionally real, so there is no problem in recognizing their mutual dependence.

evaṃ vidyād upādānaṃ vyutsargād iti karmaṇaḥ |
kartuś ca karmakartṛbhyāṃ śeṣān bhāvān vibhāvayet ||13||

13. Appropriation [and the appropriator] should be known thus
 through the abandonment of object and agent.
 All remaining existents should be considered in accordance
 with object and agent.

The argument generalizes to all existing things. Appropriation is the activity through which constituents of a causal series come to consider other parts of the same causal series as their "own." Its correct analysis is thus of paramount importance for Buddhists. This is the subject of the next chapter.

9. An Analysis of What Is Prior

THE "PRIOR" of this chapter is the person, the subject who is thought to underlie and so exist prior to the various sense faculties and states that persons are thought to possess. While common sense holds there to be such a thing, most Buddhists deny this. Not all, however; the Buddhist school known as Pudgalavāda ("Personalism") claims that such an entity must exist. This chapter is meant to refute this view. It proceeds by investigating the relation between the person and its faculties and states.* The opponent claims not only that the person must exist since the faculties and states cannot exist without a subject but also that the person exists distinct from faculties and states. The refutation turns on the point that if it can exist separately from them, then they can exist separately from it, in which case there is no ground for positing the person as a distinct entity. In outline the argument proceeds as follows:

9.1–2 Statement of opponent's thesis and reason: Person exists prior to faculties and states since they depend on a bearer.

9.3–5 Refutation of opponent's argument: Dependence requires simultaneous existence of the dependent and its basis.

*This is the relation known as "appropriation" (*upādāna*) that is thought to hold between appropriator (the person) and what is to be appropriated (the *skandhas*). The alternative title for the chapter given by Buddhapālita and Bhāviveka is "An Analysis of What Is to be Appropriated and the Appropriator."

9.6 Opponent's response: Person exists prior to faculties and states taken individually, not all together.

9.7–9 Refutation of opponent's response

9.10 Refutation of alternative proposal that person depends for its existence not on its faculties and states but on the material elements of which it is composed

9.11 Consequent refutation of faculties and states, given the refutation of person

9.12 Ultimate conclusion: We should not say that the person either does or does not exist.

darśanaśravaṇādīni vedanādīni cāpy atha /
bhavanti yasya prāg ebhyaḥ so 'stīty eke vadanty uta //1//

1. Some [opponents] say, "Vision, hearing, and the rest [of the sense faculties], as well as feeling and the rest [of the mental constituents]—
that to which they belong exists before them.

kathaṃ hy avidyamānasya darśanādi bhaviṣyati /
bhāvasya tasmāt prāg ebhyaḥ so 'sti bhāvo vyavasthitaḥ //2//

2. "How indeed will vision and so on come to belong to a nonexistent entity?
Hence before they occur there exists an established entity."

Bhāviveka and Candrakīrti identify the "some" of verse 1 as belonging to a Pudgalavāda or "Personalist" school such as the Saṃmitīyas. These Buddhists claim that since appropriation requires an appropriator (just as action requires an agent), there must be some underlying thing to which the sense faculties and the mental constituents belong.

This something they identify as the person (*pudgala*). Since they hold that it must exist prior to vision, feeling, etc., this chapter is called an analysis of "what is prior." The Pudgalavādins claim that the person (*pudgala*) differs from the self (*ātman*) in that (1) the person does not exist ultimately (those who believe in a self hold it to be ultimately real); and (2) the person is named and conceptualized in dependence on the five skandhas (a self would be named and conceptualized on the basis of its own intrinsic nature). For more on their view see SNS as well as AKB 9.

darśanaśravaṇādibhyo vedanādibhya eva ca /
yaḥ prāg vyavasthito bhāvaḥ kena prajñapyate 'tha saḥ //3//

3. [Reply:] But this entity that is established prior to vision, hearing, etc., and feeling, etc., by means of what is it conceived?

If the person is real then it must have some nature on the basis of which it may be named and conceptualized. The first possibility that will be considered here is that its nature is independent of the senses and mental contents that it is said to underlie. This was not the view of the Pudgalavādins. It is being examined here just to make certain that all possibilities are considered.

vināpi darśanādīni yadi cāsau vyavasthitaḥ /
amūny api bhaviṣyanti vinā tena na saṃśayaḥ //4//

4. If this is established even without vision, etc., then no doubt they will exist without this as well.

ajyate kenacit kaścit kiṃcit kenacid ajyate /
kutaḥ kiṃcid vinā kaścit kiṃcit kaṃcid vinā kutaḥ //5//

5. Someone is made manifest by means of something [that manifests it], something [that manifests] is manifested by someone [underlying].
How can someone [be made manifest] without something [that manifests]; how can something be manifested without someone [whom it manifests]?

If the nature of the person is distinct from the natures of the senses and mental contents, then, verse 4 points out, each can exist independently of the other. But the Personalists' argument for the existence of the person was that vision and the rest cannot exist without an underlying entity. They are said to manifest it, and manifestation requires that manifestor and manifested exist simultaneously: The idea of a manifestor is the idea of something evident to the senses that reveals the existence of some non-evident underlying thing the existence of which is required in order to explain the occurrence of the manifestor.

sarvebhyo darśanādibhyaḥ kaścit pūrvo na vidyate /
ajyate darśanādīnām anyena punar anyadā //6//

6. [The opponent:] No one whatsoever exists prior to all of vision and the rest taken together.
By means of one or another of the faculties of vision and the rest [the underlying person] is made manifest at different times.

For the reason given in verses 4–5, the Personalists want to claim that the person is named and conceptualized in dependence on the sense faculties and mental constituents ("vision and the rest"). The question they must then confront is why the person is not a mere conceptual fiction. To answer that they need to show that the person is in some sense independent of vision and the rest. Here they concede that a person could not exist prior to all of vision, etc., taken collectively. But, they point out, the person that exists prior to vision might be named and conceptualized in dependence on hearing, the one that exists prior to hearing might be named and conceptualized in dependence on smell, and so forth.

sarvebhyo darśanādibhyo yadi pūrvo na vidyate /
ekaikasmāt katham pūrvo darśanādeḥ sa vidyate //7//

7. [Reply:] If the person does not exist prior to all of vision and the rest [taken together],
how does the person exist prior to each of vision and the rest taken individually?

As Candrakīrti says, "If there is no forest prior to all the trees, then it likewise does not exist prior to each of them individually" (LVP p. 192). Suppose we plant a tree in a forest. We might then say that the tree is now one part of the forest though the forest existed before that tree. Candrakīrti is saying this cannot be ultimately true. If it were true, then we would have to say that the same forest existed before another of its trees was planted and so on. In the next two verses Nāgārjuna will pose the question whether it is the same forest that exists before and after we add a new tree.

draṣṭā sa eva sa śrotā sa eva yadi vedakaḥ /
ekaikasmād bhavet pūrvam evaṃ caitan na yujyate //8//

8. If precisely the one that is the seer is also the hearer and the feeler,
then it would exist prior to each individually, which is not possible.

The existence of this person prior to each kind of cognition individually is not possible, says Buddhapālita, because it would then follow that the being that exists prior to seeing is the hearer and feeler, like someone who goes out through different (sensory) windows. And as Bhāviveka asks, how can something be both a hearer and a feeler in one and the same instant? To be a hearer, something must hear; to be a smeller, something must smell; etc. And these faculties cannot all be exercised simultaneously. But we can also see the difficulty by asking whether the person who exists prior to seeing is the same as the one that exists prior to hearing. If the person could exist prior to one of the senses, then why not prior to two? But this leads to the hypothesis that the person could exist prior to *all* of vision and the rest, which has already been rejected in verses 3–5.

draṣṭānya eva śrotānyo vedako 'nyaḥ punar yadi /
sati syād draṣṭari śrotā bahutvaṃ cātmanāṃ bhavet //9//

9. But if the seer were itself distinct from the hearer and from the feeler,
then when there was a seer there would also be a hearer, there would be a multiplicity of subjects.

The alternative is to suppose that what exists prior to vision is a hearer, and a smeller, and a taster, etc., each one distinct from the rest. But this is clearly not what the opponent wants, since then it would be one person who sees, another who hears, and so on. In that case persons could never taste what they saw.

The term that we translate as "subject" is *ātman*. It is of course well known that this term is usually translated as "self" and that all Buddhists deny there is such a thing as the self. But here and in the next chapter it is being used to characterize the Pudgalavādin view, and this is why it would be incorrect to translate it as "self" in this context. These Personalists agree with all other Buddhists that there is no such thing as a self understood as a substance that endures through different life-stages and stands in thoroughgoing relation with the skandhas that it owns or possesses. They claim, though, that while there is no self, there must exist something that stands in the relation of appropriation to the skandhas—something that regards the skandhas as its own. Nāgārjuna's use of *ātman* here reflects the fact that in ordinary Sanskrit this word is also used as a reflexive pronoun. To speak of the subject of states like those of seeing and hearing is to speak of something that is aware of its own states. Of course all other Buddhists, including Nāgārjuna, disagree with the Personalists when they claim there must be such a subject and that its existence is compatible with the nonexistence of a self. Still fairness requires that the investigation of their claim be carried out in a neutral language.

darśanaśravaṇādīni vedanādīni cāpy atha /
bhavanti yebhyas teṣv eṣa bhūteṣv api na vidyate //10//

10. Those elements from which seeing, hearing, and the rest, and feeling and the rest,
come into existence, this entity does not exist among them.

According to Candrakīrti, the opponent has pointed out that seeing and the rest arise on the basis of the five skandhas, which are in turn based on the four elements (see 4.1). So perhaps the prior being is named and conceptualized on the basis of the four elements. The difficulty with this proposal, says Bhāviveka, is that if all these things are real (and not just different ways of conceptualizing the four elements), then they must be thought of as existing in succession: First there are the four elements, then the five external sense-field āyatanas (see 4.1), then seeing and the rest. So the person who the opponent supposes to exist prior to seeing and the rest does not exist at the time there is seeing and the rest. The appropriator must exist not only prior to what is appropriated but also simultaneously with the appropriated. And if they exist simultaneously, as do the pot and the atoms in which it inheres, then the appropriator is not ultimately real.

darśanaśravaṇādīni vedanādīni cāpy atha |
na vidyate ced yasya sa na vidyanta imāny api ||11||

11. Seeing, hearing, and the rest, and feeling and the rest—
 if that to which these belong does not exist, surely they too do not exist.

If on the other hand we say that there is nothing to which the senses and the mental contents belong, then it makes no sense to say that these exist either, for they are understood as what is appropriated. We cannot, for instance, understand what it would mean for there to be vision without someone whose vision it was; vision is something that serves a purpose for something else. But notice that this does not license an inference to the existence of a real subject of vision and so on. See the next verse.

prāk ca yo darśanādibhyaḥ sāṃprataṃ cordhvam eva ca |
na vidyate 'sti nāstīti nivṛttās tatra kalpanāḥ ||12||

12. What entity is prior to seeing and the rest, what entity is simultaneous, and what entity comes after—
 these do not exist; the concepts of existence and nonexistence no longer apply there.

We cannot say that there exists the prior entity imagined by the opponent, but we also cannot say that it does not exist (see v. 11). Nāgārjuna thinks it goes without saying that there is no third possibility here: that this prior entity somehow both exists and does not exist. As for the possibility that they might be simultaneous, this is refuted by the fact that ultimately real things existing simultaneously cannot be in a relation of dependency. (Recall that the opponent claims this entity is named and conceptualized in dependence on seeing and the rest and that they exist in dependence on it.) The same difficulty rules out the possibility that the entity exists after vision and the rest do.

Notice the care with which Nāgārjuna states the conclusion of the chapter: "The concepts of existence and nonexistence no longer apply there." We think that either the subject of vision does exist or it does not. Nāgārjuna is telling us that neither thought is well formed.

10. An Analysis of Fire and Fuel

THE LAST TWO chapters have shown difficulties with the notion of an appropriator, a notion that the Pudgalavādins rely on to establish their theory that there is a person who appropriates the five skandhas, karma, and the like. Here the opponent proposes a new analogy to explain how appropriator and what it appropriates can be in a relation of mutual dependence and yet both be ultimately real. The analogy is the example of fire and fuel. (See AKB 9 for another discussion of this analogy.) As Candrakīrti explains the example, fire is dependent on fuel (since there is no fire without fuel), but fire is ultimately real (since it has the intrinsic nature of heat). Yet fuel, while also being real in its own right, is composed of the four elements and so depends on the fire element.

10.1ab	Refutation of possibility that fire is identical with fuel
10.1cd–5	Refutation of possibility that fire is distinct from fuel
10.6	Opponent proposes alternative way of understanding the fire-fuel relation.
10.7	Refutation of this proposal
10.8–10	Refutation of mutual dependence of fire and fuel
10.11	Refutation of dependence of fire on fuel based on the problem of the three times
10.12	Conclusion: Fire is neither dependent on nor independent of fuel; fuel is neither dependent on nor independent of fire.

10.13ab Fire does not arise from itself or from another.
10.13cd Fuel is not burned in any of the three times.
10.14 Summary using fivefold examination: Fire is not identical with fuel, is not distinct from fuel, does not possess fuel, does not have fuel as locus, is not locus of fuel.
10.15 Generalization to case of person and the appropriated
10.16 Conclusion: Person and the appropriated can be neither identical nor distinct.

yadīndhanaṃ sa ced agnir ekatvaṃ kartṛkarmaṇoḥ |
anyaś ced indhanād agnir indhanād apy ṛte bhavet ||1||

1. If the fuel were identical with the fire, then agent and object would be one.
   If fire were distinct from fuel, then there would be fire without fuel.

nityapradīpta eva syād apradīpanahetukaḥ |
punarārambhavaiyarthyam evaṃ cākarmakaḥ sati ||2||

2. Fire would be always alight; it would be without a cause of lighting.
   A second beginning is pointless, and if it were so it would be devoid of object.

If fire and fuel are ultimately real, then they must be either identical or distinct; either the fire is really nothing but fuel, or it is a separately existing thing. The first hypothesis must be rejected on the grounds that it makes the agent (that which does the burning) and the object (that which is burned) one and the same thing. This is absurd, for there is a difference between a potter and a pot, between the forester who chops wood and the wood that is chopped.

If fire were a separately existing thing, however, then it would be possible for fire to exist apart from any fuel. This would mean (1) that fire could continue to exist after the fuel had been exhausted, so it would always stay alight. This would also mean (2) that there can be no such thing as lighting or starting a fire. And this would (3) make pointless any attempt to start a fire by finding fuel, since that would be trying to begin something that has already begun. Moreover, (4) fire would be devoid of an object, something on which its activity is exercised. Points 1–3 are all made explicit in the next verse.

paratra nirapekṣatvād apradīpanahetukaḥ /
punarārambhavaiyarthyaṃ nityadīptaḥ prasajyate //3//

3. Because it is not dependent on another, it is without a cause of lighting.
   It being permanently alight, it would follow that restarting is pointless.

Fire that is not dependent on something else for its existence would not require anything in order to come to be lit. In that case it would always be lit, and so the action of lighting a fire could not bring it about that a previously nonexistent fire came into existence. Since we know that there is such a thing as starting a fire, these consequences are quite absurd, and the hypothesis that fire is quite distinct from fuel must be rejected.

tatraitat syād idhyamānam indhanaṃ bhavatīti cet /
kenedhyatām indhanaṃ tat tāvanmātram idaṃ yadā //4//

4. If you were then to say, "Fuel is that which is being burned," then by what [distinct entity] is that fuel to be burned when it is [fuel] only as long as it is being burned?

The opponent claims that fuel and fire can still be independent provided we define fuel as that which is burned by fire. Presumably then fire can be said to be distinct from fuel and yet dependent on it. The point of this verse is that if fuel is by definition what is burned by fire, then fuel can be said to exist only when there is fire. So fuel is not independent of fire after all, and the difficulty pointed out in verse 1 will recur.

anyo na prāpsyate 'prāpto na dhakṣyaty adahan punaḥ /
na nirvāsyaty anirvāṇaḥ sthāsyate vā svaliṅgavān //5//

5. If fire is other than fuel, it will not touch [fuel]; not having touched, it will not burn it up; and if it does not burn it up,
it will not go out. If it will not go out, then it will endure precisely as something with its own mark.

"With its own mark" means having an intrinsic nature. The argument, according to Candrakīrti, is that just as light does not destroy darkness that it has not reached or come in contact with (see 7.10–11), so fire that is distinct from fuel will not touch fuel, will not burn it, and so will not exhaust it. This in turn means that fire will not go out, since exhausting its fuel is the cause of a fire's going out. It will endure as something whose nature it is to be alight. To this the opponent responds in the next verse.

anya evendhanād agnir indhanaṃ prāpnuyād yadi /
strī saṃprāpnoti puruṣaṃ puruṣaś ca striyaṃ yathā //6//

6. [Objection:] Fire could touch fuel even though distinct from fuel,
just as a woman touches a man, and a man touches a woman.

anya evendhanād agnir prāpnuyāt kāmam indhanam |
agnīndhane yadi syātām anyonyena tiraskṛte ||7||

7. [Reply:] Fire, being distinct from fuel, would surely be able to touch fuel
if fire and fuel were mutually independent.

The example of a woman and a man is put forward by the opponent to show that two distinct things can come into something like the relation of mutual interaction found in the case of fire and fuel. The difficulty with this example is that we know the man and the woman can exist separately. But we never see fire that is not in contact with fuel. And as for fuel, while it may seem to exist separately, it is called fuel only by virtue of its relation to fire; we see fuel as something that is potentially fire.

The term that we translate as "touch," *pra+√āp*, actually means "to reach," and by extension "to obtain." There is a kind of play on words involved in the opponent's example of the man and the woman, since when someone is said to obtain another in marriage, there is physical contact between the two. This is why we have chosen to use "touch," since this preserves the equivocation: "Touch" can be used to mean either coming into physical contact or being intimate.

The opponent concedes that the case of fire and fuel is indeed different from that of woman and man. Fire and fuel are mutually dependent in the sense that each depends for its existence on that of the other. This is not true of the woman and man who enter into a relationship. But why, the opponent asks, can't fire and fuel still have their own intrinsic natures? After all, if they are in a relationship of mutual dependence they must exist, for there can be no relation of mutual dependence between unreal things like the son and daughter of a barren woman. The answer is given in the next three verses.

yadīndhanam apekṣyāgnir apekṣyāgniṃ yadīndhanam /
katarat pūrvaniṣpannaṃ yad apekṣyāgnir indhanam //8//

8. If fire depends on fuel and fuel depends on fire,
which of the two is arisen first, fuel or the fire that is dependent on that?

The argument against mutual dependence of fire and fuel involves investigating the question of whether they exist simultaneously or else in succession. Suppose they exist in succession, and it is fuel that exists first. Candrakīrti says there would follow the absurd consequences that fuel could exist unlit and things like grass would all count as fuel. These consequences might not strike us as absurd. Buddhapālita says we must understand the dependence of fuel on fire as conceptual. By this he seems to mean that we see something as fuel only because we anticipate the arising of fire. But this would seem to leave open the possibility that fuel might exist in the unlit state. What Buddhapālita's comment brings out, however, is that when we think of fuel as something that can exist both before the fire and also when there is fire, this "fuel" is something we have conceptually constructed. Anything that could exist in either the unlit state or the lit state must be made of parts. So if by "fuel" we mean something ultimately real, and fuel is related to fire, fuel could only exist when there is fire.

yadīndhanam apekṣyāgnir agneḥ siddhasya sādhanam /
evaṃ satīndhanaṃ cāpi bhaviṣyati niragnikam //9//

9. If fire is dependent on fuel, then there is the establishing of an already established fire.
If so then also fuel would come to be without relation to fire.

Candrakīrti explains the argument of 9ab as follows. Suppose that fuel exists before fire and fire is dependent on fuel. But fire cannot be dependent on fuel if fire does not exist. So fire must already exist. But to say fire depends on fuel is to say that it is established by fuel. And if it already exists when fuel exists, then fuel's establishing fire would be the establishing of something that is already established—that is, already exists. The argument of 9cd is that fuel must likewise exist in order to be dependent on fire. But a fuel that already exists when fire does cannot be dependent on that fire.

The expression that we translate as "establishing of what is already established," *siddhasya sādhana*, is also the name of a fallacy in Indian logic: the proving of something that is already accepted as proven. Here, as elsewhere in MMK, Nāgārjuna is using the term "establish" (*siddhi*) to mean not "prove" but rather "bring about." But it seems likely that he chose the expression he uses here with its other logical use in mind as well.

The opponent now agrees that mutual dependence is incompatible with one of the pair existing before the other. But why not say that the two things arise simultaneously, each in dependence on the other?

yo 'pekṣya sidhyate bhāvas tam evāpekṣya sidhyati /
yadi yo 'pekṣitavyaḥ sa sidhyatāṃ kam apekṣya kaḥ //10//

10. If an entity *x* is established in dependence [on something else *y*], and in dependence on that very entity *x* there is established that *y* on which *x*'s establishment depends, then what is dependent on what?

If fire truly depends on fuel, then fuel must first exist before there can be fire. But if fuel in turn depends on fire, it cannot exist prior to fire. The mutual dependence that the opponent claims to hold between fire and fuel (or between person and skandhas) appears to be incoherent.

yo 'pekṣya sidhyate bhāvaḥ so 'siddho 'pekṣate katham /
athāpy apekṣate siddhas tv apekṣāsya na yujyate //11//

11. The entity that is established in dependence [on something else], how does it, before being established, depend [on that]?
But if it is something established that is dependent [on something else], it is not right to say that it depends [on something else].

What is it that is established in dependence on something else? Before something is brought into existence it cannot be said to be dependent on something else. But if it already exists, how can it be called dependent? For it to be dependent is for it to stand in need of something else for its existence.

apekṣyendhanam agnir na nānapekṣyāgnir indhanam /
apekṣyendhanam agniṃ na nānapekṣyāgnim indhanam //12//

12. Fire is not dependent on fuel; fire is not independent of fuel.
Fuel is not dependent on fire; fuel is not independent of fire.

This summarizes the reasoning so far. Bhāviveka is careful to point out that each of the four possibilities (fire is dependent on fuel, etc.) has been negated. He thereby calls attention to the fact that nothing is being affirmed about fire, fuel, or their relation. The point has been merely to rule out all the statements we might think are ultimately true concerning the fire and fuel. This might also be expressed by saying, "We cannot say that fire is dependent on fuel, . . ."

āgacchaty anyato nāgnir indhane 'gnir na vidyate /
atrendhane śeṣam uktaṃ gamyamānagatāgataiḥ //13//

13. Fire does not come from something else; fire is not found in fuel.

> As for fuel, the same can be said of it as was said of the presently being traversed, the traversed, and the not yet traversed.

In 13ab, Nāgārjuna returns to the two views of causation discussed earlier, *asatkāryavāda*, the view that the effect arises from something else (that cause and effect are distinct things), and *satkāryavāda*, the view that the effect arises from itself insofar as it already exists in unmanifest form in the cause (see 1.1–2). The difficulty with the first view as applied to the case of fire and fuel is that then fire would be uncaused. To say that fire exists distinct from fuel is to say that fire can exist without fuel.

But the second view, discussed in 13b, might seem more promising. The opponent claims there is fire already in the fuel but in unmanifest form. But under the right circumstances, such as rubbing two pieces of fuel together, this fire can be made manifest. As Candrakīrti represents it, the argument against this hypothesis is simple. Manifestation is said to be an effect of the rubbing. As an effect, does it exist in its cause or not? If not, then the *satkāryavāda* hypothesis has been abandoned. This means that the opponent, like all *asatkāryavādin*s, now owes us an explanation of why the rubbing produces manifestation of fire and not some other effect. If it does exist in its cause, then it must be in unmanifest form. What then makes this manifestation become manifest? This is the start of an infinite regress.

In 13cd, Nāgārjuna claims that the logic of the three-times argument against going (see 2.1) also applies to the fuel considered as that which is burned. Candrakīrti provides a verse to explain:

> The already burned is not what is being burned up; the not yet burned is not what is being burned up;
> the presently being burned that is distinct from the burned and the not yet burned is not what is being burned up.

As usual, the third option is rejected on the grounds that there is no third time between past and future in which the activity of being burned up can take place.

indhanaṃ punar agnir na nāgnir anyatra cendhanāt |
nāgnir indhanavān nāgnāv indhanāni na teṣu saḥ ||14||

14. Again, fire is not fuel, fire is not elsewhere than where fuel is,
fire does not possess fuel, fuel is not in fire, and fire is not in fuel.

This verse summarizes the results of the chapter using the device of the fivefold examination, which is elsewhere used to consider the relation between the person and the skandhas (e.g., at 16.2, 22.1, and MA 6.150). Two things *x* and *y* might be (1) identical, (2) distinct, (3) *x* might possess *y*, (4) *y* might have *x* as its locus, or (5) *x* might have *y* as its locus. As the commentators explain, (1) fire is not fuel because this would lead to the problem of identifying agent and action discussed in verse 1ab. Fire is not (2) distinct from fuel and located elsewhere, as this leads to the difficulty of fire's being independent that is discussed in verses 1cd–4. If (3) fire possesses fuel, this is either (a) as two distinct things, like the cow and its owner, or (b) as one and the same thing, like the chariot and its parts. Option 3a is ruled out by the fact that fire never appears distinct from fuel, while 3b would mean that fire is not ultimately real. Theses (4) and (5) are both ruled out by the fact that they require fire and fuel to be distinct, which has been shown to be impossible.

agnīndhanābhyāṃ vyākhyāta ātmopādānayoḥ kramaḥ |
sarvo niravaśeṣeṇa sārdhaṃ ghaṭapaṭādibhiḥ ||15||

15. All ways without remainder of explaining subject and the
appropriated, along with the pot, the cloth, and the like,
are to be understood in terms of fire and fuel.

Recall that the Pudgalavādins introduced the fire-fuel example as a way of understanding their claim that the person (*pudgala*) is the subject that appropriates the skandhas. Nāgārjuna says that since the fire-fuel example has been refuted, the Pudgalavādin claim about the person as appropriator has likewise been refuted. The same analysis also applies to such examples as the relation between pot and clay, cloth and threads, and so forth.

On the use of the term "subject" here see the comments on 9.9. The term we here translate as "the appropriated" is *upādāna*, which is commonly rendered "appropriation." As this term is used in the twelvefold chain of dependent origination, it means the act of appropriation—coming to consider certain skandhas in a causal series to be "me" or "mine." But in the present context it is used to refer to what are elsewhere called the *upādāna* skandhas, those elements that are appropriated—that is, considered to be "me" or "mine."

It is also worth noting that the same word is widely used to denote what Western philosophers call the material cause of an object, that out of which the object is composed. So for instance the clay counts as the *upādāna*-cause of the pot, the threads as the *upādāna*-cause of the cloth. Of course most Buddhists would deny that the cloth exists over and above the threads as anything more than a conceptual construction. But the Pudgalavādins claim that in addition to the *upādāna* skandhas, there is the subject or person that appropriates them.

ātmanaś ca satattvaṃ ye bhāvānāṃ ca pṛthak pṛthak /
nirdiśanti na tān manye śāsanasyārthakovidān //16//

16. They are not considered by us to be wise instructors in the teachings of the Buddha who describe the subject and existents [i.e., the appropriated] in terms of identity and difference.

Recall that the Pudgalavādin introduced the fire-fuel example in order to illustrate just how the relation of person as appropriator to the appropriated skandhas might work. Investigation has revealed that it cannot be ultimately true that fire and fuel stand in anything like the appropriator-appropriated relation, whether they are identical or distinct. Just as fire and fuel cannot be said to be either identical or distinct, so the appropriating subject and the existing states that are to be appropriated, such as vision and feeling, cannot be described as identical or distinct either.

11. An Analysis of the Prior and Posterior Parts (of Saṃsāra)

SAṂSĀRA, the cycle of rebirth, is said by the Buddha to be without a discernible prior limit or beginning at S II.178ff. It is unclear whether this means that the series of lives actually has no beginning (has gone on from all past eternity) or just that we could never determine that any past life is the first. (It might be that I can remember no life earlier than life *n* simply due to failure of memory.) Nāgārjuna seems to be operating with the first way of understanding this claim: My present life is just the latest in a series that has no beginning. Presumably this is because whatever was posited as the beginning of the series would be posited as itself without cause, and it is assumed that everything conditioned (like birth) has a cause, so it makes no sense to suppose there could be a first life in the series of lives.

This declaration of the Buddha's is here taken to mean that saṃsāra is also without end. This is somewhat puzzling, since nirvāṇa is said to be an end to rebirth for those individuals who attain it. And presumably what bodhisattvas aspire to is bringing about the end of rebirth for all sentient beings, so that the end of saṃsāra is at least possible in principle. What the Buddha actually says in the Saṃyutta Nikāya passages is that saṃsāra has no prior limit, which situation he describes as making saṃsāra "without first and last" (*anavarāgra*). Perhaps all he means by this is that the number of lives one has lived is nondenumerable, which is not the same thing as saying that there is no end to the series of lives one will live. To see this compare the claim that there is no beginning to the series of negative integers (no matter how far back one counts, there is always a larger negative number), which is true, with the claim that there is no end to the series, which is false (the series ends at -1).

Nāgārjuna will use this claim about the prior and posterior phases of rebirth as the starting point for an attack on the notion that within each life there are real stages called birth, aging, and death. This notion was developed by Ābhidharmikas as part of their account of rebirth and suffering. But it also came to be applied to the existence in time of all ultimately real things. Thus the three phases of origination, duration, and cessation (see chapter 7) are sometimes characterized as birth, old age, and death. In verses 7–8 Nāgārjuna will generalize the argument to all existing things.

According to Candrakīrti, however, the target of the present chapter is once again the Pudgalavādin, who takes the existence of saṃsāra to prove that there must be something that is reborn, namely the person. The point of the chapter is, he holds, to show that saṃsāra cannot be ultimately real, that it could at best be conventionally real. In that case the inference from the occurrence of saṃsāra to the existence of a person undergoing rebirth can only be valid conventionally and not ultimately, as the Pudgalavādin wants; all Buddhists agree that it is conventionally true that persons undergo rebirth. The thread of the argument is as follows:

11.1 Saṃsāra is without beginning and end.

11.2 No series lacking beginning and end can have a middle and so cannot constitute a series.

11.3–6 Argument: Birth cannot precede old age and death, cannot come after old age and death, cannot be simultaneous with old age and death, and so cannot make up a series.

11.7–8 Generalization to all cases involving succession

pūrvā prajñāyate koṭir nety uvāca mahāmuniḥ /
saṃsāro 'navarāgro hi nāsyādir nāpi paścimam //1//

1. The Great Sage declared that the prior part of saṃsāra cannot be discerned;
saṃsāra is without first and last—it has no beginning and end.

naivāgraṃ nāvaraṃ yasya tasya madhyaṃ kuto bhavet /
tasmān nātropapadyante pūrvāparasahakramāḥ //2//

2. How could there be a middle of that which lacks a beginning and an end?
Thus here there cannot be series in which one precedes another, one succeeds another, or two occur simultaneously.

The argument of 1–2ab is that something can be in the middle only if it comes between the beginning and the end in a series. Since the series of births is said to lack a first and last, it cannot contain a middle either. The reasoning might be put as follows: The middle is the midpoint in a series, equidistant from the endpoints of the series. But if the series goes on indefinitely in each direction, every point could be said to be equidistant from the ends of the series, which are infinitely far from any point. And if every point in the series could equally be called the midpoint, then none of them really is. So if the series of lives has no prior and posterior limits, the present life cannot be called one life in the series of lives.

Candrakīrti takes this to show that saṃsāra can only be conventionally real, something dependent on useful ways of conceptualizing the world. He compares it to the case of the whirling firebrand, where we see a circle of fire that doesn't really exist. It might be thought that even if the series of lives had no beginning, middle, or end, it could still be true that one life comes between two other lives. So it might seem as if there could still be a real saṃsāra. But this assumes that distinct lives occur earlier and later in time. In order for this to be ultimately true, there must be a real time in which lives can occur. This assumption will be discussed in chapter 19. But if this assumption turns out to be false, then a given life could be part of a series only through its relations to other lives: Its occurring at a particular place in the series is a property that it can only have by borrowing.

From this it is said to follow that there is no sequence of birth (prior), death (posterior), and aging (present) in a single life. The reasoning for this conclusion is given in verses 3–6.

pūrvaṃ jātir yadi bhavej jarāmaraṇam uttaram |
nirjarāmaraṇā jātir bhavej jāyeta cāmṛtaḥ ||3||

3. If birth were prior and old age and death were posterior,
there would be birth without old age and death, and one who
had not died would be born.

If birth were seen as the first in the series, it would be uncaused. But according to the explanation of rebirth given in the doctrine of dependent origination, birth is caused by old age and death.

paścāj jātir yadi bhavej jarāmaraṇam āditaḥ |
ahetukam ajātasya syāj jarāmaraṇaṃ katham ||4||

4. Suppose birth were later and old age and death came first;
how could there be a causeless old age and death of one who is
not born?

If the series began with old age and death (as cause of rebirth), then since these would not themselves have birth as cause, they would be causeless. Since nothing is without cause, this must be ruled out.

na jarāmaraṇaṃ caiva jātiś ca saha yujyate |
mriyeta jāyamānaś ca syāc cāhetukatobhayoḥ ||5||

5. And it is indeed not right that birth be simultaneous with old age and death.
That which is undergoing birth would at the same time die, and both would be without cause.

We cannot say that the two arise together in mutual reciprocal dependence. First, being born and dying are incompatible, like light and dark, so they cannot occur together. Second, if they arose simultaneously, some third thing would be needed to explain their origination. As Candrakīrti puts it, the two horns of a cow, which arise simultaneously, do not mutually cause one another. Since no such cause of both seems to be forthcoming, they would thus appear to originate without cause, which is impossible.

yatra na prabhavanty ete pūrvāparasahakramāḥ |
prapañcayanti tāṃ jātiṃ taj jarāmaraṇaṃ ca kim ||6||

6. Where there cannot be series in which *x* precedes *y*, *x* succeeds *y*, or *x* and *y* occur simultaneously,
how could they hypostatize: "This is birth and that is old age and death"?

The reasoning has been that by the laws of dependent origination (which the opponent Pudgalavādin must accept), no event can count as the absolute beginning of the life of a person. For any event in such a life must have as its cause another prior event in the life of the person. One way to avoid this conclusion is to suppose that there is a first moment in the life of a person that is caused by some prior event that is not an event in the life of a person. (This would be like solving the problem of "the chicken or the egg" by saying that there was an egg that was not caused by a chicken.) But this would mean denying dependent origination as the correct account of saṃsāra. One might still want to claim that birth in this life came before death in this life while aging in this life occurs in between the two. But this assumes that we can speak of this life as coming in the middle of a series of lives that includes past and future lives. And the argument of verse 2 was that this cannot be ultimately true.

The verb that we here translate as "hypostatize," *pra*+√*pañc*, literally means to be prolix or excessively wordy, but in the Buddhist context it comes to have a specialized meaning. In the Nikāyas it is used to mean the tendency to develop a variety of names and concepts whereby one may think and speak about an object that one finds desirable or undesirable (see M I.111–12). This tendency is said to play an important role in bondage to saṃsāra, insofar as it fuels the defilements of desire, aversion, and delusion. Thus it comes to refer to the drawing of conceptual distinctions, but in a way that connotes that there is something problematic about the process in question. In the Madhyamaka context the problem is identified as one of reification: taking what may be perfectly useful conceptual distinctions to indicate ultimately real entities and properties. For an especially clear instance of this usage, see chapter 18.

kāryaṃ ca kāraṇaṃ caiva lakṣyaṃ lakṣaṇam eva ca |
vedanā vedakaś caiva santy arthā ye ca kecana ||7||
pūrvā na vidyate koṭiḥ saṃsārasya na kevalam |
sarveṣām api bhāvānāṃ pūrvā koṭī na vidyate ||8||

7. Effect and cause, as well as the characterized and the
 characteristic,
 feeling and that which feels, and whatever other things
 there are,
8. Not only is there no prior part of saṃsāra,
 there is as well no prior part of any existents.

The analysis of this chapter applies not only to living things but to anything the existence of which involves successive parts. So this supplements the earlier analyses of effect and cause (chapter 1), thing characterized and characteristic (chapter 5), and feeling and that which feels (chapter 9). These all involve succession in time, which cannot be accounted for without positing an absolute beginning, a posit that would be irrational. So there can be no account of how such things come to exist.

12. An Analysis of Suffering

THE SECOND of the Buddha's four noble truths proclaims that suffering originates in dependence on causes. The question raised here is the following. How is suffering related to its cause; is it self-caused, is it caused by something distinct from itself, by both, or by neither? (These four alternatives are discussed by the Buddha at S II.18–19.) Beginning in verse 4 the opponent introduces the hypothesis that it is caused by a person. Then the hypothesis that it is self-caused becomes the view that it is caused by the person who experiences it in this life, while the alternative is that it is caused by someone else in a distinct life. Since all Ābhidharmikas save the Pudgalavādins claim that the person is only conventionally real (is a mere conceptual fiction), this opponent must be a Pudgalavādin. (Pudgalavāda claims it is absurd to hold that there could be suffering without someone who feels it.) The first and second hypotheses (that suffering is self-caused and other-caused) are discussed in verses 2–8, and the third and fourth in verse 9.

12.1 Assertion: Suffering is not self-made, not made by someone else, not both self- and other-made, not without cause.

12.2–4 Refutation of suffering being self-made

12.5–8 Refutation of suffering being made by another

12.9 Refutations of suffering being made by both self and other, and being causeless

12.10 Application of the same strategy to refute external objects

svayaṃ kṛtaṃ parakṛtaṃ dvābhyāṃ kṛtam ahetukam /
duḥkham ity eka icchanti tac ca kāryaṃ na yujyate //1//

1. Some say that suffering is self-made, some that it is made by another, some that it is made by both, and some that it is without cause; but it is not correct to think of suffering as an effect.

The final part of this verse states the conclusion for which Nāgārjuna will argue: that it cannot be ultimately correct to think of suffering as an effect, something that originates either from itself, something else, both, or neither. The argument for this conclusion begins with the next verse.

svayaṃ kṛtaṃ yadi bhavet pratītya na tato bhavet /
skandhān imān amī skandhāḥ saṃbhavanti pratītya hi //2//

2. If it were self-made then it would not be dependent [which is absurd],
for these skandhas originate dependent on those [past] skandhas.

For the doctrine of the five skandhas see 4.1. The five skandhas, when taken as objects of appropriation (i.e., when considered as "me" or "mine"), are said to all be of the nature of suffering. If it is the skandhas that are suffering, then to say that suffering is self-made would be to say that the skandhas are self-made, that they exist independently of all else. But the skandhas are all impermanent: They originate in dependence on causes and conditions, namely prior (equally impermanent) skandhas. So suffering cannot be self-made. If it were it would be eternal, and there would be no path to its cessation.

yady amībhya ime 'nye syur ebhyo vāmī pare yadi |
bhavet parakṛtaṃ duḥkhaṃ parair ebhir amī kṛtāḥ ||3||

3. If these were distinct from those, or those were other than these,
then suffering would be produced by another, for these would be made by those others.

The hypothesis here is that the suffering that is made up of the present skandhas is caused by distinct skandhas in the preceding life. This is a way of understanding what it would mean for suffering to be "made by another," that is, caused by something distinct from that very suffering. According to Candrakīrti, the argument against this is that a causal relation between distinct things is never seen. In support of this he cites a later verse, 18.10. The argument will be that if cause and effect were distinct, then anything could be the cause of anything else, so that we could just as well make a pot from a pail of milk as from a lump of clay. Since there must be some relation between cause and effect, it follows that the suffering consisting in the present skandhas cannot be brought about by distinct earlier skandhas.

At this point the Pudgalavādin objects that by "suffering is self-made" is not meant that a given occurrence of suffering is made by that very suffering itself. What is meant is instead that suffering is made by the very person who suffers; it is not inflicted on that person by some distinct person. Nāgārjuna replies:

svapudgalakṛtaṃ duḥkhaṃ yadi duḥkhaṃ punar vinā |
svapudgalaḥ sa katamo yena duḥkhaṃ svayaṃ kṛtam ||4||

4. If suffering is made by persons themselves, then who is that person without suffering by whom suffering is self-made?

The difficulty is that the Pudgalavādin holds the person to be named and conceptualized in dependence on the skandhas. Since it is in these skandhas that suffering is found, this amounts to saying that the person is named and conceptualized in dependence on suffering. Now when the Pudgalavādin says the person is named and conceptualized in dependence on *x*, this means that the person is never found apart from the occurrence of *x*. And this would seem to mean that the person just consists in *x*. So the Pudgalavādin position is that the person just consists in suffering. If the person just consists in suffering, then the hypothesis that suffering is made by the person herself really means that suffering is self-caused. That hypothesis was rejected in verse 2. Since it is already agreed that suffering cannot be caused by that very suffering, the Pudgalavādin owes us an explanation as to who this person is by whom suffering could be said to be "self-made." Who is this "the person herself" who exists apart from suffering?

The alternative for the Pudgalavādin is to say that suffering is "made by another" in the sense of being made by a distinct person from the person whose suffering it is. This hypothesis is explored in the next four verses.

parapudgalajaṃ duḥkhaṃ yadi yasmai pradīyate /
pareṇa kṛtvā tad duḥkhaṃ sa duḥkhena vinā kutaḥ //5//

5. If suffering [of person *y*] is made by another person *x*, then how, suffering having been made by that other person *x*, would there be this [person *y*] without suffering to whom the suffering is bestowed?

The second alternative is that suffering is made by one person in one life and bestowed on another person in another life. This would appear to make karma unfair, since then one person is being rewarded or punished for the good and bad deeds of someone else. But the problem Nāgārjuna brings up is that suffering can't be bestowed on someone who doesn't exist. In order for it to be possible for *x* to give something to *y*, *y* must exist prior to the giving. And if someone exists before the suffering is bestowed, then that person exists without suffering. This contradicts the Pudgalavāda position that the person is named and conceptualized in dependence on the skandhas, and hence on suffering.

parapudgalajaṃ duḥkhaṃ yadi kaḥ parapudgalaḥ /
vinā duḥkhena yaḥ kṛtvā parasmai prahiṇoti tat //6//

6. If suffering is generated by a distinct person, who is this distinct person
who, while without suffering, having made it, bestows it on another?

Moreover, who is the person who bestows the suffering? Such a one cannot be without suffering. Was the suffering bestowed on the person by another? The difficulty with this is taken up in the next verse.

svayaṃ kṛtasyāprasiddher duḥkhaṃ parakṛtaṃ kutaḥ /
paro hi duḥkhaṃ yat kuryāt tat tasya syāt svayaṃ kṛtam //7//

7. The self-made being unestablished, how can suffering be made by another?
For the suffering the other made would surely be self-made with respect to that other person.

If it is a person in one life who makes the suffering responsible for the suffering of the person in another life, then who makes the suffering responsible for the existence of the former person? If the person is named and conceptualized in dependence on skandhas, and these exist because of prior suffering, then we have the start of an infinite regress. The only way to avoid this infinite regress is to say that the suffering whereby the former person exists is self-made. And this has already been shown to be impossible.

na tāvat svakṛtaṃ duḥkhaṃ na hi tenaiva tat kṛtam /
paro nātmakṛtaś cet syād duḥkhaṃ parakṛtaṃ katham //8//

8. Suffering is, first of all, not self-made, not at all is that made just by that.
If the other could not be self-made, how would suffering be made by the other?

This summarizes the argument against suffering's being either self-made or other-made. As Candrakīrti points out, it is contradictory to suppose that something could produce itself. But without something that is self-caused, how will we ever find that which produces something else?

syād ubhābhyāṃ kṛtaṃ duḥkhaṃ syād ekaikakṛtaṃ yadi /
parākārāsvayaṃkāraṃ duḥkham āhetukaṃ kutaḥ //9/

9. Suffering might be made by both self and other if it were made by one or the other.
And how can there be a suffering not caused by self or other, or that is causeless?

The third hypothesis, that suffering is made both by the sufferer him- or herself and by someone else, inherits the defects of the first and second hypotheses. It also has the difficulty that the terms "self" and "other" are mutually incompatible. The fourth hypothesis would have us believe that suffering arises for no reason whatsoever. As the *Akutobhayā* comments laconically, this would be "a big mistake."

na kevalaṃ hi duḥkhasya cāturvidhyaṃ na vidyate /
bāhyānām api bhāvānāṃ cāturvidhyaṃ na vidyate //10//

10. Not only can suffering not be found under any of the four possibilities,
external objects also cannot be found under any of the four possibilities.

According to Buddhapālita the argument against external objects would go as follows: Matter is either caused by itself, or by something distinct, or by both, or else it is uncaused. But matter cannot be self-caused, since nothing is; matter cannot be caused by something distinct, since that would be self-made; and so forth.

13. An Analysis of the Composite

THE SUBJECT of this chapter is, according to Candrakīrti, what is *saṃskṛta*. Literally this word means "made through a coming together"—that is, composite or compounded—but there is an ambiguity here. This could mean something that is composite in the sense of being made of parts, like a chariot. Or it could mean something that is produced through the coming together of a set of causes and conditions. Buddhists all agree that anything that is composite in the first sense is not ultimately real, that it lacks intrinsic nature. But Ābhidharmikas hold that while dharmas are composite in the second sense, they are not composite in the first sense. And so, they claim, there is no difficulty holding that dharmas are ultimately real. Mādhyamikas disagree. They claim that anything that is composite in the second sense is just as empty as something composite in the first sense. And since everything thought of as real is the product of causes and conditions, this means that everything is without intrinsic nature. This dispute is examined here through the lens of competing interpretations of a remark of the Buddha's.

The importance of this chapter is often overlooked. This may be in part because of the title Candrakīrti assigned to it, "An Analysis of the Composite." The *Akutobhayā* and Bhāviveka call it instead "An Analysis of Reality (*tattva*)," while Buddhapālita calls the chapter "An Analysis of Emptiness." Now since Mādhyamikas hold that everything composite is empty, and that all of reality is characterized by emptiness, these three titles all indicate the same fact. But the importance of that fact might be more evident under a different title. The outline of the chapter's argument is as follows:

13.1–2	Appeal to Buddha's teachings in support of emptiness
13.3–4ab	Objection: Fact of alteration is evidence that not all things are empty in the Madhyamaka sense.
13.4cd–6	Reply: There could be no alteration of non-empty things.
13.7	Diagnosis: Objection wrongly assumes that emptiness must be a property of real things.
13.8	Conclusion: Emptiness removes all metaphysical views, including emptiness itself understood as a metaphysical view; emptiness is itself empty.

tan mṛṣā moṣadharma yad bhagavān ity abhāṣata /
sarve ca moṣadharmāṇaḥ saṃskārās tena te mṛṣā //1//

1. The Blessed One said that whatever is deceptive in nature is vain
and that all composite things being deceptive in nature, they are vain.

The commentators give a full quotation from an unnamed sūtra: "Indeed the ultimate truth, O monks, is that nirvāṇa is not deceptive in nature. Whatever things are composite, those are deceptive in nature and vain." (Close parallels are to be found at M III.245, M II.261, S III.142, and Sn 160–61.) The Buddha's point seems to have been that since anything composite is impermanent, to hanker after it would be useless and foolish. Composite things are deceptive in that they falsely appear as if they might endure. Only nirvāṇa, the one noncomposite thing, is truly worth striving for.

tan mṛṣā moṣadharma yad yadi kiṃ tatra muṣyate |
etat tūktaṃ bhagavatā śūnyatāparidīpakam ||2||

2. If the Buddha's statement "Whatever is deceptive in nature is vain" is true, then what is there about which one is deceived?
This was said by the Blessed One for the illumination of emptiness.

According to the *Akutobhayā*, the question in 2ab is triggered by the fact that to say all composite things are deceptive in nature and vain is to say that they are not ultimately real. But in that case there is nothing that is genuinely deceptive, nothing about which we are genuinely mistaken. So the Buddha must have been getting at some deeper point in saying this. And according to the Mādhyamika this deeper point is that all composite things are empty or devoid of intrinsic nature.

The *Akutobhayā* has the opponent then object that in this sūtra the Buddha is not teaching the emptiness of all dharmas but rather just the emptiness of the person: The person is not ultimately real, something with intrinsic nature, because it is "composite" in the first sense of being a whole made of parts. It is then vain because, being composite in this sense, it must be impermanent. This is an instance of a characteristic dispute between Abhidharma and Mahāyāna: Both agree that there are things that are empty or devoid of intrinsic nature, but they disagree as to what things are empty. The former teaches that the person is devoid of intrinsic nature (*pudgalanairātmya*) and so is not ultimately real, while the latter teaches that all things are empty or devoid of intrinsic nature (*dharmanairātmya*). And as Candrakīrti points out, the opponent rejects the latter interpretation on the grounds that it leads to nihilism, the clearly false view that nothing whatsoever exists. The opponent gives an argument for his own interpretation of the sūtra in verses 3–4ab.

bhāvānāṃ niḥsvabhāvatvam anyathābhāvadarśanāt |
nāsvabhāvaś ca bhāvo 'sti bhāvānāṃ śūnyatā yataḥ ||3||

3. [Objection:] For existents there is lack of intrinsic nature,
because they are seen to alter.
There is no [ultimately real] existent that is without intrinsic
nature, due to the emptiness of existents.

The *Akutobhayā* explains that in 3ab and 3d the "existents" are the person and other things that are composite in the first sense, while the "existents" in 3c are dharmas, things that are only composite in the second sense. In 3ab the opponent is explaining why persons and other composite things must be said to be empty, while in 3c the opponent claims dharmas could not be empty of intrinsic nature. Composite things can be said to be empty because they undergo alteration. Something can change only if one part of it remains the same while another changes. So anything that changes must have parts, and thus must be without its own intrinsic nature. But it could not be true that all things, including dharmas, are empty. For then there wouldn't be anything to be empty. The Mādhyamika and the opponent agree that anything that is empty in the sense of being devoid of intrinsic nature is not ultimately real. But the Mādhyamika claims that all things are empty in this sense. The opponent thinks this is incoherent. Candrakīrti represents the opponent as saying: "There is no existent devoid of intrinsic nature. Emptiness is regarded by you as the attribute of existents. But the bearer of the attribute being nonexistent, there cannot be the attribute dependent on it. Indeed the son of a barren woman being nonexistent, black color cannot be attributed to him. Therefore the intrinsic nature of existents does indeed exist" (LVP p. 240). If anything at all is empty, there must be ultimately real things, and these must be non-empty. The opponent continues the objection in the first half of verse 4.

kasya syād anyathābhāvaḥ svabhāvaś cen na vidyate /
kasya syād anyathābhāvaḥ svabhāvo yadi vidyate //4//

4. Of what would there be alteration if intrinsic nature were not real?
[Reply:] Of what would there be alteration if intrinsic nature *were* real?

According to the *Akutobhayā*, the opponent is arguing in 4ab that there must be dharmas with intrinsic nature in order for there to be the type of alteration known as "change of situation." The Vaibhāṣikas claimed that dharmas exist in all three times (past, present, and future), but a dharma's functioning varies depending on its temporal situation: A dharma situated in the present is functioning, a dharma situated in the past has functioned, and a dharma situated in the future will function. The Vaibhāṣikas hold that this must be true if we are to explain why composite entities like persons seem to undergo alteration. And, they argue in 4ab, there could not be change of situation unless there really were dharmas to undergo the change of situation. A real dharma must have an intrinsic nature throughout the three times, so it cannot be that all things are empty.

Nāgārjuna replies in verse 4cd that there couldn't be any alteration if there were things with intrinsic nature. The argument for this will come in the next two verses. But Candrakīrti provides the useful example of the heat of fire: Since there is no fire that is not hot, heat is the intrinsic nature of fire. He will later (in 15.2) give the heat of water as an example of a property that is not the intrinsic nature of that which has the property. (Both examples should be understood in terms of our ordinary conceptions of these substances and not in terms of any sophisticated theory of the elements developed by Abhidharma schools.) Reflection on why the heat of hot water could not be intrinsic to water will help us better understand the argument.

We know that water need not be hot to exist. So we say that heat is an extrinsic property of water, because we think that the cause of water's being hot is distinct from the cause of water's existing. This means that water can undergo alteration from being cold to being hot. But now when water undergoes this alteration, there must be something about it that makes it continue to be water—first cold water and then hot water. Suppose we were to call this something the intrinsic nature of water—say, wetness. Now we have given water two natures, an extrinsic nature (either being hot or being cold) and an intrinsic nature (wetness). But this in turn means that water (at least water as commonly understood) cannot be an ultimately real thing. For something with two natures is something with parts, something composite in the first sense. We have arrived at our conception of water by bundling together two distinct properties, which shows that water is something that is conceptually constructed.

Now the Vaibhāṣika view of "change of situation" purportedly concerns dharmas, things with natures that are simple. But the fact that these dharmas are said to undergo "change of situation" shows that this cannot be true. For just as with the example of water, there must be one part that remains the same through time and another part that changes over time. In the case of fire (understood now as a dharma), the first would be heat, while the second would be its functional status (not yet functioning, presently functioning, no longer functioning). But this would show that heat is not actually the intrinsic nature of fire. For only ultimately real things have intrinsic natures, and this would show that fire is not ultimately real. Alteration is only possible for things that are composite, not for the ultimately real things with intrinsic nature. "When intrinsic nature must thus be undeviating, then due to its lack of deviation there could be no alteration; for cold is not found in fire. Thus if intrinsic nature of existents were accepted, then there would be no alteration. And the alteration of these is found, so there is no intrinsic nature" (LVP p. 241).

tasyaiva nānyathābhāvo nāpy anyasyaiva yujyate |
yuvā na jīryate yasmād yasmāj jīrṇo na jīryate ||5||

5. It is not correct to say that alteration pertains to the thing
itself that is said to alter or to what is distinct.
For a youth does not age, nor does the aged one age.

If a youth were ultimately real, its intrinsic nature would be youthfulness. Aging is the destruction of youthfulness, so a real youth could not be what ages. An old person is distinct from a youth, lacking youthfulness, so it likewise cannot be what ages. If we say that it is the person who ages, first being a youth and then later being aged, we implicitly accept that a person is composite in the first sense, and so not ultimately real. For we would then be thinking of a person as something that always has the nature of person-ness but sometimes has the property of being youthful and at other times has the property of being aged. So at any given time the person has at least two natures, which would make the person something that is made up of parts.

The opponent now proposes a new example, milk changing into curds. We do, after all, say that milk becomes curds. This suggests that there is one thing that undergoes alteration from one state to another.

tasya ced anyathābhāvaḥ kṣīram eva bhaved dadhi |
kṣīrād anyasya kasyātha dadhibhāvo bhaviṣyati ||6||

6. If alteration pertained to it, then milk itself would be curds.
On the alternative, what else but milk would come to have
the nature of curds?

Suppose that milk and curds were ultimately real. Milk is liquid, while curds are solid. So if it were milk that underwent the alteration into curds, the solidity of curds would already be in milk. Since this is false (if it were true then it would be pointless to make curds), we can reject the hypothesis that it is milk that undergoes the alteration. But the alternative is to suppose that it is something distinct from milk that undergoes alteration. This is contrary to our experience: We can't produce curds from water, for instance. Notice that the argument is an application of the refutation from chapter 1 of production either from itself or from another.

The opponent now repeats the objection first lodged in verse 3, to the effect that denying intrinsic nature is tantamount to nihilism. But the objection is put in a new way. It is now put as the claim that it would be incoherent to claim that all things are empty. As Candrakīrti puts it, "There is no existent whatsoever that is without intrinsic nature, and you claim there is the emptiness of existents. Therefore there is a locus of emptiness as something with intrinsic nature" (LVP p. 245). Nāgārjuna's reply to this objection is contained in the next two verses.

yady aśūnyaṃ bhavet kiṃcit syāc chūnyam iti api kiṃcana |
na kiṃcid asty aśūnyaṃ ca kutaḥ śūnyaṃ bhaviṣyati ||7||

7. If something that is non-empty existed, then something that is empty might also exist.
Nothing whatsoever exists that is non-empty; then how will the empty come to exist?

While both sides agree that some things, such as chariots and persons, are empty of intrinsic nature, the opponent holds that, for there to be emptiness, there must be ultimately real things to serve as the ground or locus of emptiness. Here Nāgārjuna agrees with the opponent that emptiness could not ultimately occur without ultimately real things that it characterized. But he does not withdraw his claim that all things are empty—that nothing whatsoever has intrinsic nature. How is this possible? As he hints in verse 8, and says explicitly in 18.11 and 24.18, the Mādhyamika does not claim that the emptiness of things is ultimately real. To say of things that they are empty is just to say that they are not ultimately real, and their not being ultimately real is not itself ultimately real.

śūnyatā sarvadṛṣṭīnāṃ proktā niḥsaraṇaṃ jinaiḥ |
yeṣāṃ tu śūnyatādṛṣṭis tān asādhyān babhāṣire ||8||

8. Emptiness is taught by the conquerors as the expedient to get rid of all [metaphysical] views.
But those for whom emptiness is a [metaphysical] view have been called incurable.

The "views" in question concern the ultimate nature of reality, or metaphysical theories. The word translated here as "expedient" literally means something that expels or purges. So emptiness is here being called a sort of purgative or physic. Candrakīrti quotes the following exchange between the Buddha and Kāśyapa at section 65 of the *Kāśyapaparivarta Sūtra*:

> "It is as if, Kāśyapa, there were a sick person, and a doctor were to give that person a physic, and that physic having gone to the gut, having eliminated all the person's bad humors, was not itself expelled. What do you think, Kāśyapa, would that person then be free of disease?"
>
> "No, lord, the illness of the person would be more intense if the physic eliminated all the bad humors but was not expelled from the gut."

So to the extent that emptiness gets rid of all metaphysical views, including itself interpreted as a metaphysical view, it might be called a meta-physic.* Buddhapālita sums up the situation more positively by describing those who do not make this error and instead see things correctly: "They see that emptiness is also empty."

* The analogy of the purgative that purges itself was also used by the Pyrrhonian skeptics of ancient Greece. See Diogenes Laertius, *Lives of Eminent Philosophers*, vol. 2 (Cambridge MA: Harvard University Press, 1931), p. 76.

14. An Analysis of Conjunction

CONJUNCTION (or contact) is the relation that occurs between a sense, like vision, and its object, such as color-and-shape, resulting in the arising of a consciousness, such as seeing a colored patch (see 3.7). The commentators represent the opponent as objecting to the arguments presented in the preceding chapters, saying that since the Buddha taught the conjunction of the senses and their sense objects, there must be ultimately real things that come in contact with each other. And thus there must be things with intrinsic nature; it cannot be that all things are empty. The whole of this chapter is given over to Nāgārjuna's response to this objection; it is structured as a refutation of the possibility of conjunction being ultimately real.

14.1–2 Assertion: No entities ever enter into relation of conjunction (contact) with one another.

14.3–4 Reason: Conjunction requires that conjoined entities be distinct, and there is no distinctness.

14.5–7 Refutation of distinctness

14.8 Conclusion: Since there is no distinctness, there can be no conjunction.

draṣṭavyaṃ darśanaṃ draṣṭā trīṇy etāni dviśo dviśaḥ |
sarvaśaś ca na saṃsargam anyonyena vrajanty uta ||1||

1. The visible object, vision, and the seer, these three, whether in pairs
   or all together, do not enter into conjunction with one another.

Candrakīrti explains that the visible object is color-and-shape, vision is the eye (understood as a power), and the seer is consciousness. This is one of six triples (one for each of the five external senses and the inner sense) that collectively make up the eighteen dhātus. On some interpretations of the doctrine of the twelvefold chain of dependent origination, there is contact among all three, and this serves as the cause of first feeling and then desire. On other interpretations, contact is between visible object and vision, with visual consciousness the result. Nāgārjuna's argument is meant to apply to all interpretations of the doctrine, hence the "whether in pairs or all together."

evaṃ rāgaś ca raktaś ca rañjanīyaṃ ca dṛśyatām |
traidhena śeṣāḥ kleśāś ca śeṣāṇy āyatanāni ca ||2||

2. So desire, the one who desires, and what is desirable should [also] be seen.
   Likewise the remaining defilements and the remaining āyatanas are to be seen by means of the threefold division [of action, agent, and object].

The three defilements (*kleśa*s) are desire, aversion, and delusion, so by "the remaining defilements" is meant the two besides desire. For the remaining āyatanas see 3.1. In all these cases there are three things involved: an active power (e.g., vision, desire), an agent (e.g., the seer, the one who desires), and an object (e.g., a visible object, a desirable object). Nāgārjuna will argue that in each case none of these three things can come into conjunction or contact with the others.

anyenānyasya saṃsargas tac cānyatvaṃ na vidyate /
draṣṭavyaprabhṛtīnāṃ yan na saṃsargaṃ vrajanty ataḥ // 3 //

3. Conjunction is of one distinct thing with another distinct thing, and distinctness does not exist
with respect to the visible object and the rest; thus they do not enter into conjunction.

Contact or conjunction requires two or more distinct things. Bhāviveka gives support by pointing out that an entity does not come in contact with itself. And as Nāgārjuna will argue, there is ultimately no such thing as one thing's being distinct from another. In that case there cannot be conjunction among the visible object and the rest.

na ca kevalam anyatvaṃ draṣṭavyāder na vidyate /
kasyacit kenacit sārdhaṃ nānyatvam upapadyate // 4 //

4. And not only is there no distinctness of the visible object and the rest,
so mutual distinctness of anything with something else is not possible.

The argument, which begins in the next verse, will generalize to the cases of all the āyatanas and defilements. Since in none of these cases can action, agent, and object be ultimately distinct from one another, they cannot be ultimately in conjunction.

anyad anyat pratītyānyan nānyad anyad ṛte 'nyataḥ /
yat pratītya ca yat tasmāt tad anyan nopapadyate // 5 //

5. What is distinct is distinct in dependence on that from which it is distinct; it is not distinct apart from that from which it is distinct.
When *x* is dependent on *y*, it does not hold that *x* is distinct from *y*.

yady anyad anyad anyasmād anyasmād apy ṛte bhavet /
tad anyad anyad anyasmād ṛte nāsti ca nāsty ataḥ // 6 //

6. If the distinct thing were distinct from that from which it is distinct, then it would be distinct [even] without that from which it is distinct.
But the distinct thing cannot be distinct without that from which it is distinct; hence there is no distinctness.

nānyasmin vidyate 'nyatvam ananyasmin na vidyate /
avidyamāne cānyatve nāsty anyad vā tad eva vā // 7 //

7. Distinctness is not found in what is distinct, nor is it found in what is nondistinct.
And distinctness not being found, there can be neither the distinct nor the nondistinct.

The argument is that the distinctness of something always involves reference to the other, that from which it is distinct. So something's distinctness cannot be an intrinsic property of that thing. Its distinctness is dependent on the existence of the other. Candrakīrti gives the example of short and long: Since something can be called short only in comparison with something else that is longer than it, something's being short is not an intrinsic property, a property that a thing could have apart from how everything else is. Distinctness "is not found under ultimate analysis"; it is not ultimately true that there are distinct things. (Note that this does not mean it is ultimately true that everything is one.) Instead distinctness is "established by worldly convention." That is, distinctness is, like the chariot, something we find in the world only because of facts about the way we talk and think.

Another way to see why distinctness could not be a property of an ultimately real thing is to consider what it would mean to call distinctness an intrinsic property. An intrinsic property is a property that something might have even if it were the only thing existing in the universe. Could such a thing be said to be distinct? For that matter, could it be said to be nondistinct? What this suggests is that in order to think of something as distinct, we must set that thing alongside other things. It is the mind's imaginative power that does this. (And likewise for the thing's being nondistinct, i.e., identical with itself.) So distinctness is a property imposed on the world through the mind's imaginative power.

na tena tasya saṃsargo nānyenānyasya yujyate /
saṃsṛjyamānaṃ saṃsṛṣṭaṃ saṃsraṣṭā ca na vidyate // 8 //

8. It is not correct to say that conjunction is of this with itself,
   nor that there is the conjunction of this with another.
   The presently being conjoined, the conjoined, and that which
   conjoins—none of these exist.

The argument of 8ab is, according to the *Akutobhayā*, that conjunction would have to either involve a thing taken separately from all else, or else be between things that are mutually distinct. As was just argued, for two things to be mutually distinct from one another, they must be brought into a relation of mutual dependence: The pot is distinct from the cloth only in dependence on the cloth's being distinct from the pot. Since two things in a relation of mutual dependence cannot be ultimately distinct, and conjunction requires distinct things, conjunction is not possible on this hypothesis. The alternative is to consider the pot without reference to the cloth. But for there to be conjunction there must be two distinct things; conjunction cannot be between a thing and itself. Hence conjunction cannot be ultimately real.

15. An Analysis of Intrinsic Nature

ACCORDING TO Abhidharma, to be ultimately real is to have intrinsic nature (*svabhāva*). Something is ultimately real just to the extent that its being what it is does not depend on the natures of other things. The test for something's having intrinsic nature is to see if it retains its nature after being either divided up or analyzed. (See AKB 6.4.) Thus the chariot is not ultimately real precisely because its nature is not to be found among its parts. In this chapter Nāgārjuna will argue that anything originating in dependence on causes and conditions must lack intrinsic nature and thus be empty. Since most Buddhists believe that all things originate in dependence on causes and conditions, this is tantamount to an argument for the claim that all things that are accepted as real by Buddhists are empty.

We here follow the usual practice of using Candrakīrti's chapter titles. But it is worth noting that the *Akutobhayā*, Buddhapālita, and Bhāviveka all use a different title: "An Analysis of the Existent and Nonexistent" (*bhāvābhāvaparīkṣā*). This may better represent the purpose of the chapter. For after Nāgārjuna establishes that anything dependently originated must be devoid of intrinsic nature, he uses this result to claim for Madhyamaka the status of being a "middle path" between the extremes of existence and nonexistence—of holding either that there are ultimately existing things or that ultimately nothing exists. In doing this he is attempting to show not only that the Madhyamaka teaching of the emptiness of all things avoids the problem of metaphysical nihilism (see chapter 13) but also that this represents a legitimate extension of the Buddha's teachings. The thread of reasoning traced by the chapter is as follows:

15.1–2 Argument: Nothing that originates in dependence on distinct causes and conditions can have intrinsic nature.

15.3 If there is no intrinsic nature, there can be no extrinsic nature.

15.4 If there is neither intrinsic nor extrinsic nature, there can be no existents.

15.5 If there is no existent, there can be no nonexistent.

15.6–7 Assertion: The Buddha's rejection of eternalism and annihilationism is the denial that ultimately things either exist or do not exist.

15.8–11 Argument for assertion

15.8–9: Anything with intrinsic nature could not cease to exist.

15.10–11: Why saying that things ultimately exist amounts to eternalism, and saying that things ultimately cease to exist amounts to annihilationism

na saṃbhavaḥ svabhāvasya yuktaḥ pratyayahetubhiḥ |
hetupratyayasaṃbhūtaḥ svabhāvaḥ kṛtako bhavet ||1||

1. It is not correct to say that intrinsic nature (*svabhāva*) is produced by means of causes and conditions.
An intrinsic nature that was produced by causes and conditions would be a product.

Candrakīrti explains the argument as follows. The intrinsic nature of a newly arisen thing cannot have already been in the causes and conditions that produced that thing. For if it were, the production of that thing would have been pointless: If there is already heat in the fuel, why bother to start a fire to obtain heat? So if there is intrinsic nature, it would have to be a product of causes and conditions. But this cannot be, for it creates a difficulty that is discussed in the next verse.

Buddhapālita's comments make it possible to interpret the verse somewhat differently. While Candrakīrti illustrates production (*saṃbhava*) with the examples of the seed producing a sprout and ignorance producing predispositions, Buddhapālita gives the example of threads and cloth. While Candrakīrti's examples involve a product that comes into existence after its cause and conditions, the relation between threads and cloth is more like that of the chariot and its parts, the relation of composition that holds between things that exist simultaneously. Understood in this way, the argument would be that the intrinsic nature of an existent could not be something that depends on its component parts and their natures, since that would turn what is supposedly an intrinsic nature into something extrinsic or borrowed from those component parts. The chariot is not an ultimate existent precisely because all its properties are borrowed from the properties of its parts. If the argument is interpreted in this way, then the problem discussed in our comments on verse 2 does not arise.

svabhāvaḥ kṛtako nāma bhaviṣyati punaḥ katham |
akṛtrimaḥ svabhāvo hi nirapekṣaḥ paratra ca ||2||

2. But how could there ever be an intrinsic nature that is a
 product?
 For intrinsic nature is not adventitious, nor is it dependent
 on something else.

The difficulty in an intrinsic nature's being a product is that the two terms are mutually contradictory. Candrakīrti explains that we ordinarily say the heat of hot water or the red color of quartz (something that is normally white) are not their intrinsic natures because these properties are products of distinct causes and conditions. Hot water is hot because of the proximity of fire; the quartz may be red because of excess iron. The water and the quartz get these properties in dependence on causes and conditions that are adventitious or extraneous to the existence of the quartz and the water. But in verse 1 it was argued that intrinsic nature would also have to be a product of causes and conditions. The fire would have to acquire its heat in dependence on the fuel, air, and friction. So heat, as a product, could not be an intrinsic nature of fire.

We might step back from the text and the commentaries for a moment and reflect on this argument. Mādhyamikas often claim that the emptiness of something follows from its being dependently originated. Candrakīrti says as much, for instance, in his comments on 1.10 (LVP p. 87), 18.7 (LVP p. 368), and 22.9 (LVP p. 440). And we will see Nāgārjuna make an equivalent claim in 24.18. But the argument presented in this verse appears to be the only one that explicitly offers support for this claim. There might be other ways to support it; for instance, if it is true that the causal relation is conceptually constructed (as chapters 1 and 20 seek to show), then one might argue that nothing that is thought to arise through causes and conditions can be ultimately real. But the present argument appears to be the only one where Nāgārjuna seeks to show that an intrinsic nature cannot be caused. The question is whether the argument succeeds.

It might be thought that it does not, since there is an important difference between the case of the quartz and the case of fire. We would call red an extrinsic or adventitious property of quartz because the cause of its being red is distinct from the cause of its coming into existence. Quartz can (and normally does) come into existence without red color. This is not true, though, of the heat of fire. Whenever fire comes into existence, heat also occurs. So it looks like the cause of the heat is just the cause of the fire. And in that case it would seem odd to say that heat is extrinsic or adventitious with respect to the fire. The fact that heat is the product of causes and conditions seems irrelevant to the question of whether it is the intrinsic nature of fire.

But there may be a way to answer this objection. What Nāgārjuna might have had in mind is that the fire must be thought of as existing distinct from the property of heat because otherwise the heat could not be thought of as something the fire "owns," something it receives from the causes and conditions and takes as its own. If the test of something's being ultimately real is that it have intrinsic nature, then the thing and its nature must be conceptually distinguishable. This conception of a dharma is actually built into one account of the term that is commonly accepted among Ābhidharmikas: that a dharma is that which bears its intrinsic nature. (See, e.g., AKB 1.2, also As §94 p. 39.) It would seem as if the consistent position for Abhidharma would be to identify a dharma with its nature (thus treating dharmas as equivalent to what philosophers now call tropes). And there were Ābhidharmikas who did espouse this view. (This is Candrakīrti's target when he discusses the example of the head of Rāhu; see LVP p. 66.) But this may not have been widely held until well after Nāgārjuna.

> *kutaḥ svabhāvasyābhāve parabhāvo bhaviṣyati /*
> *svabhāvaḥ parabhāvasya parabhāvo hi kathyate //3//*

3. Given the nonexistence of intrinsic nature, how will there be
   extrinsic nature (*parabhāva*)?
   For extrinsic nature is said to be the intrinsic nature of
   another existent (*parabhāva*).

Extrinsic nature is nature that is borrowed from something distinct, such as the heat of water or the shape of the chariot. Nāgārjuna claims that having proven there is no intrinsic nature, he can also conclude there is no extrinsic nature. There are two ways to understand the argument. (1) In order to say that heat is the extrinsic nature of water, we need to first establish what water is. We can't say that heat is a merely adventitious property of water unless we know what water is essentially, what it has to be like to be water. And this requires that water have an intrinsic nature. (2) In order for the chariot to borrow its shape from its parts, those parts must themselves exist. And for them to exist ultimately they must have intrinsic natures. Thus if nothing has intrinsic nature, nothing can be said to have extrinsic nature either. Nothing can borrow a nature unless there is something that owns a nature.

svabhāvaparabhāvābhyām ṛte bhāvaḥ kutaḥ punaḥ |
svabhāve parabhāve ca sati bhāvo hi sidhyati ||4||

4. Further, without intrinsic nature and extrinsic nature how can there be an existent (*bhāva*)?
For an existent is established given the existence of either intrinsic nature or extrinsic nature.

Something can be called an existent only if it has some nature, either intrinsic or extrinsic. And since neither sort is coherent, it follows that there can ultimately be no existents. But there may be a play on words here as well: The Sanskrit word *bhāva* can mean either "nature" or "existent."

bhāvasya ced aprasiddhir abhāvo naiva sidhyati |
bhāvasya hy anyathābhāvam abhāvaṃ bruvate janāḥ ||5||

5. If the existent is unestablished, then the nonexistent (*abhāva*) too is not established.
For people proclaim the nonexistent to be the alteration of the existent.

It is tempting to take the conclusion of verse 4 to mean that nothing whatsoever exists, that all is nonexistent. But Nāgārjuna denies this. For an action of mine to be impolite, it must be possible that certain actions are polite. Without at least the possibility of politeness, there can be no impoliteness. Likewise for existence and nonexistence. For it to be ultimately true that all is nonexistent, it must at least be possible for there to be ultimate existents. But that requires that we be able to make sense of intrinsic nature. The argument of this chapter so far has been that we cannot do that on terms acceptable to the Buddhist.

svabhāvaṃ parabhāvaṃ ca bhāvaṃ cābhāvam eva ca |
ye paśyanti na paśyanti te tattvaṃ buddhaśāsane ||6||

6. Intrinsic nature and extrinsic nature, existent and nonexistent—
who see these do not see the truth of the Buddha's teachings.

kātyāyanāvavāde cāstīti nāstīti cobhayam |
pratiṣiddhaṃ bhagavatā bhāvābhāvavibhāvinā ||7||

7. In "The Instructing of Katyāyana" both "it exists" and "it does not exist"
are denied by the Blessed One, who clearly perceives the existent and the nonexistent.

The reference is to the Sanskrit parallel of *Kaccāyanagotta Sutta* (S II.17, III.134–35). There the Buddha tells Katyāyana that his is a middle path between the two extreme views of existence and nonexistence. Ābhidharmikas interpret this text as rejecting two views about the person: that there is a self, so that persons exist permanently; and that since there is no self, the person is annihilated or becomes nonexistent (at the end of a life, or even at the end of the present moment).

The middle path is that while there is no self, there is a causal series of skandhas that is conveniently designated as a person.

Nāgārjuna holds that while the Abhidharma claim about persons is not incorrect, there is a deeper meaning to the Buddha's teaching in the sūtra. This is that there is a middle path between the extremes of holding that there are ultimately existing things and holding that ultimately nothing exists. And as all the commentators make clear, to call the doctrine of emptiness a middle path is to say that one can deny each extreme view without lapsing into the other. How one does this is a matter of some dispute. But Candrakīrti quotes the *Samādhirāja Sūtra*:

> "It exists" and "it does not exist" are both extremes; "pure" and "impure" are both extremes.
> The wise man, avoiding both extremes, likewise does not take a stand in the middle. (LVP p. 270)

This suggests that the Madhyamaka middle path is not a "moderate" or compromise position lying on the same continuum as the two extremes. Instead it must involve rejecting some underlying presupposition that generates the continuum.

The disagreement over the interpretation of the sūtra is a variant on the dispute between Abhidharma and Mahāyāna over emptiness: Is it of all dharmas, or only of persons? (See 13.2.) The Ābhidharmika claims that if all dharmas were empty, then the absurd consequence of nihilism (universal nonexistence) would follow. Nāgārjuna may be seen as here responding to that charge.

yady astitvaṃ prakṛtyā syān na bhaved asya nāstitā /
prakṛter anyathābhāvo na hi jātūpapadyate //8//

8. If something existed by essential nature (*prakṛti*), then there would not be the nonexistence of such a thing.

For it never holds that there is the alteration of essential nature.

prakṛtau kasya vāsatyām anyathātvaṃ bhaviṣyati /
prakṛtau kasya vā satyām anyathātvaṃ bhaviṣyati //9//

9. [Objection:] If essential nature did not exist, of what would there be the fact of alteration?
[Reply:] If essential nature did exist, of what would there be the fact of alteration?

By "essential nature"(*prakṛti*) is here meant just intrinsic nature. A new argument: If there were things that ultimately existed because they had intrinsic nature, they could not cease to exist. If intrinsic nature is not dependent on causes and conditions, then something's having that nature is not dependent on any other factor. But this should mean that there could be no reason for it to lose that nature—and thus cease to exist. So the doctrine that there are ultimately real things with intrinsic nature leads unwittingly to the conclusion that what exists is eternal and unchanging.

astīti śāśvatagrāho nāstīty ucchedadarśanam /
tasmād astitvanāstitve nāśrayeta vicakṣaṇaḥ //10//

10. "It exists" is an eternalist view; "It does not exist" is an annihilationist idea.
Therefore the wise one should not have recourse to either existence or nonexistence.

asti yad dhi svabhāvena na tan nāstīti śāśvatam /
nāstīdānīm abhūt pūrvam ity ucchedaḥ prasajyate //11//

11. For whatever exists by its intrinsic nature does not become nonexistent; eternalism then follows.
"It does not exist now [but] it existed previously"—from this, annihilation follows.

The two extreme views the Buddha refers to in "The Instructing of Katyāyana" are also called eternalism and annihilationism. (For more on these, see the comments on 17.10.) Nāgārjuna here interprets these to refer respectively to the view that things exist having intrinsic nature and the view that the lack of intrinsic nature means that things are utterly unreal. The argument is that the first leads to the conclusion that ultimately real things are eternal, while the second leads to the conclusion that ultimately nothing whatsoever exists. So even if the Buddha did not explicitly claim that his was a middle path between the existence and the nonexistence of entities in general and was instead only discussing the existence or nonexistence of the person, Nāgārjuna takes this to be a plausible extension of the Buddha's remarks to Katyāyana.

16. An Analysis of Bondage and Liberation

IN RESPONSE to the conclusion of the last chapter, the opponent retorts that there must be intrinsic nature, since there would be no bondage to the wheel of saṃsāra and no liberation from saṃsāra unless there were existing things undergoing rebirth. There are two possibilities as to what might be reborn: first, the composite things or *saṃskāra*s, those impermanent psychophysical elements (the skandhas) that originate in dependence on prior causes and conditions (and are thus composite or *saṃskṛta* in the sense examined in chapter 13); and second, the person (*pudgala*) that is thought of as consisting of the composite elements. In this chapter both possibilities are examined. Here is the thread of the argument:

16.1a–c	Refutation of the claim that it is psychophysical elements that are reborn
16.1d–3	Refutation of the claim that it is the person that is reborn
16.4–5	Refutation of the possibility that either the elements or the person is what is liberated
16.6	Bondage cannot be explained by appropriation.
16.7–8	Refutation of the possibility of bondage and liberation in any of the three times.
16.9–10	Soteriological consequences of the refutation of bondage and liberation

16.9: Paradox of liberation: The thought that one might attain liberation prevents one from achieving it.
16.10: Resolution of paradox: Ultimately there is neither rebirth nor liberation.

saṃskārāḥ saṃsaranti cen na nityāḥ saṃsaranti te /
saṃsaranti ca nānityāḥ sattve 'py eṣa samaḥ kramaḥ //1//

1. If it is composite things that undergo rebirth, they are not reborn as permanent entities
nor as impermanent entities; if it is the living being that is reborn, the method [of refutation] is the same.

Suppose it were the composite psychophysical elements that underwent rebirth. They must be either permanent or else impermanent. If the psychophysical elements were permanent, then they would be changeless. And anything that is changeless does not perform any function; an entity does something only by changing in some way. But being reborn involves doing something: going from one life to another on the basis of one's actions in the one life. So permanent psychophysical elements could not be what is reborn. But neither could impermanent psychophysical elements. To say these are impermanent would be to say they do not endure from one moment to the next. In that case they can neither undergo alteration nor be causally efficacious. (Compare the reasoning of 1.6–7.) And for the same reason that a changeless permanent thing cannot go through rebirth, so an impermanent changeless thing could not be said to be reborn either.

This might make it seem as if it must be not the elements but the person who is reborn. If the person or living being is what is made up of the psychophysical elements, then it might seem as if it is just the right sort of thing for rebirth. For then it could serve as the enduring thing that has different collections of impermanent psychophysical elements as its constituents at different times. So it could both endure and undergo alteration. But Nāgārjuna denies that this solution will work, since the same reasoning applies to it as to the hypothesis that it is composite things that are reborn. If the person is permanent, then it performs no function. And if it is impermanent, then it is likewise not causally efficacious. The argument against its being the person who is reborn continues in the next two verses.

pudgalaḥ saṃsarati cet skandhāyatanadhātuṣu /
pañcadhā mṛgyamāṇo 'sau nāsti kaḥ saṃsariṣyati //2//

2. If it is said that it is the person that is reborn, it—being investigated in the fivefold manner with respect to the skandhas, āyatanas, and dhātus—does not exist; who then will be reborn?

For the skandhas see chapter 4, for the āyatanas see chapter 3, and for the dhātus see chapter 5. According to Candrakīrti, the five possibilities are: (1) The person has the intrinsic nature of the skandhas, etc. (i.e., the person is identical with the psychophysical elements); (2) the person is distinct from them; (3) the person exists possessing the skandhas, etc.; (4) the person is in the skandhas, etc.; (5) the skandhas and so on exist in the person. And he refers us to the analysis of fire and fuel for the reasoning involved in rejecting each. (See 10.14.)

upādānād upādānaṃ saṃsaran vibhavo bhavet /
vibhavaś cānupādānaḥ kaḥ sa kiṃ saṃsariṣyati //3//

3. Being reborn from one appropriation [i.e., state of being] to another, it would be extinct.
And being extinct and without appropriation, who is it that will be reborn to what?

According to the *Akutobhayā*, the argument is that the person who is thought to undergo rebirth does so either with the basis of appropriated psychophysical elements or else without this as basis. Suppose (3ab) the person who undergoes rebirth has appropriated psychophysical elements as a basis of appropriation. But it is different elements that the person would depend on in the prior life and in the present life. And rebirth means going from one life to another. So the person would be without appropriated elements when undergoing rebirth and thus would be extinct or deprived of the state of being (*vibhava*). Thus there is no person who is reborn. The alternative (3c) is that the person who undergoes rebirth is without skandhas to serve as basis of appropriation. But there can be no such thing as a person without any basis of psychophysical elements. We can see this from the fact that when some Buddhists (just which is a matter of some controversy) supply the idea of an intermediate state of being (*antarābhava*) to fill the gap between death and rebirth, this "being" is always furnished with skandhas that are thought to pertain to it. To be utterly without any psychophysical elements whatsoever seems tantamount to being utterly extinct. Hence the question of 3d: Who is this person and where is it that he or she is going?

saṃskārāṇāṃ na nirvāṇaṃ kathaṃcid upapadyate /
sattvasyāpi na nirvāṇaṃ kathaṃcid upapadyate //4//

4. The nirvāṇa of composite things is not in any way possible.
Nor is the nirvāṇa of a living being in any way possible.

Buddhapālita explains that the same reasoning applies to the attainment of nirvāṇa as was just used in the case of rebirth. Regardless of whether it were the composite elements or it were the person that attained nirvāṇa, this would be either as permanent or as impermanent entities. But permanent things do not undergo change, while impermanent things perform no function.

na badhyante na mucyanta udayavyayadharmiṇaḥ /
saṃskārāḥ pūrvavat sattvo badhyate na na mucyate //5//

5. The composite things, whose nature it is to come to be and
   pass away, are neither bound nor liberated.
   As before, a living being is neither bound nor liberated.

Neither bondage nor liberation can pertain to the composite elements, because their transitory nature means that they do not abide in any state or condition. The living being or person is neither bound nor liberated because, as was said in verse 2, it is not to be found in any of the five ways it might be related to the composite elements.

bandhanaṃ ced upādānaṃ sopādāno na badhyate /
badhyate nānupādānaḥ kimavastho 'tha badhyate //6//

6. If binding means appropriating, then what has appropriation
   is not bound.
   Something without appropriation is not bound. Then in
   what state is one bound?

Suppose that bondage to saṃsāra comes about through appropriation—taking the psychophysical elements as "me" and "mine." Then what is it that is bound, something in the state of having appropriated the composite things or something without such appropriation? It cannot be something that has appropriation as its nature, for such a thing has already been bound and so cannot be bound again. But neither can it be something that is without appropriation, for such a thing is by nature unbound, like the enlightened one.

badhnīyād bandhanaṃ kāmaṃ bandhyāt pūrvaṃ bhaved yadi /
na cāsti tac cheṣam uktaṃ gamyamānagatāgataiḥ //7//

7. If there were binding prior to what is to be bound, then it would assuredly bind [what is to be bound].
But that does not exist; the rest of [the argument is to be understood in terms of] what was said with presently being traversed, the traversed, and the not yet traversed.

Binding requires an agent, something that, due to ignorance, desire, and the like, engages in appropriation and thus brings about bondage to saṃsāra. The difficulty is that prior to binding there is no such agent; ignorance, desire, and the like are devoid of locus.

Thus binding cannot occur before there is something that is bound. Nor, clearly, can binding occur after there is something bound, since this would be superfluous. And the third possibility—that binding occurs at some third time when there is neither what is bound nor what is not yet bound—is ruled out by the argument of the three times, as was worked out in the analysis of motion in chapter 2. Buddhapālita applies the logic of that chapter to the case of bondage thus: "The already bound is not bound. The not-yet bound is not bound. The presently being bound that is distinct from the already bound and the not-yet bound is not bound" (P vol. 2, p. 11).

baddho na mucyate tāvad abaddho naiva mucyate |
syātāṃ baddhe mucyamāne yugapad bandhamokṣaṇe ||8||

8. It is not, on the one hand, the bound that is liberated; nor indeed is the not-yet bound liberated.
If the bound were undergoing liberation, there would be simultaneous binding and liberation.

Who or what is liberated? It cannot be something that is bound, for if its nature is to be bound, then it cannot be liberated without ceasing to exist. Nor can it be something that is not yet bound, for in that case liberation would be pointless. We may then think that there must be a third possibility here, that what is bound undergoes a process of liberation. And Buddhapālita concedes that this is what people do say. But that fact should tell us that this can be true only conventionally, not ultimately. Since bondage and liberation are opposed states, something that is bound could undergo a process of becoming liberated only if there could be one portion of it that was still bound while another portion was now liberated. So the subject of this process of undergoing liberation is something with parts. And so it is a mere conceptual fiction, not something ultimately real. What is ultimately real is without parts. Hence it would have to be either bound or liberated.

nirvāsyāmy anupādāno nirvāṇaṃ me bhaviṣyati |
iti yeṣāṃ grahas teṣām upādānamahāgrahaḥ ||9||

9. "Being without appropriation, I shall be released; nirvāṇa will be mine."
For those who grasp things in this way, there is the great grasping of appropriation.

If release from saṃsāra comes about through the cessation of appropriation—through ceasing to have thoughts of "I" and "mine"—then the desire for one's own liberation constitutes an obstacle to its attainment. This is the Buddhist formulation of the so-called paradox of liberation. This paradox is recognized by virtually all schools of Indian philosophy concerned with release from suffering and rebirth. Here the paradox is put in terms of the notion that when one has the thought, "I shall be released," one is identifying with and appropriating the psychophysical elements—which is just what causes bondage to saṃsāra.

na nirvāṇasamāropo na saṃsārāpakarṣaṇam |
yatra kas tatra saṃsāro nirvāṇaṃ kiṃ vikalpyate ||10||

10. Where nirvāṇa is not reified nor saṃsāra rejected,
 what saṃsāra is there, what nirvāṇa is falsely imagined?

The argument of this chapter has shown that there can be no such thing as the overcoming of ignorance and attaining of nirvāṇa. Or to be more precise, it cannot be ultimately true that there is such a process. And in the absence of such a process, it is difficult to see how there could be the two states of saṃsāra and nirvāṇa. Hence the suggested conclusion: that we cease attempting to conceptualize the two and no longer take up attitudes of desire and aversion respectively toward them. But this is ambiguous. It might be taken to mean that while saṃsāra and nirvāṇa are ultimately real, their nature is ungraspable. Or it might mean that the very idea of ultimately real things is incoherent. Nāgārjuna will have more to say on this question at 25.19–20.

17. An Analysis of Action and Fruit

THIS CHAPTER examines the relation between an action (*karman*) and its consequence or fruit (*phala*), the relation specified by what are now commonly called the laws of karma. Note the word *karman* is being used quite differently here than in chapter 8: There it was used in the Grammarians' sense of the object or goal of an action, whereas here it means the action itself. The first five verses lay out the common understanding of the relation between action and fruit shared by several schools. In verse 6 a question is raised concerning how this can be compatible with the doctrine of impermanence. The following thirteen verses give solutions proposed by different schools. Then beginning in verse 21 Nāgārjuna subjects these to his own critical examination.

17.1–5	Presentation of orthodox understanding of action and its classification
17.6	Difficulty for the orthodox theory: What endures between time of action and time of fruit to guarantee that the action is appropriately rewarded or punished?
17.7–11	Solution 1: the seed hypothesis
17.12	Objection to the seed hypothesis
17.13–20	Solution 2: the hypothesis of the unperishing
17.21	Nāgārjuna's assertion: Action is without intrinsic nature.
17.22–25	Reasons for assertion that action is without intrinsic nature

17.26 Emptiness of action and the defilements
17.27 Emptiness of the body/person
17.28 Objection: Action must exist, since there are agents and enjoyers.
17.29–30 Reply: There is neither action, nor agent; there is neither fruit nor enjoyer.
17.31–33 Conclusion: Action, fruit, and all associated with them are illusory.

ātmasaṃyamakaṃ cetaḥ parānugrāhakaṃ ca yat /
maitraṃ sa dharmas tad bījaṃ phalasya pretya ceha ca //1//

1. Self-control, being thoughtful of others,
and friendliness—these states of mind are meritorious and
the seeds of fruit both hereafter and here.

The laws of karma have to do with the relation between an action and its consequences for the agent. But by "action" is meant more than a mere bodily movement such as breathing or blinking, which are typically done without thought. It is the state of mind behind an action that determines what sort of fruit the agent will reap. Here are detailed the states of mind that result in such good fruits as human rebirth, both in this life ("here") and in future lives ("hereafter"). By implication, the opposed states of mind yield unpleasant consequences for the agent.

cetanā cetayitvā ca karmoktaṃ paramarṣiṇā /
tasyānekavidho bhedaḥ karmaṇaḥ parikīrtitaḥ //2//

2. Action was said by the Supreme Sage to be volition and what
is brought about by volition.

He has proclaimed there to be many distinct varieties of
action.

Bhāviveka explains "Supreme Sage" to include not only the Buddha but also the śrāvakas (the "hearers," those who have become enlightened through hearing the Buddha's teachings), pratyekabuddhas, and bodhisattvas. Candrakīrti takes the term to refer to just the Buddha. Anticipating the next verse, he explains "what is brought about by volition" is a bodily or verbal action that follows a volition.

tatra yac cetanety uktaṃ karma tan mānasaṃ smṛtam |
cetayitvā ca yat tūktaṃ tat tu kāyikavācikam ||3||

3. Of these, that which is called "volition" is known as mental
action.
And that which is called "what is brought about by volition"
is bodily and verbal action.

The two varieties of action mentioned in verse 2 are described. Volitions are purely mental in nature; the disposition of friendliness—wishing for the welfare of others—would be an example of a volition. The second variety, "what is brought about by volition," includes what would count as actions in the normal sense of the term, namely bodily movements and speech. But as Bhāviveka makes clear, these count as actions only if they occur intentionally (i.e., are caused by a volition).

vāg viṣpando 'viratayo yāś cāvijñaptisaṃjñitāḥ |
avijñaptaya evānyāḥ smṛtā viratayas tathā ||4||
paribhogānvayaṃ puṇyam apuṇyaṃ ca tathāvidham |
cetanā ceti saptaite dharmāḥ karmāñjanāḥ smṛtāḥ ||5||

4. Speech, gesture, what is known as the unmanifest unrestrained,
   likewise the other unmanifest called the restrained,
5. merit connected with utilization, demerit connected with
   utilization,
   and volition—these seven dharmas are said to be types of
   action.

In order to explain how volition, speech, and bodily actions could give rise to fruits much later (such as in another life), some Ābhidharmikas developed a theory of seven varieties of action dharma involved in the causal chain leading from volition to fruit. Since the idea behind much Abhidarma theorizing is to assist individuals in making progress toward enlightenment, these states were classified in terms of whether they produced fruits conducive to liberation (and so were "meritorious") or not (and so counted as "demeritorious"). In verse 2, speech and gesture were identified as the two varieties of action called "what is brought about by volition." Both involve activity that is evident to others. And this publicly manifest activity results from the occurrence of a volition.

In addition, four types of unmanifest action dharmas are mentioned. The first and second are involved in the situation in which a volition that normally leads to speech or gesture does not do so owing to some external circumstance such as lack of opportunity. These unmanifest action dharmas are meant to explain how an earlier volition can bring about a much later act when there is no manifest connecting link. In what is called the unrestrained unmanifest, the volition is bad in nature, while the restrained unmanifest involves a good volition. (By "restraint" is meant the sort of abstaining or refraining from wrong action that is central to the taking of monastic vows.) For the first sort, Candrakīrti gives the example of someone who resolves to make his or her livelihood by killing (e.g., by fishing) but has not yet caught any fish and so has not performed the bodily act of killing. It is a series of unmanifest unrestrained action dharmas that explains how the original intention can lead to the later act even when no connecting link is manifest to anyone in the interim. The restrained unmanifest action dharma is used to explain the opposite sort of case—formation of an intention to perform some good act coupled with lack of opportunity to carry out the intention.

The fifth and sixth dharmas, also unmanifest action dharmas, involve what is called "utilization" (*paribhoga*), by which is meant specifically the use of something donated to a worthy cause such as the Saṃgha. Such gifts were thought to generate a special sort of karmic merit, so it is perhaps not surprising to find a category of dharmas devoted to accounting for their efficacy. The idea of "merit connected with utilization" has support in the Nikāyas, where the Buddha is reported to have said that when a monk uses an item donated to the Saṃgha, this results in enhanced karmic merit for the donor (A II.54). The dharma known as "merit connected with utilization" is meant to explain, at the level of dharmas, the mechanism that brings this about. The second sort, "demerit connected with utilization," has to do with the case where a donated object is given with bad intention: Candrakīrti gives the example of having a temple constructed where living beings are killed (perhaps in sacrifice). The idea seems to be that the bad karma incurred by making such a donation with that intention is compounded whenever such a killing is carried out by others.

This account matches the classification of action given by the Vaibhāṣika school:

I. Volition
II. Action brought about by volition
  1. Manifest action brought about by volition
    a. Speech
    b. Bodily action (gesture)
  2. Unmanifest action brought about by volition
    a. Productive of speech
      i. Restrained
      ii. Unrestrained

iii. Neither restrained nor unrestrained
b. Productive of bodily action
i. Restrained
ii. Unrestrained
iii. Neither restrained nor unrestrained

Types II.1a and II.1b are both subdivided into the meritorious and the demeritorious. Types II.2a.i and II.2b.i, flowing as they do from intentions governed by the sort of restraint characteristic of good conduct, are always meritorious. Types II.2a.ii and II.2b.ii are always demeritorious since they flow from the opposite sort of intention. Types II.2a.iii and II.2b.iii, which represent situations involving the use of a donation, may be either meritorious or demeritorious. Also included in the Vaibhāṣika classification but not mentioned here are unmanifest action dharmas involved in meditative states.

tiṣṭhaty ā pākakālāc cet karma tan nityatām iyāt /
niruddhaṃ cen niruddhaṃ sat kiṃ phalaṃ janayiṣyati //6//

6. If the action endures to the time of maturation, then it would be permanent.
If it is destroyed, then being destroyed, what fruit will it produce?

In this verse a difficulty is raised for anyone who accepts the account of karma outlined in verses 1–5. According to the general law of karma, an action gives rise to a fruit. But the fruit typically occurs some time after the action—often in another lifetime. The question then is how an action that occurs at one time can bring about a fruit at a later time. One possibility is that the action endures from the time of its occurrence until its maturation, when the fruit arises. But if the action endures, then it is eternal. For if something does not perish at one moment, there can be no reason why it should perish at some other moment. So if it endures for some time, then it will endure for all time. And something eternal cannot produce anything. The alternative is to say that the action goes out of existence immediately upon its occurrence. But in this case it would seem impossible for it to produce a fruit that occurs later.

Different Abhidharma schools proposed various solutions to this problem. One such solution is that of the Vaibhāṣikas, who held that each dharma exists in all three times. (See 13.4.) In that case the action is still existent in some sense when the fruit comes into existence. But their solution is not taken up here. Instead Nāgārjuna first presents the seeds hypothesis that was later associated with the Sautrāntika school and then the view of the Pudgalavādins.

yo 'ṅkuraprabhṛtir bījāt saṃtāno 'bhipravartate /
tataḥ phalam ṛte bījāt sa ca nābhipravartate //7//

7. A series starting with the sprout proceeds from a seed,
a fruit proceeds from that series, and without the seed the series does not come forth.

bījāc ca yasmāt saṃtānaḥ saṃtānāc ca phalodbhavaḥ /
bījapūrvaṃ phalaṃ tasmān nocchinnaṃ nāpi śāśvatam //8//

8. Since the series is from the seed, and the fruit is arisen from the series,
the fruit has the seed as its predecessor; thus it [the seed] is neither annihilated nor eternal.

yas tasmāc cittasaṃtānaś cetaso 'bhipravartate /
tataḥ phalam ṛte cittāt sa ca nābhipravartate //9//

9. Likewise a mental series proceeds from a mental element,
a fruit proceeds from that series, and without the mental element, the series does not come forth.

cittāc ca yasmāt saṃtānaḥ saṃtānāc ca phalodbhavaḥ |
karmapūrvaṃ phalaṃ tasmān nocchinnaṃ nāpi śāśvatam ||10||

10. Since the series is from the mental element, and the fruit is arisen from the series,
the fruit has the action as its predecessor; thus the action is neither annihilated nor eternal.

The idea is that just as a mango seed can serve to bring a mango into existence even though the seed goes out of existence long before the mango appears, so an action can cause a karmic fruit to occur long after the action took place. In the case of the mango seed, there is a causal series of intermediary entities: the sprout, the sapling, the young tree, and the flowering tree. Under the right conditions, the last entity in this series gives rise to the mango fruit. But since this series was started by the seed, we can say that the fruit has the seed as its ultimate cause. By the same token, an action can cause a type of mental event called a karmic trace. Since every existing thing is momentary, this karmic trace will only exist for a moment. But it will cause a successor karmic trace of the same sort. And this in turn will cause another trace like itself. This causal series will continue until such time as conditions are appropriate for the ripening of the karmic trace, at which time the karmic fruit will appear. The proximate cause of this fruit is the immediately preceding karmic trace. But this trace owes its existence to its predecessor, and so on, backward along the series to the action. So the action may be called the ultimate cause of the karmic fruit.

The Buddha called his view a middle path between the extremes of eternalism and annihilationism. One thing this has been taken to mean is that a Buddhist account of the person reconciles the continued existence of a person over one or more lifetimes with the absence of any permanent or eternal constituent of the person. The dilemma posed in verse 6 in effect asks how this reconciliation can take place. If no part of the person endures, how can an action in one life produce a fruit in another life? And if the action in this life is annihilated prior to the fruit that comes in the next life, then the one who enjoys that fruit does not deserve it, since he or she is not the one who acted. The solution that would come to be associated with Sautrāntika posits a causal series to mediate between action and karmic fruit. Since it is just such a series that is conveniently designated as a person, it is conventionally true that the person who acted in the one life enjoys the fruit of that action in another life. At the same time, ultimately nothing endures; what we call a "person" is just a series of momentary entities and events. The series endures—it is not annihilated—but its constituent elements are momentary, each going out of existence the moment after it was produced. (For other examples of this strategy see Mil 40–50; see also Vism 553–55.)

dharmasya sādhanopāyāḥ śuklāḥ karmapathā daśa /
phalaṃ kāmaguṇāḥ pañca dharmasya pretya ceha ca //11//

11. There are ten pure paths of action that are means for establishing the meritorious.
The fruit of the meritorious is the objects of the five senses, both hereafter and here.

bahavaś ca mahāntaś ca doṣāḥ syur yadi kalpanā /
syād eṣā tena naivaiṣā kalpanātropapadyate //12//

12. [Objection:] There would be many gross errors on this hypothesis
of yours; so this hypothesis [of a seed-generated series] does not hold here.

The objection in verse 12 is said to come not from Nāgārjuna but from another opponent. According to Buddhapālita, Bhāviveka, and Candrakīrti, the difficulty being raised for the view just presented is that the example of the seed-fruit series is not sufficiently like the case of the action-fruit connection. For the seed of a mango will only produce a mango tree, never an oak tree. But a given action may in one case yield human rebirth, in another divine rebirth; in one case the fruit may be pleasant, in another case it may be painful; and so on.

imāṃ punaḥ pravakṣyāmi kalpanāṃ yātra yojyate /
buddhaiḥ pratyekabuddhaiś ca śrāvakaiś cānuvarṇitām //13//

13. I, however, shall here propose the following hypothesis that is suitable
and that has been expounded by buddhas, pratyekabuddhas, and śrāvakas.

pattraṃ yathāvipraṇāśas tathārṇam iva karma ca /
caturvidho dhātutaḥ sa prakṛtyāvyākṛtaś ca saḥ //14//

14. The unperishing is like the pledge pen, the action is like the debt.
It is fourfold with respect to sphere, and it is by nature indeterminate.

"The unperishing" is a dharma that is said to result from an action that does not immediately produce its karmic fruit. The analogy here is to the pen with which one pledges to repay a debt and, by extension, to the written record of one's debt. While the action of incurring the debt by signing the pledge is in the past, the record remains as long as the debt has not been repaid, and it serves as the immediate cause of the repayment. So by analogy there is an "unperishing" that occurs following an action; it abides until such time as the fruit arises. One may thus think of it as a sort of karmic debt. The *Akutobhayā* tells us that its four varieties have to do with the cosmic sphere in which it may be operative: that of desire (the mundane world) or one of the three transmundane spheres attained in meditation—those of form, formlessness, and the undefiled. It is indeterminate in nature insofar as it is not in and of itself conducive toward either pleasure or pain. As Candrakīrti explains this, if the karmic debt incurred by acts conducive to pain were itself conducive to pain, it could not exist in those who have overcome desire. And if the karmic debt incurred by acts conducive to pleasure were itself conducive to pleasure, then it could not be found in those whose roots of good conduct have all been destroyed. Its indeterminacy thus reflects the complexity of the workings of karma—the complexity that this opponent used against the seeds hypothesis in verse 12.

prahāṇato na praheyo bhāvanāheya eva vā |
tasmād avipraṇāśena jāyate karmaṇāṃ phalam ||15||

15. It is not to be relinquished by abandonment; it is to be
avoided only by meditation or otherwise.
Thus the fruit of actions is produced by the unperishing.

The unperishing, one's karmic debt, is not left behind just by understanding the four noble truths—that is, understanding how all acts of appropriation lead to suffering. Such understanding leads to the abandonment of those ways of being, such as the life of the householder, that generate new karmic debt. But it does not by itself eliminate the unperishing dharmas generated by actions in the present life prior to one's attaining understanding. This karmic debt can only be escaped in one of two ways: through the path of meditation or "otherwise"—which the commentators explain as rebirth on a different plane of existence, something attained by advanced practitioners approaching liberation. Short of these, such dharmas will produce the appropriate fruit.

prahāṇataḥ praheyaḥ syāt karmaṇaḥ saṃkrameṇa vā /
yadi doṣāḥ prasajyeraṃs tatra karmavadhādayaḥ //16//

16. If it were to be relinquished by abandonment or by transference of the action,
various difficulties would result, including the disappearance of the [past] action.

Two hypotheses concerning how one's karmic debt might be evaded are here argued against. The first is the one already rejected in verse 15, that abandonment—what the commentators refer to as the "path of understanding"—could bring about the destruction of the imperishable dharmas generated by one's actions. The second is that one leaves behind all one's karmic debts at death, when there is transference to a new life. (This is "normal" death and rebirth, as opposed to the sort of rebirth in a higher plane of existence mentioned in verse 15.) To suppose that mere abandonment of the mundane way of life or transference to existence in a new life could free one from one's karmic debts is to suggest that a past action might have no fruit or that the fruit that arises in one's life might not be due to one's own past actions. To these opponents such ideas are deeply threatening to the moral order.

sarveṣāṃ visabhāgānāṃ sabhāgānāṃ ca karmaṇām /
pratisaṃdhau sadhātūnām eka utpadyate tu saḥ //17//

17. At the moment of rebirth there occurs a single [unperishing] with respect to all actions of the same sphere, both dissimilar and similar.

karmaṇaḥ karmaṇo dṛṣṭe dharma utpadyate tu saḥ /
dviprakārasya sarvasya vipakve 'pi ca tiṣṭhati //18//

18. It arises with respect to all the individual actions of the two different sorts in this world, and even though the fruit be ripened, it persists.

In the rebirth process there is a kind of "karmic debt consolidator" for all past actions, whether karmically meritorious, demeritorious, or neutral. So while each of the many actions one performed in this life that have not yet borne their fruit are still present at the time of death, these are then expunged by the one unperishing that consolidates their respective efficacies and determines the nature of the new life. So the many unperishings may be said to cease, just as one's many old debts are repaid when one takes out a debt-consolidation loan. But as this theorist warned in verse 16, this should not be thought of as the relinquishment of one's actions.

The commentators are not sure whether the two different sorts of action referred to in verse 18 are: volition and what is brought about by volition (see v. 2); or that conducive to pleasure and that not conducive to pleasure; or the pure (leading to liberation) and the impure (not leading to liberation).

phalavyatikramād vā sa maraṇād vā nirudhyate /
anāsravaṃ sāsravaṃ ca vibhāgaṃ tatra lakṣayet //19//

19. It is destroyed either by going beyond the fruit or by death. In the latter case it shows itself as the distinct states of pure and impure.

While the fruits of one's actions cannot be evaded, the unperishing can be destroyed. Here we are told that there are two ways this might happen. "Going beyond the fruit" means winning release from saṃsāra by means of the path of meditation discussed in verse 15. Destruction by death refers to the fact that the many individual karmic debts accumulated in a lifetime are eliminated by the "karmic debt consolidator" at the time of rebirth. Depending on the overall tenor of the actions in the preceding life, the new life will be either pure or impure. For this one unperishing determines all the significant facts about the situation into which one is born, including the station of one's family, the nature of one's body and sense faculties, place and time, and so on.

śūnyatā ca na cocchedaḥ saṃsāraś ca na śāśvatam |
karmaṇo 'vipraṇāśaś ca dharmo buddhena deśitaḥ ||20||

20. There is emptiness but there is no annihilation; there is saṃsāra but there is no eternity.
And the unperishing dharma of action was taught by the Buddha.

This opponent claims his is the orthodox Buddhist view. First and foremost, he claims it was taught by the Buddha that there is such an entity as the unperishing dharma. (He no doubt has in mind the verse that is cited in the commentaries on verse 21.) And since he agrees that it is destroyed (as discussed in verse 19), it does not exist intrinsically and so can be said to be empty or devoid of intrinsic nature. Yet while it is subject to destruction and consequently empty, the wrong view of annihilationism is avoided, since one's karmic debts remain until they are fulfilled. This in turn shows how there can be rebirth without the existence of an eternal entity such as an enduring self. So the doctrine of the unperishing plays a role in reconciling some core Buddhist teachings.

At this point we are to imagine Nāgārjuna entering the discussion. The Ābhidharmika opponents have given their different accounts of the relation between action and fruit. These accounts presuppose the real existence of action and fruit and some sort of real connection between them. Nāgārjuna retorts that no action is to be found. The opponent then asks why this is. Nāgārjuna responds:

karma notpadyate kasmān niḥsvabhāvaṃ yatas tataḥ |
yasmāc ca tad anutpannaṃ na tasmād vipraṇaśyati ||21||

21. Why is an action not arisen? Because it is without intrinsic nature.
And since it is unarisen, it does not perish.

Ultimately no action is to be found because all actions are empty or devoid of intrinsic nature. The evidence for this claim will be developed in subsequent verses. But the opponent has a more immediate concern. In a verse cited by both Bhāviveka and Candrakīrti (P vol. 2, pp. 37–38) the Buddha is represented as saying:

> Actions do not perish even after billions of cosmic epochs;
> the right set of conditions and the right time having been attained, they assuredly produce fruit for living things.

If an action does not perish, then it must surely be real and so have intrinsic nature; hence Nāgārjuna's claim in 21b cannot be correct. To this Nāgārjuna then replies that an action is said not to perish because ultimately no actions arise. Something that never occurred in the first place cannot be said to perish. The Buddha's claim about actions must be taken as a mere *façon de parler* and not as a description of the ultimate truth about action and fruit.

karma svabhāvataś cet syāc chāśvataṃ syād asaṃśayam |
akṛtaṃ ca bhavet karma kriyate na hi śāśvatam ||22||

22. If the action were something with intrinsic nature, then it would doubtless be eternal.
And the action would be undone, for the eternal is not something that is done.

Candrakīrti explains that the action would be eternal if it had intrinsic nature because anything with intrinsic nature cannot undergo alteration of nature. It then follows that the action would never be done or performed. This is so because in order for the action to be done, it must alter from the state of being undone to the state of being done. But the eternal is changeless, so it could not undergo this alteration.

akṛtābhyāgamabhayaṃ syāt karmākṛtakaṃ yadi /
abrahmacaryavāsaś ca doṣas tatra prasajyate //23//

23. If the action were not done [by the agent], then there is the concern that there would be a result of what was not done [by the agent],
and there then follows the fault of incontinence.

To call an action "undone" means, in this context, not done by the person currently reaping the fruit. From this there then follows the absurd result called "the state of incontinence." The commentators have slightly different accounts of what this fault is. According to Candrakīrti, it means that someone who has lived a faultless life of continent behavior might still reap the fruit of incontinence. According to the other commentators the absurd result is that someone who has lived a life of incontinence might reap the fruit of continence, and so make progress toward nirvāṇa.

vyavahārā virudhyante sarva eva na saṃśayaḥ /
puṇyapāpakṛtāṃ naiva pravibhāgaś ca yujyate //24//

24. Without doubt this would contradict all worldly conduct.
And it would not be correct to distinguish between those who have done the meritorious and those who have done wrong.

If the fruit of an action could come from an undone action, then such worldly pursuits as farming and weaving would be undermined. For one would be as likely to get a crop by not sowing as by sowing. Likewise the karmic laws that specify which actions should be done and which should not would be undermined. For the assumption behind recommending certain actions as meritorious and others as wrong is that doing actions of the first sort brings about pleasant fruit while doing actions of the second sort brings about unpleasant fruit. If the fruit can arise from an undone action, then this assumption is undermined. The *Akutobhayā* adds that this holds as well for the distinction between actions that are wholesome (conducive to nirvāṇa) and unwholesome (not conducive to nirvāṇa).

tad vipakvavipākaṃ ca punar eva vipakṣyati /
karma vyavasthitaṃ yasmāt tasmāt svābhāvikaṃ yadi //25//

25. And that action that has already ripened will produce a fruit yet again
if it follows from the action's being determinate that it is endowed with an intrinsic nature.

The action-fruit connection depends on there being determinate kinds of actions: An action of this sort leads to this kind of fruit, an action of that sort leads to that kind of fruit, and so on. The opponent takes the determinacy of an action to consist in its having its own nature. Nāgārjuna's point here is that in that case the action must always have that nature. And from this he claims it follows that even when the action has produced its fruit, it will continue to have the nature that led to its producing that fruit. So an action that has already produced its fruit will continue to produce more such fruit.

Our translation reflects the reading of 25cd given by three commentators. Candrakīrti understands it somewhat differently: "... if it follows from an action's having intrinsic nature that it is determinate." But the underlying logic of the argument is not significantly affected, since "being determinate" and "having intrinsic nature" are virtually synonymous for the opponent.

karma kleśātmakaṃ cedaṃ te ca kleśā na tattvataḥ /
na cet te tattvataḥ kleśāḥ karma syāt tattvataḥ katham //26//

26. You hold that action is by nature defiled and the defilements are not ultimately real.
If for you the defilements are not real, how would action be ultimately real?

The defilements are desire, aversion, and delusion. All unwholesome actions are said to be conducive to remaining in saṃsāra by virtue of their being caused by one or another of these defilements. But as Nāgārjuna will argue in chapter 23, the defilements cannot themselves be said to be ultimately real. One argument for this will be that the defilements are all themselves based on the mistaken view that there is an agent of actions. Since it is not ultimately true that there is a self (see 18.6), it cannot be ultimately true that there are defilements. The present argument is that, given this result about the defilements, it makes no sense to suppose that actions are ultimately real.

karma kleśāś ca dehānāṃ pratyayāḥ samudāhṛtāḥ /
karma kleśāś ca te śūnyā yadi deheṣu kā kathā //27//

27. Action and the defilements are described as conditions for the arising of the body.
If action and the defilements are empty, then what is to be said of the body?

According to the twelve-link chain of dependent origination, the occurrence of the body in a new life is dependent on the actions and their root defilements in the prior life. The argument so far has been that the defilements and action lack intrinsic nature and thus are empty. This verse extends that result to the body that is said to be their product.

The opponent now seeks to defend his view by citing the teachings of the Buddha, who appears to have accepted the existence of beings that are both agent and enjoyer when he spoke of something that is "enclosed in ignorance and bound by thirst."

avidyānivṛto jantus tṛṣṇāsaṃyojanaś ca yaḥ /
sa bhoktā sa ca na kartur anyo na ca sa eva saḥ //28//

28. [Objection:] The person who is enclosed in ignorance and bound by thirst,
that person is the enjoyer; but that one is neither someone other than the agent nor someone identical with the agent.

The Buddha said that beings are "enclosed in ignorance and bound by thirst." (The passage quoted by both the *Akutobhayā* and Candrakīrti, and identified by the *Akutobhayā* as from the "Anavarāgra Sūtra," is found at S II.178.) And as the context makes clear, such beings must be both agent of the action and enjoyer of the fruit of the action. For in the twelve-link formula of dependent origination, ignorance is said to occur in one life while thirst is a fruit that results from that ignorance in the succeeding life. But the Buddha also said (e.g., at S II.76) that the person who acts and the person who reaps the fruit are neither the same person nor are they distinct persons. Since agent and enjoyer are said by the Buddha to exist, the opponent reasons that action must likewise exist.

na pratyayasamutpannaṃ nāpratyayasamutthitam /
asti yasmād idaṃ karma tasmāt kartāpi nāsty ataḥ //29//

29. [Reply:] Since the action does not exist dependent on conditions and does not exist having sprung up without dependence on conditions, therefore the agent also does not exist.

If actions are empty (v. 27), it cannot be ultimately true that they arise—whether their arising is dependent on conditions or is unconditioned. But in the absence of ultimately real actions, there cannot be an agent of those actions.

To this it might be added that when the opponent sought to support his view by quoting the Buddha, he missed an important point. When the Buddha said that agent and enjoyer are neither identical nor distinct, this was not a way of saying that there is a real agent who bears some sort of indeterminate relation to a real enjoyer. Instead this was a way of saying that, strictly speaking, there is no such thing as the agent (or the enjoyer, either). This is the Buddha's "middle path" solution discussed above in the comments on verse 10.

karma cen nāsti kartā ca kutaḥ syāt karmajaṃ phalam /
asaty atha phale bhoktā kuta eva bhaviṣyati //30//

30. If there is neither action nor agent, how would there be the fruit born of the action?
Moreover if the fruit does not exist, how will there be its enjoyer?

Something is a karmic fruit only if it arises in dependence on an action. So if there ultimately are no actions, there likewise can be no ultimately real fruits. And something is the enjoyer of a fruit only if there are fruits to be enjoyed.

yathā nirmitakaṃ śāstā nirmimītārddhisaṃpadā |
nirmito nirmimītānyaṃ sa ca nirmitakaḥ punaḥ ||31||
tathā nirmitakākāraḥ kartā yat karma tatkṛtam |
tadyathā nirmitenānyo nirmito nirmitas tathā ||32||

31. Just as the Teacher by his supernatural power fabricates a magical being
that in turn fabricates yet another magical being,
32. so with regard to the agent, which has the form of a magical being, and the action that is done by it,
it is like the case where a second magical being is fabricated by a magical being.

kleśāḥ karmāṇi dehāś ca kartāraś ca phalāni ca |
gandharvanagarākārā marīcisvapnasaṃnibhāḥ ||33||

33. Defilements, actions, and bodies, agents, and fruits,
are similar to the city of the gandharvas; they are like a mirage, a dream.

For the city of the gandharvas see 7.34. The guiding image of these three verses is that of a buddha endowed with supernatural powers that are of use in teaching the Dharma. Among these powers is that of making the audience see a magician who then produces various magical illusions. These illusions are thus products of something that is itself a magical illusion. Applied to the subject matter of this chapter, the analogy gives the result that agent and enjoyer of fruit are mere appearances that merely appear to produce the apparent action and enjoy the apparent fruit respectively, and that all these appearances are useful for attaining the end of the Buddha's teachings: nirvāṇa.

18. An Analysis of the Self

WHILE WE FOLLOW Candrakīrti in calling this chapter an analysis of the self, the commentators introduce it as being concerned with the nature of reality. The connection between these two topics is as follows. Buddhists all agree that there is nothing in reality that is the basis of our sense of "I" and "mine." They agree that it is our mistaken belief in the existence of something behind this sense of "I" and "mine" that brings about suffering. So they should all agree that reality is characterized by the absence of self. The question is, what is this reality that falsely appears as if it included a self? For Abhidharma, the answer is that reality is just the impermanent, impersonal dharmas. Abhidharma holds that there must be such a reality on which the false belief in "I" and "mine" is superimposed. Madhyamaka agrees that belief in "I" and "mine" is false. But Madhyamaka disputes the claim that there must be dharmas, things with intrinsic nature, underlying this false belief. (The dual focus of this chapter is reflected in the name given it by Buddhapālita and Bhāviveka, "An Analysis of the Self and Dharmas.") The argument proceeds by examining the common ground shared by both sides—rejection of a self—and then exploring the consequences of this for our conception of reality.

It begins with what looks like a perfectly orthodox account of the doctrine of nonself and the role its realization plays in the cessation of suffering. But in verse 5 a new note is struck: Liberation requires realization of the emptiness of all things. In the remainder of the chapter Nāgārjuna tries to show that this central Madhyamaka claim is fully in line with the core teachings of the Buddha. This will involve attempting to dispel what for the Mādhyamika are misconceptions about those teachings, such as that the doctrine of nonself was meant to represent a description of the ultimate nature of reality, or that the ultimate nature of reality is to be grasped through a kind of nonconceptual intuition. In three pairs of verses he will present a core Buddhist teaching first in positive terms and then purely negatively; the first represents how other Buddhists have understood the doctrine, the second is the Madhyamaka understanding. In each case the suggestion will be that while other interpretations of the teaching in question all have their place in the path to liberation, the Madhyamaka stance represents the culmination. In outline the chapter may be represented as follows:

18.1–3 Establishment of nonself
- 18.1: Refutation of the self
- 18.2: Refutation of what belongs to the self
- 18.3: Refutation of the person

18.4 Soteriological consequences of nonself: liberation

18.5 Liberation requires realization of emptiness

18.6–11 Madhyamaka as expressing core elements of the Buddha's teachings
- 18.6–7: The Buddha's graded teachings on the self, with cessation of hypostatization through realization of emptiness as the final step
- 18.8–9: The Buddha's graded teachings about the nature of reality, with the realization that reality lacks an ultimate nature being the final step
- 18.10: How emptiness establishes the Buddha's middle path between eternalism and annihilationism
- 18.11: The Buddha's teachings themselves characterized by emptiness

18.12 Significance of pratyekabuddhas to correct understanding of the Buddha's teachings

ātmā skandhā yadi bhaved udayavyayabhāg bhavet /
skandhebhyo 'nyo yadi bhaved bhaved askandhalakṣaṇaḥ //1//

1. If the self were the skandhas, it would participate in coming to be and passing away.
If it were something other than the skandhas, it would be something having the defining characteristic of a non-skandha.

For the skandha classification see chapter 4. Candrakīrti tells us that by "self" (*ātman*) is meant the object of the sense of "I." He also says that while elsewhere the relation between self and skandhas is examined using the fivefold schema that was used in looking at the relation between fire and fuel (see 10.14, 16.2), here the analysis will consider just the two possibilities of identity and distinctness. To say that the self is identical with the skandhas is to say that the self is nothing more than these psychophysical elements, in the same way in which a pile of bricks is just the individual bricks. The argument against the self being identical with the skandhas is simply that since they come into and go out of existence many times over the course of a single life (and likewise over the course of rebirth), one would have many selves over time. This clearly conflicts with our sense of an "I," for we each take ourselves to be a single entity that endures over time. The argument against the self being distinct from the skandhas is that it should then be grasped as something with its own intrinsic nature, distinct from the intrinsic natures of the five skandhas. Yet no such thing is ever grasped in our experience of persons.

ātmany asati cātmīyaṃ kuta eva bhaviṣyati /
nirmamo nirahaṃkāraḥ śamād ātmātmanīyayoḥ //2//

2. The self not existing, how will there be "what belongs to the self"?
There is no "mine" and no "I" because of the cessation of self
and that which pertains to the self.

Our ordinary conception of the person involves the notion of an "I" and also the notion of the "mine." The "I" is conceptualized as the subject or owner, while the "mine" is what this "I" appropriates or takes as its own. The commentators explain that by "mine" or "what belongs to the self" is here meant specifically the five appropriation skandhas—those psychophysical elements that are the basis of identification. The argument here is that if there is no self, there can likewise be no appropriation skandhas, which are by definition elements that the person appropriates. And, says the *Akutobhayā*, the nonexistence of the self and what belongs to the self is the defining characteristic of reality. Notice, however, that this need not be taken to mean that there are no skandhas. All this argument seems to show is that if there are skandhas, they do not have the property of being appropriated by the self.

nirmamo nirahaṃkāro yaś ca so 'pi na vidyate /
nirmamaṃ nirahaṃkāraṃ yaḥ paśyati na paśyati //3//

3. And who is without "mine" and "I"-sense, he is not found.
One who sees that which is without "mine" and "I"-sense
does not see.

This verse comes in response to an objection: If reality is devoid of "I" and "mine," then those who know reality are themselves devoid of "I" and "mine." But in order for this to be true, there must be such beings who are lacking in all sense of "I" and "mine." And for there to be such beings, there must be a self and the skandhas that that self appropriates.

This objection in effect says that the Buddhist thesis of nonself cannot coherently be stated, for if it were true then it would be false.

The response to this objection is that only defective vision could make one see a person where there is no self and no appropriation skandhas. For the person is named and conceptualized in dependence on the skandhas that are thought of as its own. So without a self and without appropriation of skandhas, how could there be any conception of a person?

> *mamety aham iti kṣīṇe bahiś cādhyātmam eva ca |*
> *nirudhyata upādānaṃ tatkṣayāj janmanaḥ kṣayaḥ ||4||*

4. The senses of "mine" and "I" based on the outer and the inner being lost,
appropriation is extinguished; because of losing that, there is the cessation of birth.

This is the standard account of nirvāṇa accepted by all Buddhists: One attains release from saṃsāra by ridding oneself of all sense of "I" and "mine"; this leads to an end of appropriation of the skandhas, hence to an end of the processes responsible for rebirth. "Outer" is explained as whatever is thought of as distinct from the self and is thus a potential object of appropriation. "Inner" is explained as whatever is taken as the core or essence of the person.

> *karmakleśakṣayān mokṣaḥ karmakleśā vikalpataḥ |*
> *te prapañcāt prapañcas tu śūnyatāyāṃ nirudhyate ||5||*

5. Liberation is attained through the destruction of actions and defilements; actions and defilements arise because of falsifying conceptualizations;
those arise from hypostatization; but hypostatization is extinguished in emptiness.

For the defilements see 14.2. By "falsifying conceptualizations" (*vikalpa*) is here meant all thoughts involving the concepts of "I" and "mine." Actions cannot arise out of the defilements without these concepts. Action based on aversion, for instance, requires the concepts of the "I" and the "not-I." Such conceptualizations in turn require the occurrence of hypostatization (*prapañca*), which is the tendency to reify what are actually just useful ways of talking. (See 11.6.) But this tendency is undermined through coming to realize the emptiness of all dharmas.

The commentators explain "emptiness" to mean the lack of intrinsic nature of all dharmas and not just the emptiness of essence that Ābhidharmikas agree characterizes the person. This is the distinctively Mādhyamika use of "emptiness," something that would not be readily accepted by Ābhidharmikas given their view that dharmas are ultimately real precisely because they bear intrinsic natures. Ābhidharmikas agree that liberation requires knowledge of emptiness but only in the sense of the emptiness of the person. Mādhyamikas claim that liberation requires knowledge of the emptiness of all dharmas. (See 13.2.) As Candrakīrti explains, "These falsifying conceptions are aroused due to various hypostatizations stemming from repeated practice over the course of beginningless births of such dichotomies as cognition and the cognized, what is expressed and expression, agent and action, instrument and act, pot and cloth, crown and chariot, *rūpa* and feeling, woman and man, profit and loss, pleasure and pain, fame and infamy, blame and praise, and so on" (LVP p. 350). All such dichotomies, in other words, contribute to suffering when we take them to reflect the nature of reality and fail to see them as mere useful tools.

ātmety api prajñapitam anātmety api deśitam /
buddhair nātmā na cānātmā kaścid ity api deśitam //6//

6. "The self" is conveyed and "nonself" is taught
by buddhas; it is taught as well that neither self nor nonself is the case.

That the Buddha sometimes explained his teachings in a way that could be taken to express belief in a self is generally acknowledged by Buddhists. But this is taken to be an example of the Buddha's pedagogical skill (*upāya*). For the occasions of such teachings involve audiences who do not acknowledge karma and rebirth and consequently believe that their good and evil deeds die with them. Since this belief led these people to conduct that bound them ever more firmly to saṃsāra, the Buddha judged it best that they first come to accept the existence of rebirth. Since rebirth is most easily understood in terms of the idea of a self that transmigrates, this led to discourses that appear to convey belief in a self. But the Buddha's pedagogical strategy was to help these people achieve a less deluded view of reality so that they would eventually be able to understand the teaching of nonself.

This orthodox understanding of the Buddha's teachings seems to suggest that nonself is the accepted view for all Buddhists. But this verse goes on to suggest otherwise. It suggests that when the Buddha taught nonself, he was likewise employing his pedagogical skill, so that this too is not to be taken as the ultimately correct account of reality. Candrakīrti explains that to so take the teaching of nonself is to overlook the Buddha's insistence that his is a "middle path." According to Candrakīrti, "self" and "nonself" are counterpoised theses, each of which is required to give the other meaning. So if the doctrine of self does not accurately represent the nature of reality, then the doctrine of nonself likewise cannot. There is then a third teaching, to the effect that there is neither self nor nonself. One might take this for Madhyamaka's final teaching on the self, what it takes to represent the ultimate truth on the matter. But if this verse and the next verse follow the pattern of verses 8 and 9 below, then all three views discussed in this verse would be "graded teachings," none of which counts as ultimately true by Madyamaka standards. (The third may, however, represent a distinctively Mahāyāna view held, for instance, by some members of the Yogācāra school.)

nivṛttam abhidhātavyaṃ nivṛttaś cittagocaraḥ |
anutpannāniruddhā hi nirvāṇam iva dharmatā ||7||

7. The domain of objects of consciousness having ceased, what is to be named is ceased.
The nature of things is to be, like nirvāṇa, without origination or cessation.

The *Akutobhayā* explains that once one has understood that *rūpa* and other dharmas are empty of intrinsic nature, one realizes that ultimately there are no objects of which to be aware. And when one is no longer aware of anything ultimately real, the temptation to employ dichotomous concepts and hypostatizing discourse concerning such things as pots and cloth, crowns and chariots, ceases. This might be taken to show that realization of emptiness (in the Madhyamaka sense) is connected to the meditational state of the "signless" (*animitta*) that the Buddha says immediately precedes the attainment of nirvāṇa (see D II.102). But it also suggests that emptiness represents the final stage on the path that other Buddhists took to culminate in insight into nonself. For while all agree that hypostatization lies at the root of the problem of suffering, only Madhyamaka appreciates that it is not just hypostatization concerning "I" and "mine" that is problematic. The realization that all things are devoid of intrinsic nature is required in order to bring to a halt our tendency to see ultimately real entities behind what are merely useful concepts.

sarvaṃ tathyaṃ na vā tathyaṃ tathyaṃ cātathyam eva ca |
naivātathyaṃ naiva tathyam etad buddhānuśāsanam ||8||

8. All is real, or all is unreal, all is both real and unreal,
all is neither unreal nor real; this is the graded teaching of the Buddha.

The "all" here refers to the skandhas, āyatanas, dhātus, and the like, things that Ābhidharmikas claim exist. Their being real would consist in their actually existing with the natures they are thought to possess (such as vision's having the power to apprehend color and shape). This verse appears to affirm at least one of the four possibilities that arise with respect to this thesis. But it does not rule out the possibility that all four might be true. And the third and fourth possibilities themselves seem to be contradictory. Moreover, the commentaries explain that all four possibilities may be affirmed. So it may seem as if Nāgārjuna is here asserting one or more contradictions.

The invocation of the notion of a "graded teaching" is meant to forestall the objection that only one of these four possibilities could be true. This notion is a variant on the idea of the Buddha's pedagogical skill that was invoked in verse 6. It involves the idea that each of the Buddha's different (and seemingly conflicting) teachings on a given topic can be placed within a hierarchy, so that all can be reconciled as leading toward some single understanding or goal.

According to the *Akutobhayā*, the hierarchy involved here is as follows: "All is real" affirms the Abhidharma theses about the skandhas and so on as conventionally true. (Ābhidharmikas would obviously disagree; they claim that their accounts of these entities are ultimately true.) "All is unreal" refers to the fact that none of these theses is ultimately true (since all these entities are empty and thus lack the intrinsic natures that they appear to possess). "All is both real and unreal" asserts that the Abhidharma theses are both conventionally true and ultimately false. And "All is neither real nor unreal" expresses the insight of the yogins, who, because they investigate reality in a way that does not involve superimposition of falsifying concepts, can find nothing to be said or thought concerning the nature of reality.

One might wonder whether the Mādhyamika is entitled to say that there is a hierarchy here. To say that there is is to suggest that each position comes closer to accurately reflecting the nature of reality than its predecessor. And it is to suggest that the last position best represents how things ultimately are. If Mādhyamikas were to say this, they would seem to contradict their claim that nothing bears an intrinsic nature. For an account to accurately reflect how things ultimately are, it would seem that it must correctly describe their intrinsic natures. If nothing bears an intrinsic nature, then no account can be true to the intrinsic natures of things. (See 13.7–8.) But perhaps the hierarchy here is not based on increasing accuracy but on increasing usefulness for achieving our goal (in this case, the cessation of suffering).

aparapratyayaṃ śāntaṃ prapañcair aprapañcitam |
nirvikalpam anānārtham etat tattvasya lakṣaṇam ||9||

9. Not to be attained by means of another, free [from intrinsic nature], not populated by hypostatization,
devoid of falsifying conceptualization, not having many separate meanings—this is the nature of reality.

While in verse 5 "falsifying conceptualization" and "hypostatization" would have been taken by an Ābhidharmika to refer to our tendency to construe experience in terms of "I" and "mine," in this verse they clearly refer to our tendency to suppose that things have intrinsic natures. In other words, while verse 5 could be understood as concerned with the "emptiness of the person" (the person's being devoid of essence), this verse is clearly concerned with the emptiness of dharmas (dharmas' lack of intrinsic nature). For Mahāyāna Buddhists, this is the most important difference between the Mahāyāna and the Abhidharma understandings of reality.

To say that the nature of reality is not to be attained by means of another is to say that one must apprehend it directly for oneself. Candrakīrti provides the example of someone who sees hairs everywhere because of an eye disorder. While such a person can come to understand that the hairs are unreal through being told so by someone with normal vision, this will not prevent the person from still seeing the hairs. Only through some sort of personal transformation can that person come to no longer see hairs everywhere. By the same token, we can come to understand that nothing actually bears the nature that it presents to us in our experience, but this alone will not prevent our experiencing things as having their natures intrinsically. It is possible to come to experience the emptiness of things directly, but this requires a kind of personal transformation.

To say that reality lacks many separate meanings is to say that all things are fundamentally of the same nature—namely, empty of intrinsic nature. But the commentators all add that this is also a consequence of reality's being grasped without using falsifying conceptualization. For if nothing has an intrinsic nature, then a correct seeing of things cannot use the natures of things in order to draw conceptual distinctions. In order to discriminate between "this" and "that," one must be able to locate some difference in the natures of the "this" and the "that." This will prove impossible if things lack their own natures.

Finally, notice that while both verse 8 and verse 9 concern the nature of reality, the views canvassed in verse 8 are said to all fall short of the final characterization of its ultimate nature, while no such qualification is made about the view put forward in verse 9. And notice as well that all the terms in verse 9 are negative.

> *pratītya yad yad bhavati na hi tāvat tad eva tat /*
> *na cānyad api tat tasmān nocchinnaṃ nāpi śāśvatam //10//*

10. When something exists dependent on something [as its cause], that is not on the one hand identical with that [cause],
but neither is it different; therefore that [cause] is neither destroyed nor eternal.

Nāgārjuna is here drawing several parallels between the Madhyamaka teaching of the emptiness of all dharmas and the Buddha's teachings concerning the person. For instance, the Buddha said that the reaper of the karmic fruit is neither identical with nor distinct from the sower of the karmic seed. And he claimed that through understanding this one could see how his account of persons avoids the extremes of eternalism and annihilationism. Nāgārjuna here claims that when one dharma causes another, the two can be neither identical nor distinct. And he says that for this reason the extremes of annihilationism and eternalism with respect to dharmas can be avoided.

The argument for the claim that the cause is neither identical with nor distinct from the effect is the one given at 1.1–7, 4.1–3, 10.1–7, and 12.2–3. If cause and effect were identical, producing the effect would be pointless. If they were distinct, then anything could be the cause of anything. That it follows from this that dharmas are neither annihilated nor eternal depends on the point that in order for something to be either eternal or subject to annihilation, it must be ultimately real. Any two ultimately real things must be either identical or else distinct. If cause and effect are neither, then it cannot be ultimately true that the cause is either eternal or subject to annihilation. The strategy here precisely parallels the Buddha's in presenting his claim that sower and reaper are neither identical not distinct.

Other Buddhists would not accept the Madhyamaka claim that cause and effect are neither identical nor distinct when applied to the case of dharmas. They would, though, agree that when there is a causal relation between two things that turn out on analysis to be neither identical nor distinct, that allows us to say that the cause is neither annihilated nor eternal. This was precisely the Buddha's strategy of the middle path: show that the person is neither subject to annihilation nor eternal by showing that because sower and reaper can be neither identical nor distinct, these can only represent hypostatizations of the elements in a causal series.

anekārtham anānārtham anucchedam aśāśvatam |
etat tal lokanāthānāṃ buddhānāṃ śāsanāmṛtam ||11||

11. Not having a single goal, not having many goals, not destroyed, not eternal:
This is the nectar of the teachings of the buddhas, lords of the world.

Typically, a classical Indian treatise on some subject begins with a statement of the goal or purpose (*artha*) of the inquiry contained in that treatise. Here the Buddha's teachings are said to have neither just a single goal nor many goals. The *Akutobhayā* and Buddhapālita give attaining heaven and attaining liberation as examples of goals that such a teaching might be thought to have. The idea here is that if all things are empty, then such things as goals cannot be ultimately real.

Candrakīrti, though, understands the word we have translated as "goal" (*artha*) differently. He takes it to here be used in its other sense of "meaning." So he takes the first line of this verse to say that the Buddha's teachings should be understood as being "free of both unity and diversity when analyzed, and beyond both eternalism and annihilationism" (LVP p. 377).

The key point in this verse, however, comes with the claim that the Buddha's teachings are neither destroyed nor eternal. If we follow the logic of verse 10, this would mean that the Buddha's teachings are empty. If for instance we take dependent origination to be central to the Buddha's middle path, then this would turn out not to represent the fixed order of how things ultimately are in themselves.

saṃbuddhānām anutpāde śrāvakāṇāṃ punaḥ kṣaye /
jñānaṃ pratyekabuddhānām asaṃsargāt pravartate //12//

12. Though the completely enlightened ones do not arise and the śrāvakas disappear,
the knowledge of the pratyekabuddhas arises independently.

A *pratyekabuddha* is someone who attains nirvāṇa entirely on his or her own, without learning the path to nirvāṇa through encountering the teachings of a buddha. This is also true of buddhas ("completely enlightened ones"). But buddhas share their realization with others while pratyekabuddhas do not. The śrāvakas, or "hearers," are those who attain liberation through following the teachings of a buddha. According to the *Akutobhayā*, Nāgārjuna brings up this trichotomy of enlightened figures in order to show that Buddhism has always recognized a kind of enlightening insight that is "not to be attained by means of another" (v. 9). But the figure of the pratyekabuddha might also serve as a concrete image illustrating the point that the Buddha's teachings are neither annihilated nor eternal. For pratyekabuddhas arise at a time when the most recent buddha's teachings have been forgotten and a new buddha has not yet appeared.

19. An Analysis of Time

ANY ACCOUNT of the ultimate nature of reality must include something concerning the status of time. On the face of it there seem to be just two possibilities: that time is itself among the things that are ultimately real and that time is a conceptual fiction constructed on the basis of facts about those things that are ultimately real. Nāgārjuna considers the first possibility in verses 1–5 and the second in verse 6.

Time consists of three phases: past, present, and future. So if time is real, then these three must likewise be real. Do they exist independently of one another, or are they in relations of mutual dependence? Buddhapālita begins his commentary on this chapter by rejecting the thesis of independence. The grounds for this rejection are that if, say, the future existed by itself, then where it existed would always be the future and never the present or the past. The result would be that time would be static and unchanging: what exists in the future would never be anything but future. In this case, since the existence of time is supposed to explain the possibility of change, an inquiry into time's nature would be futile. So if there is time, we must conclude that the three phases of time exist dependent on one another: something is, for instance, the present or future only by virtue of occurring later than the past.

In outline the argument proceeds as follows:

Assumption: Time must either (a) itself be ultimately real, or else (b) exist dependent on the existence of entities.

Suppose (a).

19.1–2 Refutation of possibility that present and future exist dependent on the past

19.3ab Refutation of possibility that present and future exist independently of the past

19.3cd Conclusion: Present and future do not exist on assumption (a).

19.4 Same strategy refutes possibility of past and present in dependence on the future, of past and future in dependence on the present; also applies to other cases of interdefined triples

19.5 Reply to implicit objection that since time can be measured it must exist: Only that which abides can be measured, and time cannot be abiding.

19.6 Refutation of (b) on the grounds that no entities ultimately exist (something established in the other chapters of this work)

pratyutpanno 'nāgataś ca yady atītam apekṣya hi /
pratyutpanno 'nāgataś ca kāle 'tīte bhaviṣyataḥ //1//

1. If the present and the future exist dependent on the past,
then present and future would be at the past time.

The difficulty with the thesis of dependence is that then present and future must exist not only in the present and future respectively but in the past as well. And the present cannot be what it is—namely the time in which what is now occurring takes place—if it exists not just now but also in the past. For if it existed in the past, then what is occurring would also be what has already occurred, which is absurd. Why, though, does the thesis of dependence require that present and future exist in the past? The next verse addresses this question.

pratyutpanno 'nāgataś ca na stas tatra punar yadi |
pratyutpanno 'nāgataś ca syātāṃ katham apekṣya tam ||2||

2. If, moreover, present and future do not exist there,
then how would present and future exist dependent on
that?

The argument is simply that there cannot be dependence of one thing on another thing unless they both exist at the same time. The son is dependent for his being a son on the father, and this relation of dependence requires that the two exist together at some time.

anapekṣya punaḥ siddhir nātītaṃ vidyate tayoḥ |
pratyutpanno 'nāgataś ca tasmāt kālo na vidyate ||3||

3. There is no establishment of the two, moreover, if they are
independent of the past.
Therefore neither present nor future time exists.

The argument for this would appear to be the one that Buddhapālita gave in framing the argument of verse 1.

etenaivāvaśiṣṭau dvau krameṇa parivartakau |
uttamādhamamadhyādīn ekatvādīṃś ca lakṣayet ||4||

4. In this manner one would regard the remaining two cases.
Thus one would regard best, worst, and middling as well as
singularity and so on.

The same reasoning can be used to show that past and future would have to exist in the present and that past and present must exist in the future, thereby demonstrating the absurdity of supposing that the three times could exist in dependence on one another. Likewise one could develop an argument along the same lines in order to demonstrate a problem with other such triads: best, worst, and middling, for instance, and singularity, duality, and plurality. Buddhapālita adds that the same reasoning would undermine the real existence of such pairs as near and far, earlier and later, cause and effect, and so forth.

nāsthito gṛhyate kālaḥ sthitaḥ kālo na vidyate /
yo gṛhyetāgṛhītaś ca kālaḥ prajñapyate katham //5//

5. A nonabiding time cannot be apprehended; an abiding time that can be apprehended does not exist. And how is a nonapprehended time conceived?

The opponent has objected to the preceding argument on the grounds that time must surely exist since it can be measured in such units as instant, moment, hour, and the like. Nāgārjuna then responds with a dilemma: Does this time that can be measured exist as something that abides or remains unchanging, or does it exist as something nonabiding, as something that undergoes change? As Buddhapālita explains, only that which is fixed or settled can be measured, so a nonabiding time could not be measured. But if we then suppose that time must abide since it can be measured, we run into the difficulty that then time becomes static, which is unacceptable. The only time that might exist and so be measured is one that cannot be apprehended and consequently cannot be measured. So if it is a fact that time can be measured, it cannot follow from this that time is real.

Candrakīrti has the opponent concede at this point that time cannot be an independently existing ultimately real thing. But the opponent thinks there is still a way to acknowledge the reality of time, namely to have it be something that is named and conceptualized on the basis of things that are ultimately real (in the same way in which the person is said to be named and conceptualized on the basis of ultimately real psychophysical elements):

> True, what is known as time does not in any sense exist as a permanent entity, distinct from *rūpa* and so on, endowed with an intrinsic nature. What then? Time, which is designated by such words as "instant" and the like, is conceptualized on the basis of conditioned entities such as *rūpa* and the like. Here there is no fault. (LVP p. 387)

The idea is that time is a derivative notion, a useful way of conceptualizing the occurrence of compounded (and thus impermanent) entities. What exist are those entities; time is our way of understanding their relations. Nāgārjuna then responds:

> *bhāvaṃ pratītya kālaś cet kālo bhāvād ṛte kutaḥ |*
> *na ca kaścana bhāvo 'sti kutaḥ kālo bhaviṣyati ||6||*

6. If time exists dependent on an existent, how will time exist in the absence of an existent?
   No existent whatsoever exists; how, then, will there be time?

The hypothesis in question requires that there be ultimately real entities. And as Candrakīrti laconically points out, this has already been refuted at some length.

20. An Analysis of the Assemblage

In this chapter Nāgārjuna returns to the relation between cause and effect. The "assemblage" referred to in the title is the conjunction of cause and conditions, this conjunction corresponding to what is now called the *total* cause. The stock illustration of this idea is the case of the production of a sprout. While we might be tempted to call the seed the cause of the sprout, this would not be true if by "cause" we meant the necessary and sufficient conditions for the sprout's production. In addition to the seed, there must be such factors as soil, moisture, and warmth before the sprout can arise. The assemblage is the set of all these factors occurring together. In Abhidharma the members of this set are called "cause and conditions" (*hetupratyaya*). The "cause" (*hetu*) usually corresponds in certain respects to what Aristotle called the material cause (in this case the seed). The "conditions" (*pratyaya*) are the other factors.

Now the causal relation is usually thought to be one of producing: To cause is to bring the effect into existence; this is what explains the effect's arising. But now that we have distinguished between what is commonly called the cause (e.g., the seed) and the aggregate of cause and conditions (e.g., the occurrence of seed together with soil, moisture, warmth, etc.), we can ask just what it is that does the producing. Is it the aggregate, or is it just one member of the aggregate, the cause, that actually does the producing? The title we use here is Candrakīrti's, but other commentators give different titles. Buddhapālita and Bhāviveka use the title "An Examination of the Assemblage and Causal Factors," and this better conveys what Nāgārjuna will do here. First he will argue that the aggregate cannot be what produces the effect. To this it might be replied that the aggregate does produce the effect in a metaphorical sense, namely by virtue of the fact that one of its components, the cause, produces the effect. And so the argument then turns to an examination of whether the cause can be said to produce the effect. Nāgārjuna will argue that cause and effect cannot be related to one another in the way that would be necessary in order for it to be literally true that cause produces effect and so metaphorically true that the aggregate produces the effect. The argument proceeds in part by examining the two possibilities for such a relation's obtaining: that the effect exists in its causal antecedents and that the effect is not to be found there. These possibilities are reflected in the two theories of causation known as *satkāryavāda* and *asatkāryavāda*, which we encountered earlier (see 1.3, 4.6, 10.13). But here the consequences of these two views are traced out in much greater detail than above.

The subject of this chapter is closely related to that of chapter 1, which asked whether existing things may be said to *arise* from cause and conditions. But the question in this chapter is whether the aggregate of cause and conditions can be said to *produce* the effect. We use "produce" here instead of "arise" because the verb Nāgārjuna uses here, √*jan*, is different than the one he used in chapter 1, *sam-ut*√*pad*. Both verbs are used to refer to the relation between producer and produced; the first applies to what produces, the second to what is produced. We see no reason to think that the change in verbs has philosophical significance.

The argumentative thread runs as follows:

20.1–8 Refutation of the assemblage of the cause and conditions
- 20.1–4: An effect neither exists nor does not exist in the assemblage.
- 20.5–6: Assemblage has no causal nature that explains pro-

duction of a distinct effect because it could neither be given to the effect nor cease with the assemblage.

20.7–8: Assemblage does not produce a distinct effect whether assemblage exists simultaneous with effect or prior to the effect.

20.9–22 Refutation of the cause

20.9–10ab: The ceased cause does not produce an effect.

20.10cd–11: The cause can be neither connected nor unconnected to its effect.

20.12–15: There can be no contact between cause and effect.

20.16: A cause is neither empty nor non-empty of effect's intrinsic nature.

20.17–18: Effect is neither empty nor non-empty of intrinsic nature.

20.19–20: Cause and effect can be neither identical nor distinct.

20.21: An effect is neither real nor unreal.

20.22: Unproductive cause is not a cause.

20.23–24 Conclusion: Assemblage of the cause and conditions does not produce an effect.

hetoś ca pratyayānāṃ ca sāmagryā jāyate yadi /
phalam asti ca sāmagryāṃ sāmagryā jāyate katham //1//

1. If the effect is produced by the assemblage of the cause and the conditions
and the effect exists in the assemblage, how will it be produced by the assemblage?

To say that the effect exists in the assemblage is to affirm *satkāryavāda*, the view that the effect exists in unmanifest form in its cause. The argument here is that in that case we cannot say that the assemblage produces the effect. In order for something to be produced, it must come into existence at a particular time, the time of production. If the sprout already exists in the assemblage of seed, soil, moisture, warmth, etc., then we cannot say that these produce the sprout. For if the sprout already exists, then they cannot bring it into existence.

hetoś ca pratyayānāṃ ca sāmagryā jāyate yadi |
phalaṃ nāsti ca sāmagryāṃ sāmagryā jāyate katham ||2||

2. If the effect is produced by the assemblage of the cause and the conditions
and the effect does not exist in the assemblage, how will it be produced by the assemblage?

If *satkāryavāda* must be denied, it would seem that we should then embrace *asatkāryavāda*. But this verse claims otherwise. The argument is that to say the effect is produced by the assemblage is to say that the one is produced from the other. And what is not existent in the assemblage cannot be produced from them, any more than sesame oil can be produced by pressing sand.

hetoś ca pratyayānāṃ ca sāmagryām asti cet phalam |
gṛhyeta nanu sāmagryāṃ sāmagryāṃ ca na gṛhyate ||3|

3. If the effect existed in the assemblage of the cause and the conditions,
would it not be perceived in the assemblage? And it is not perceived in the assemblage.

No matter how closely we look, we shall never find a sprout among the seed, soil, moisture, warmth, etc. Thus there are no grounds for maintaining that the effect exists in the assemblage. Of course, as Candrakīrti points out, the supporter of *satkāryavāda* will maintain that there are inferential grounds, such as the fact that one cannot produce sesame oil from sand or curds from a water pot. And as Bhāviveka recognizes, the Sāṃkhya will also claim that the reason we do not perceive the effect in the assemblage is that it has not yet been made manifest. But, says Bhāviveka, the manifestation theory has already been refuted. (See 10.13.) And, says Candrakīrti, the sesame-seeds inference is an argument against *asatkāryavāda*; it is not directly an argument for *satkāryavāda*. It would be such an inferential ground for holding *satkāryavāda* only if the two theories exhausted the possibilities, so that one or the other had to be true. And this is just what the Mādhyamika denies.

hetoś ca pratyayānāṃ ca sāmagryāṃ nāsti cet phalam /
hetavaḥ pratyayāś ca syur ahetupratyayaiḥ samāḥ //4//

4. If the effect did not exist in the assemblage of the cause and the conditions,
then causes and conditions would be the same as noncauses and nonconditions.

The most fundamental difficulty for *asatkāryavāda* is to explain why we can produce a pot but not curds by throwing and firing clay. The assemblage of the clay, the throwing, and the firing counts as cause and conditions with respect to the pot but counts as noncause and nonconditions with respect to the curds. According to *asatkāryavāda*, neither the pot nor the curds exists in the assemblage. What then explains the difference?

hetuṃ phalasya dattvā ca yadi hetur niruddhaṃ ca /
yad dattaṃ yan nirudhaṃ ca hetor ātmadvayaṃ bhavet //5//

5. If the cause, having given its causal character to the effect,
were to cease,
there would be a double nature of the cause—what is given
and what is ceased.

On the Buddhist formulation of *asatkāryavāda*, the cause goes out of existence when the effect is produced. (See 1.5–6.) The opponent might try to answer the difficulty raised in verse 4 by claiming that the cause transfers its causal capacity to the effect when it goes out of existence. But to say this is to attribute to the cause two distinct natures: the nature whereby it is said to have gone out of existence and the nature whereby it is said to have causal capacity. For if it only had a single nature, then that nature would cease when it went out of existence and would not continue on as the nature of the effect. The difficulty Candrakīrti sees with this hypothesis is that the two natures have contradictory characters: The nature that is transferred to the effect is enduring, while the nature that ceases with the cause is transitory. And one thing cannot have two contradictory natures.

hetuṃ phalasyādattvā ca yadi hetur nirudhyate |
hetau niruddhe jātaṃ tat phalam āhetukaṃ bhavet ||6||

6. And if the cause were to cease without having given its causal
character to the effect,
the effect, being produced when the cause is extinguished,
would be without cause.

If the opponent seeks to avoid the above difficulty by claiming that the cause has a single nature that perishes with it, then we are back to the problem of explaining why just these causes and conditions produced this effect. For then the *asatkāryavādin* can no longer explain this by claiming that the cause has a causal capacity that it gives to the effect.

So on this formulation the effect could perfectly well arise from any aggregate of causes and conditions.

phalaṃ sahaiva sāmagryā yadi prādurbhavet punaḥ /
ekakālau prasajyete janako yaś ca janyate //7//

7. If the effect were to become manifest simultaneously with the assemblage,
it would follow that the producer and that which is produced are simultaneous.

If the opponent seeks to avoid the last-mentioned difficulty by having assemblage and effect occur simultaneously, then as Buddhapālita points out, it would be impossible to say which is the cause and which the effect. The father is said to cause the son precisely because the father exists prior to the son.

pūrvam eva ca sāmagryāḥ phalaṃ prādurbhaved yadi /
hetupratyayanirmuktaṃ phalam āhetukaṃ bhavet //8//

8. And if the effect were to become manifest before the assemblage,
then the effect, being devoid of cause and conditions, would be without cause.

The third possibility, besides those of effect succeeding assemblage (vv. 5–6) and effect being simultaneous with assemblage (v. 7), is that the effect occurs before the assemblage. This has the obvious defect that in that case the assemblage cannot possibly cause the effect, which must then be considered to arise causelessly. The argument of these four verses is another instance of the three-times schema applied to the case of causation, parallel to that of 1.5–6.

niruddhe cet phalaṃ hetau hetoḥ saṃkramaṇaṃ bhavet |
pūrvajātasya hetoś ca punarjanma prasajyate ||9||

9. If it were held that, the cause having ceased, there were transference of the cause to the effect,
it would follow that there is another birth of a cause that had already been produced.

At this point, according to the commentators, a new opponent (identified by Bhāviveka as a Sāṃkhya) enters the discussion. This opponent agrees that the aggregate does not produce the effect; instead the effect is produced by the cause (*hetu*). The hypothesis under scrutiny here is that when the cause ceases, its nature is transferred to the effect. But as Candrakīrti points out, this is just like saying that the cause has changed into the dress of an effect. It thus conflicts with the fundamental Buddhist tenet that nothing is permanent, for it is saying that something endures through the change of clothing from that of cause to that of effect. And since the opponent holds that the effect is produced or born, this birth will be its second, for the effect is just the cause in new clothing, and the cause was previously produced. This is likewise an absurd consequence. Buddhist philosophers agree with Locke, who said that a given thing can only have one beginning of existence. (See *An Essay Concerning Human Understanding* II.27.1.)

janayet phalam utpannaṃ niruddho 'staṃgataḥ katham |
hetus tiṣṭhann api kathaṃ phalena janayed vṛtaḥ ||10||

10. How could what is ceased and ended produce an arisen effect?
How, on the other hand, could a cause that is connected with the effect, though enduring, produce the effect?

Suppose the opponent were to respond to the above difficulty by reverting to the view that the cause goes out of existence before the effect comes into existence. In that case the cause cannot be what is responsible for the nature of the effect. For an entity that no longer exists can do nothing. If, in order to remedy this defect, the opponent were to claim that cause and effect stand in some sort of relation that makes possible the cause's determining the nature of the effect, then they must exist together. And if they exist together while the cause brings about the determination of the effect's nature, then the effect must have already come into existence before the cause produced it. So once again the cause cannot be what produces the effect.

athāvṛtaḥ phalenāsau katamaj janayet phalam |
na hy adṛṣṭvā na dṛṣṭvā ca hetur janayate phalam ||11||

11. And if unconnected with the effect, what sort of effect will that produce?
The cause will not produce the effect whether it has seen or not seen [the object].

Here 11ab continues the line of argument of verse 10. An opponent who agrees that the cause cannot have the appropriate sort of connection to the effect must then concede that the cause cannot determine the nature of the effect. Thus there is no reason why it should produce any one sort of effect rather than some other.

According to the *Akutobhayā* and Bhāviveka, 11cd introduces an example to make a related point. The example is the production of visual consciousness by the sense faculty of vision. The question is whether vision produces this effect having already itself seen what is visible or having not seen it. If one says the former, then vision's production of visual consciousness will be production of what has already arisen, since its having seen the visible just is an instance of visual consciousness. As for the alternative that vision produces visual consciousness without having seen the visible object, in that case anything whatever might be seen, regardless of what vision has come in contact with. Suppose my eyes come in contact with a patch of blue and this contact results in visual consciousness. If my vision produces this visual consciousness without having itself seen blue, why should the resulting visual consciousness be of blue and not of red, which is equally unseen by my vision?

nātītasya hy atītena phalasya saha hetunā /
nājātena na jātena saṃgatir jātu vidyate //12//

12. Never is there contact of a past effect with a past cause,
with a future cause, nor with a present cause.

nājātasya hy ajātena phalasya saha hetunā /
nātītena na jātena saṃgatir jātu vidyate //13//

13. Never is there contact of a future effect with a future cause,
with a past cause, nor with a present cause.

na jātasya hi jātena phalasya saha hetunā /
nājātena na naṣṭena saṃgatir jātu vidyate //14//

14. Never is there contact of a present effect with a present cause,
with a future cause, nor with a cause that has perished.

For the cause to determine the effect, there must obtain some relation of contact between the two. And this requires that they exist together. Things that are past and things that are future do not exist: Past things no longer exist, while future things do not yet exist. This explains why real contact is ruled out in all cases where one or both of the relata are either past or future. The one remaining case is where both are presently occurring. The difficulty with this, the commentators explain, is that cause and effect are never simultaneous. So the overall argument here is essentially the same as that of 1.5–6.

asatyāṃ saṃgatau hetuḥ kathaṃ janayate phalam /
satyāṃ vā saṃgatau hetuḥ kathaṃ janayate phalam //15//

15. In the absence of contact, how could a cause produce an effect?
But then if there is contact, how could a cause produce an effect?

This verse summarizes the reasoning of the preceding three verses. The production relation that must hold between cause and effect requires that both exist together. Yet when they do exist together, the production of the effect becomes superfluous, since it already exists.

hetuḥ phalena śūnyaś cet kathaṃ janayate phalam /
hetuḥ phalenāśūnyaś cet kathaṃ janayate phalam //16//

16. If the cause is empty of the effect, how will it produce the effect?
If the cause is not empty of the effect, how will it produce the effect?

To say that the cause is empty (or devoid) of the effect is to say that the intrinsic nature of the effect is not found in the cause. The reason for rejecting this hypothesis is the same as in verse 4: In that case the alleged cause is no different from other factors that we agree are non-causes. The alternative is to say that the intrinsic nature of the effect is found in the cause. But in this case the effect already exists, since its existence is just the occurrence of its intrinsic nature. So in this case the cause cannot be said to produce the effect.

phalaṃ notpatsyate 'śūnyam aśūnyaṃ na nirotsyate /
aniruddham anutpannam aśūnyaṃ tad bhaviṣyati //17//

17. A non-empty effect will not arise, a non-empty effect will not cease.
Being non-empty, it will be unceased and unarisen.

To say the effect is non-empty is to say it bears its own intrinsic nature. The argument for the claim that something with intrinsic nature can neither arise nor cease was given in chapter 15.

katham utpatsyate śūnyaṃ kathaṃ śūnyaṃ nirotsyate |
śūnyam apy aniruddhaṃ tad anutpannaṃ prasajyate ||18||

18. How will what is empty arise? How will what is empty cease?
It follows that what is empty is also unceased and unarisen.

Since what is empty or devoid of intrinsic nature is not ultimately real, it cannot be ultimately true that an effect that is empty arises or ceases.

hetoḥ phalasya caikatvaṃ na hi jātūpapadyate |
hetoḥ phalasya cānyatvaṃ na hi jātūpapadyate ||19||

19. It can never hold that cause and effect are one.
It can never hold that cause and effect are distinct.

ekatve phalahetvoḥ syād aikyaṃ janakajanyayoḥ |
pṛthaktve phalahetvoḥ syāt tulyo hetur ahetunā ||20||

20. Given oneness of cause and effect, there would be unity of producer and product.
Given separateness of cause and effect, there would be equivalence of cause and noncause.

Are cause and effect identical or are they distinct? If they are identical, then father is identical with son, vision is identical with visual consciousness, seed is identical with sprout, and so on. If, on the other hand, they are distinct, then once again the cause is no different from a noncause, and the effect would be utterly independent of the cause.

phalaṃ svabhāvasadbhūtaṃ kiṃ hetur janayiṣyati |
phalaṃ svabhāvāsadbhūtaṃ kiṃ hetur janayiṣyati ||21||

21. How will a cause produce an intrinsically real effect?
How will a cause produce an intrinsically unreal effect?

The argument here is essentially the same as that of verses 17–18.

na cājanayamānasya hetutvam upapadyate |
hetutvānupapattau ca phalaṃ kasya bhaviṣyati ||22||

22. If something is not producing [an effect], it cannot be the cause.
And if it cannot be the cause, whose effect will [the effect] be?

Something has the nature of a cause only if it actively produces. No adequate account of production seems to be forthcoming. But something can be an effect only if it is produced by a cause. Hence there can likewise be no effects.

na ca pratyayahetūnām iyam ātmānam ātmanā |
yā sāmagrī janayate sā kathaṃ janayet phalam ||23||

23. If an assemblage of cause and conditions does not produce itself by means of itself, how could it produce an effect?

Should the opponent object that the argument has strayed from the original hypothesis—that the assemblage produces the effect—to the different view that a single cause produces the effect, the response is that the assemblage is not itself ultimately real, being a whole made of parts. As such it is incapable of performing any real function.

na sāmagrīkṛtaṃ phalaṃ nāsāmagrīkṛtaṃ phalam |
asti pratyayasāmagrī kuta eva phalaṃ vinā ||24||

24. The effect not being made by the assemblage, the effect is also not made without the assemblage.
How indeed can there be an assemblage in the absence of an effect?

Since the assemblage is not itself a real entity, it cannot be what produced the effect. But to say that the effect is produced without the assemblage is to say that the effect is uncaused, which is impossible. For by "the assemblage" is meant the occurring together of cause and conditions. So one cannot say that there is an effect. And in this case one equally cannot say that there is an assemblage of cause and conditions. The existence of such an assemblage obviously depends on their together possessing the capacity to produce an effect, and we are unable to find an effect.

21. An Analysis of Arising and Dissolution (of Existents)

According to all the commentators, the opponent now reverts to the topic of chapter 19, time, insisting that it must be real since there really occur the arising and dissolution of existents. Since arising and dissolution cannot take place without differences in time, and such differences cannot exist unless time exists, the opponent claims time must be ultimately real. What follows is an investigation of the notion that there can be such things as the arising (coming into existence) and dissolution (cessation or disappearance) of existing things. Given impermanence, if there are real entities then there must be arising and dissolution. What the chapter seeks to determine is what it would mean for entities to exist under conditions of impermanence. As comes out explicitly in verse 14, however, the underlying concern is with what the Buddha meant when he warned against the extreme views of eternalism and annihilationism (see 15.6–11, 17.10, 18.10). Something that does not undergo arising and dissolution is eternal, while anything that does undergo arising and dissolution is, upon its dissolution, annihilated. Ābhidharmikas take the Buddha's warning to apply just to partite entities, like the person, and use the idea that dharmas undergo arising and dissolution as part of their account of the impermanence of persons. Nāgārjuna will here call that attempt into question.

21.1 Assertion: Arising and dissolution occur neither together nor separately.

21.2–7 Reasons for assertion

21.8 Mutual dependence of arising and dissolution and the entity they characterize

21.9 Arising and dissolution can characterize neither the empty nor the non-empty.

21.10 Arising and dissolution are neither identical nor distinct.

21.11 Arising and dissolution are illusory because there can be no existent they characterize.

21.12–13 An existent can be produced neither from an existent nor from a nonexistent, neither from itself nor from what is other.

21.14 Existence of entities requires that one hold one of the extreme views of eternalism and annihilationism.

21.15 Opponent: The two extremes are avoided by acknowledging a series of existents in which dissolution of one existent is always followed by arising of another.

21.16–17 Reply: This proposal still amounts to embracing either eternalism or annihilationism.

21.18–21 Dissolution of cause cannot precede arising of effect, dissolution of cause cannot succeed arising of effect, dissolution of cause and arising of effect cannot be simultaneous, and hence there can be no such thing as a causal series of existents.

vinā vā saha vā nāsti vibhavaḥ saṃbhavena vai /
vinā vā saha vā nāsti saṃbhavo vibhavena vai //1//

1. Dissolution does not at all exist either with or without arising.

Arising does not at all exist either with or without dissolution.

Dissolution is the going out of existence of an existing entity. Arising is its coming into existence. Each member of the pair occurs either separately or else accompanied by the other. Nāgārjuna claims that none of the four resulting hypotheses holds. The reasons are given in the next four verses.

bhaviṣyati kathaṃ nāma vibhavaḥ saṃbhavaṃ vinā /
vinaiva janma maraṇaṃ vibhavo nodbhavaṃ vinā //2//

2. How could there ever be dissolution without arising?
There is no death without [prior] birth, [and likewise] there is no dissolution without origination.

Dissolution or cessation can only occur to something that exists, and nothing exists that has not undergone arising, just as no one dies who was not first born.

saṃbhavenaiva vibhavaḥ kathaṃ saha bhaviṣyati /
na janma maraṇaṃ caiva tulyakālaṃ hi vidyate //3//

3. How could there be dissolution together with arising?
For death and birth do not take place at the same time.

In verse 2 it was argued that dissolution is dependent for its occurrence on arising, hence that dissolution cannot occur distinct from arising. It is now argued that it cannot occur together with arising either, since the two have opposed natures.

Of course one might want to object that the dependence obtaining between arising and dissolution need not require that the two occur simultaneously; the opponent may claim that although dissolution is dependent on arising, the arising of the entity occurs earlier than the dissolution. But recall that the opponent wishes to establish the real existence of time based on the existence of arising and dissolution. To claim that arising and dissolution may occur at distinct times is to presuppose the reality of time. So the opponent cannot object to the argument in this way.

bhaviṣyati kathaṃ nāma saṃbhavo vibhavaṃ vinā /
anityatā hi bhāveṣu na kadācin na vidyate //4//

4. How indeed will there be arising without dissolution?
For never is there not found impermanence among existents.

Having shown that dissolution cannot occur either together with or apart from arising, the argument now turns to the case of arising. To say that arising occurs without dissolution is to say that something that comes into existence never goes out of existence. This violates the fundamental fact about the world at the heart of the Buddha's teachings: that all is impermanent.

saṃbhavo vibhavenaiva kathaṃ saha bhaviṣyati /
na janma maraṇaṃ caiva tulyakālaṃ hi vidyate //5//

5. How indeed will there occur arising together with dissolution?
For death and birth do not take place at the same time.

Arising cannot occur without dissolution, but it also cannot occur together with dissolution. The reason is the same as in verse 3.

sahānyonyena vā siddhir vinānyonyena vā yayoḥ /
na vidyate tayoḥ siddhiḥ kathaṃ nu khalu vidyate //6//

6. Concerning these two things that are not established either as together or separate from one another, how will their establishment ever occur?

Since it is difficult to see what other possibility there might be besides arising and dissolution occurring conjointly or distinctly, it is reasonable to conclude that they cannot be ultimately real. Thus their occurrence cannot be used in support of the claim that time exists.

kṣayasya saṃbhavo nāsti nākṣayasyāsti saṃbhavaḥ |
kṣayasya vibhavo nāsti vibhavo nākṣayasya ca ||7||

7. There is no arising of what is characterized by destruction; nor is there the arising of what is not characterized by destruction.
There is no dissolution of what is characterized by destruction, nor again the dissolution of what is not characterized by destruction.

Candrakīrti explains the argument as follows. Arising and dissolution are events that occur to existing things. And existing things are either characterized by destruction or not characterized by destruction. We may thus ask whether arising and dissolution are to be understood as belonging to an existent that is characterized by destruction or is not characterized by destruction. Something characterized by destruction, however, could not be the locus of arising, since arising and destruction are mutually incompatible. And since there can be no arising of such a thing, there likewise cannot be its dissolution. As for what is not characterized by destruction, there can be no origination of something whose nature it is to never be nonexistent. And the dissolution of such a thing is likewise impossible, since it lacks the nature of something that can be both existent and nonexistent.

saṃbhavaṃ vibhavaṃ caiva vinā bhāvo na vidyate |
saṃbhavo vibhavaś caiva vinā bhāvaṃ na vidyate || 8 ||

8. An existent does not occur without arising and dissolution.
Arising and dissolution do not occur without an existent.

We here follow the order given in Y 352, which reverses the order of 8ab and 8cd as given in LVP, since Ye's ordering is supported by the *Akutobhayā*, Buddhapālita, and Bhāviveka. Arising and dissolution are properties, and properties require a locus. In this case the locus must be an existent entity, for only an existent can be characterized by arising and dissolution. The difficulty is that while arising and dissolution are properties of an existent, it is also true that an impermanent existent cannot occur without them. There is thus a relation of mutual dependence between an existent and its properties of arising and dissolution: Neither can exist without the other.

saṃbhavo vibhavaś caiva na śūnyasyopapadyate |
saṃbhavo vibhavaś caiva nāśūnyasyopapadyate || 9 ||

9. Arising and dissolution do not hold with respect to that which is empty.
Arising and dissolution do not hold with respect to that which is non-empty.

That which is empty is devoid of intrinsic nature and so is not ultimately real. So arising and dissolution cannot characterize a being that is empty. But neither can it characterize what is not empty—that is, what has intrinsic nature. According to Candrakīrti, the reason is that since there is nothing that is not empty, arising and dissolution would then be without a locus. But the *Akutobhayā* explains the argument differently: What is non-empty has a fixed, determinate nature, and this is incompatible with arising and dissolution.

saṃbhavo vibhavaś caiva naika ity upapadyate |
saṃbhavo vibhavaś caiva na nānety upapadyate ||10||

10. It does not hold that arising and dissolution are one.
It does not hold that arising and dissolution are distinct.

The two states must, if they are real, be either identical or distinct. They cannot be identical, since arising conflicts with the nature of dissolution. But neither can they be distinct. For there is invariable concomitance between arising and dissolution: Wherever there is the one, the other is also found. And if they were distinct, it would be possible to find an occurrence of the one without the other.

dṛśyate saṃbhavaś caiva vibhavaś ceti te bhavet |
dṛśyate saṃbhavaś caiva mohād vibhava eva ca ||11||

11. If you maintained that arising and dissolution of existents are indeed seen,
arising and dissolution are only seen because of delusion.

We observe the arising and dissolution of things in everyday life, so there seems to be some reason to think that they are real phenomena. But the Mādhyamika says this is a mere appearance generated by the delusion that fuels our bondage to saṃsāra. The reason why this appearance is deceptive, the commentators suggest, is that arising and dissolution must pertain to an existent, and an existent could only be produced from an existent or from a nonexistent. But neither possibility is tenable, as is argued in the next verse.

na bhāvāj jāyate bhāvo 'bhāvo bhāvān na jāyate |
nābhāvāj jāyate bhāvo 'bhāvo 'bhāvān na jāyate ||12||

12. An existent is not produced from an existent, nor is a nonexistent produced from an existent.
An existent is not produced from a nonexistent, nor is a nonexistent produced from a nonexistent.

We here follow the order given in Y 354, which reverses the order of 12ab and 12cd as given in LVP, since Ye's ordering is supported by the *Akutobhayā*, Buddhapālita, and Bhāviveka. According to Candrakīrti, the first possibility is ruled out on the grounds that then cause and effect would be simultaneous (since only presently existing things are existent), and production would be pointless since the entity that is supposed to be the effect would already exist. As for the second possibility, since nonexistence is incompatible with existence, this is equivalent to saying that there could be darkness in the light. The third possibility is ruled out on the grounds that then the daughter of a barren woman could produce a real son. The fourth is ruled out on the grounds that the cause-effect relationship cannot hold between two unreal things.

na svato jāyate bhāvaḥ parato naiva jāyate |
na svataḥ parataś caiva jāyate jāyate kutaḥ ||13||

13. Not from itself nor from what is other is an existent produced,
and neither is it produced from both itself and what is other;
from what, then, is it produced?

The *Akutobhayā* gives as grounds for rejecting the first possibility that a ceaseless arising would be pointless. The idea is that if a thing produced itself, it would always be in the process of producing itself; but the arising of an entity should be something that only occurs at one time. This is also said to lead to an infinite regress. As for the second possibility, Buddhapālita explains that something *y* can be distinct from a given existent *x* only if the entity *x* itself exists, in which case production is once again pointless. The third possibility must also be rejected, since it inherits all the problems of both the first and the second.

bhāvam abhyupapannasya śāśvatocchedadarśanam /
prasajyate sa bhāvo hi nityo 'nityo 'pi vā bhavet //14//

14. For one who acknowledges the existent, there would follow either eternalism or annihilationism, for an existent would be either permanent or impermanent.

If one holds that there are ultimately real existents, then they must be either permanent or impermanent. But if they are permanent, then one holds that there are eternal existents. And if they are impermanent, then one holds that there is the annihilation of existents. And the views known as eternalism and annihilationism were said by the Buddha to be extremes to be avoided. (See also 15.6–11, 17.10, 18.10.)

Note, however, that on the Abhidharma interpretation of this warning, it applies only to such existents or "beings" as persons and not to what Abhidharmas hold to be ultimately real, namely the dharmas. On their understanding, eternalism is the view that the person exists eternally (in the form of a self), and annihilationism is the view that the person is annihilated at death (or upon the cessation of the present psychophysical elements). For them, the middle path between these two extreme views is the position that there is a causal series of impermanent dharmas, all of which are empty of the nature of a self. Nāgārjuna claims instead that the middle path involves avoiding the extremes of eternalism and annihilationism with respect not just to persons but to all things. In place of the Abhidharma doctrine of the emptiness of persons (*pudgalanairātmya*), he advocates the emptiness of dharmas (*dharmanairātmya*) as the true middle path.

bhāvam abhyupapannasya naivocchedo na śāśvatam /
udayavyayasaṃtānaḥ phalahetvor bhavaḥ sa hi //15//

15. [Objection:] For one who acknowledges existents there
would be neither annihilation nor eternity,
for a state of being is a series consisting of the arising and passing away of effect and cause.

The opponent here proposes a way out of the dilemma posed by Nāgārjuna in verse 14: In a causal series such as a state of being (*bhava*) or individual life, the effect arises upon the passing away or dissolution of its cause. For instance, the present psychophysical elements or skandhas making up an adult human being came into existence due to the passing away of earlier psychophysical elements that made up that human as a child. Thus the fault of eternalism is avoided, since each existent entity passes away, but the fault of annihilationism is also avoided, since something new is always being produced.

udayavyayasaṃtānaḥ phalahetvor bhavaḥ sa cet /
vyayasyāpunarutpatter hetūcchedaḥ prasajyate //16//

16. [Reply:] If a state of being is a series consisting of the arising
and passing away of effect and cause,
then annihilation of the cause follows, for there is no re-arising of what passes away.

Nāgārjuna responds that this strategy will not help the opponent avoid the fault of annihilationism, since the dissolution of the cause at each step in the series is precisely the annihilation of that existent. It cannot be claimed that the cause is not annihilated due to its giving birth to the effect. For the effect must be a distinct existent if it is to be the product of the cause. So the effect cannot be seen as the cause reborn.

sadbhāvasya svabhāvena nāsadbhāvaś ca yujyate /
nirvāṇakāle cocchedaḥ praśamād bhavasaṃtateḥ //17//

17. There cannot be said to be the nonexistence of what exists
intrinsically.
And at the time of nirvāṇa there would be annihilation, since
the series of states of being ceases.

Moreover, on the opponent's interpretation of the middle path, cause and effect are ultimately real entities and thus have intrinsic nature. Such entities cannot cease to exist, since cessation would involve a change in their nature, which is ruled out for ultimately real entities. (See 13.4cd–6.) Thus the fault of eternalism has not been avoided. In addition, when the arhat attains nirvāṇa, or final cessation, the causal series of psychophysical elements ceases and there is no rebirth. In this case the opponent cannot say that the fault of annihilationism has been avoided, for there is no successor effect in the series.

carame na niruddhe ca prathamo yujyate bhavaḥ |
carame nāniruddhe ca prathamo yujyate bhavaḥ ||18||

18. It is not correct to say that the first moment of the new state
of being occurs when the last moment of the old state of
being has ceased.
Nor is it correct to say that the first moment of the new state
of being occurs when the last moment of the old state of
being has not ceased.

The final moment of one state of being is said to be the cause of the first moment of the new state of being. Does the first moment of the new state of being occur upon the cessation of the last moment of the old state of being, or does it occur before the cessation of the last moment? It cannot be upon cessation, since then the last moment will be no more causally efficacious than the last moment in the life of an arhat. But neither can it be prior to cessation, for then the old state of being has not ceased, so this could not count as rebirth.

nirudhyamāne carame prathamo yadi jāyate |
nirudhyamāna ekaḥ syāj jāyamāno 'paro bhavet ||19||

19. If the first moment of the new state of being were produced when the last moment of the old state of being were ceasing,
what was ceasing would be one thing and what was being born would be another.

It is presumably one being that undergoes rebirth. But if the last moment of the old life were undergoing cessation at the same time that the first moment of the new life were being produced, there would be an overlap of the two lives. And there cannot be overlap between different periods in the life of a single being. So there would be two beings involved in rebirth, not one.

na cen nirudhyamānaś ca jāyamānaś ca yujyate |
sārdhaṃ ca mriyate yeṣu teṣu skandheṣu jāyate ||20||

20. It is not correct to suppose that ceasing and being born are simultaneous.
Would one be born in just those skandhas in which one died?

The opponent might think to avoid the difficulty pointed out in verse 19 by supposing that it is a single being who simultaneously undergoes death and rebirth. The difficulty with this hypothesis is that for it to be the same being, the same skandhas must be involved in both events. And if death and rebirth were simultaneous, then these skandhas would simultaneously undergo death and birth. Since the death and birth processes are quite the opposite of one another, this is quite impossible.

evaṃ triṣv api kāleṣu na yuktā bhavasaṃtatiḥ |
yā nāsti triṣu kāleṣu kutaḥ sā bhavasaṃtatiḥ ||21||

21. Thus in none of the three times can there be a series of states of being.
How can it be a series of states of being if it does not exist in the three times?

Verse 18ab rejects the possibility that the first moment occurs after the cessation of the last moment. Verse 18cd rejects the possibility that the first moment occurs before the cessation of the last moment. In verses 19–20 the third possible time—simultaneous cessation and production—was considered and rejected. Thus the notion that existence involves a series of causes and effects cannot help the opponent avoid the faults of eternalism and annihilationism.

22. An Analysis of the Tathāgata

TATHĀGATA is an epithet for the Buddha (or a buddha). Candrakīrti introduces this chapter by having the opponent object that the causal series of lives must be ultimately real, since otherwise there could be no Tathāgata. The argument is that without such a series, there could be no rebirth, and without rebirth there could not be the countless lives of practice that are said to be necessary to attain the virtues and the skills of a buddha.

Nāgārjuna's response will be that ultimately there can be no such thing as the Tathāgata. That is, the Buddha will turn out to be just as empty as the psychophysical elements on which he is thought to depend. This will in turn provide an opportunity to revisit the question of eternalism and annihilationism that was discussed in chapters 15, 17, 18, and 21. The thread of the argument is as follows:

22.1–10 The emptiness of the Tathāgata
- 22.1: A Tathāgata with intrinsic nature is not found under the fivefold analysis.
- 22.2–8: The Tathāgata cannot depend on the skandhas.
  - 22.2–4: A Tathāgata without intrinsic nature cannot depend on the skandhas, whether identical with or distinct from them.
  - 22.5–7: A Tathāgata that is neither identical with nor distinct from the skandhas cannot depend on the skandhas.

22.8: Conclusion: Given the failure of the fivefold analysis, the Tathāgata cannot depend on the skandhas.
22.9–10: The skandhas on which the Tathāgata is thought to depend are empty, so both being empty, the one cannot depend on the other.

22.11 Tetralemma concerning emptiness: Even emptiness is only conventionally true.

22.12–14 Realizing the emptiness of the Tathāgata brings to an end all hypostatization concerning the Tathāgata.

22.15–16 Implications of the emptiness of the Tathāgata
22.15: Those who hypostatize the Tathāgata do not see him.
22.16: The Tathāgata being empty, the world too is empty.

skandhā na nānyaḥ skandhebhyo nāsmin skandhā na teṣu saḥ |
tathāgataḥ skandhavān na katamo 'tra tathāgataḥ ||1||

1. The Tathāgata is neither identical with the skandhas nor distinct from the skandhas; the skandhas are not in him nor is he in them;
he does not exist possessing the skandhas. What Tathāgata, then, is there?

Here the Tathāgata is subjected to the same fivefold examination that was applied to the person or living being earlier. (See 10.14, 16.2.) Candrakīrti's commentary quotes extensively from previous discussions in chapters 10 and 18.

buddhaḥ skandhān upādāya yadi nāsti svabhāvataḥ |
svabhāvataś ca yo nāsti kutaḥ sa parabhāvataḥ ||2||

2. If the Buddha is dependent on the skandhas, then he does not exist intrinsically.
But how can someone who does not exist intrinsically exist extrinsically?

Given the failure of the fivefold examination to turn up an ultimately real Buddha, one might suppose that the Tathāgata is named and conceptualized on the basis of the five skandhas. But to say this is to say that the Buddha lacks intrinsic nature and so fails to exist ultimately. Given this, one cannot claim that the Tathāgata exists dependent on other things that do have intrinsic nature. The reason is given in the next verse.

pratītya parabhāvaṃ yaḥ so 'nātmety upapadyate /
yaś cānātmā sa ca kathaṃ bhaviṣyati tathāgataḥ //3//

3. It is possible that one who is dependent on extrinsic nature is without an essence.
But how will one who is devoid of essence become the Tathāgata?

The commentators compare that which lacks its own nature and only exists by virtue of borrowing its nature from other entities to a magically created being and a reflection in a mirror. The term that we here translate as "without an essence," namely *anātman*, also means "without self." But Candrakīrti explains that here it means being without intrinsic nature or essence. As he understands the argument, in order for the Tathāgata to derive its nature from other things (such as the skandhas), it must first exist. And in order for it to exist, it must have a nature of its own, an essence. So since it lacks its own nature, it cannot be in a position to borrow a nature from other entities.

yadi nāsti svabhāvaś ca parabhāvaḥ kathaṃ bhavet |
svabhāvaparabhāvābhyām ṛte kaḥ sa tathāgataḥ ||4||

4. And if there is no intrinsic nature, how will there be an extrinsic nature?
Besides intrinsic nature and extrinsic nature, what Tathāgata is there?

Presumably a real entity must either have its own nature or else have a nature it borrows from other reals. Since neither possibility is tenable, it should follow that we cannot make out a sense in which there might be a real Tathāgata. But now a new opponent, identified by Bhāviveka as a Vātsīputrīya (a Pudgalavādin), enters the discussion, claiming that the Tathāgata has an inexpressible status of being neither identical with nor distinct from the skandhas. The Tathāgata, though named and conceptualized in dependence on the skandhas (and so presumably having only conventional existence), is nonetheless ultimately real.

skandhān yady anupādāya bhavet kaścit tathāgataḥ |
sa idānīm upādadyād upādāya tato bhavet ||5||

5. If there were some Tathāgata not dependent on the skandhas, then he could attain dependence [on the skandhas]; thus he would be dependent.

For this hypothesis to work, it must be the case that this indescribable Tathāgata exists prior to being conceived in dependence on the skandhas. For it is only if he exists independently of this relation that he can come into the relation of being named and conceptualized in dependence on the skandhas.

skandhāṃś cāpy anupādāya nāsti kaścit tathāgataḥ |
yaś ca nāsty anupādāya sa upādāsyate katham ||6||

6. But there is no Tathāgata whatsoever without dependence on the skandhas.
   And how will one who does not exist without dependence come to depend on them?

Such a Tathāgata that is without any dependence on the skandhas for its being named and conceptualized does not exist. And since it does not exist, it is unable to come into a relation of dependence on the skandhas.

na bhavaty anupādattam upādānaṃ ca kiṃcana |
na cāsti nirupādānaḥ kathaṃcana tathāgataḥ ||7||

7. Something cannot be what is depended upon without having been depended upon [by someone].
   Nor can it be that the Tathāgata somehow exists devoid of what he depends on.

The *Akutobhayā* and Buddhapālita explain the argument as being based on the beginninglessness of saṃsāra. For there to be the relation of dependence, there must be that which is dependent and that on which it depends. In the present case what is dependent would be the Tathāgata, and what it is dependent on is the skandhas. But because the round of rebirths in saṃsāra is without beginning, there cannot be the relation of prior and posterior between the skandhas and the Tathāgata that is required for the relation to hold. There is no moment in the past about which we could say that before that moment there were the skandhas but no Tathāgata. For if saṃsāra is beginningless, then there is no first birth of the Tathāgata. And in order for the Tathāgata to be dependent on the skandhas, the skandhas must be prior to the Tathāgata.

The term that is here and in the next three verses translated as "what is depended on" is *upādāna*, which was translated earlier (e.g., at 3.7, 8.13, 10.15, etc.) as "appropriation." Both here and elsewhere, *upādāna* refers to those skandhas in dependence on which a person is named and conceptualized. Unenlightened beings, however, identify with those skandhas that serve as the grounds of their sense of "I," and this identifying can also be called "appropriating." Presumably the Tathāgata, as an enlightened being, does not identify with those skandhas in dependence on which he is named and conceptualized. So it may be inappropriate to call those skandhas associated with the Tathāgata an appropriation. That is why we have chosen to use the more neutral "what is depended on" in this chapter.

tattvānyatvena yo nāsti mṛgyamāṇaś ca pañcadhā /
upādānena sa kathaṃ prajñapyeta tathāgataḥ //8//

8. Being something that does not exist as either identical with
   or distinct from [the skandhas] when investigated in any of
   the five ways [mentioned in verse 1 of this chapter],
   how is the Tathāgata conceptualized by means of what he
   depends on?

No real Tathāgata has been found by considering the five ways in which he might stand in relation to what is real, the skandhas. Nor is there any other way in which such a being might be found. Hence it makes no sense to speak of a real Tathāgata.

yad apīdam upādānaṃ tat svabhāvān na vidyate /
svabhāvataś ca yan nāsti kutas tat parabhāvataḥ //9//

9. Moreover that on which he depends does not exist by virtue
   of intrinsic nature.
   And how can what does not exist intrinsically exist
   extrinsically?

Candrakīrti explains that "that on which he depends" is the five skandhas, that which the Tathāgata is said to be dependent on. These do not exist by virtue of intrinsic nature because, being dependently originated, they lack intrinsic nature. From this it is said to follow that the skandhas likewise do not exist extrinsically. The argument is the same as that given in verses 2–3.

evaṃ śūnyam upādānam upādātā ca sarvaśaḥ |
prajñapyeta ca śūnyena kathaṃ śūnyas tathāgataḥ ||10||

10. Thus both that on which he depends and the one who is
 dependent are altogether empty.
 And how is an empty Tathāgata to be conceptualized by
 means of something empty?

Both the Tathāgata and that on which he supposedly depends for his being conceptualized (the skandhas) are empty or devoid of the nature required to be real. Thus the claim that the Tathāgata is named and conceptualized in dependence on the skandhas turns out to be utterly without meaning.

śūnyam ity apy avaktayam aśūnyam iti vā bhavet |
ubhayaṃ nobhayaṃ ceti prajñaptyarthaṃ tu kathyate ||11||

11. "It is empty" is not to be said, nor "It is non-empty,"
 nor that it is both, nor that it is neither; ["empty"] is said only
 for the sake of instruction.

When a Mādhyamika says that things are empty, this is not to be understood as stating the ultimate truth about the ultimate nature of reality. Instead this is just a useful pedagogical device, a way of instructing others who happen to believe there is such a thing as the ultimate truth about the ultimate nature of reality. So the claim made here is in effect the same as the claim Nāgārjuna will make at 24.18, that emptiness is itself empty.

Here as elsewhere, Nāgārjuna employs the device known as the tetralemma (*catuṣkoṭi*) to express his point. He considers all four possible views concerning emptiness, only to reject them all. But as Bhāviveka reminds us, and as Candrakīrti pointed out in his comments on 18.6, when the Buddha rejects all four possibilities with respect to such questions as whether the world is eternal (e.g., at M I.484–85, 431), this is because while each may prove useful for certain purposes under certain circumstances, all share a presupposition that is false (see M I.486–87). Candrakīrti suggests that what we have here is another instance of a "graded teaching," with each of the four possibilities representing a view held by certain philosophers. (See 18.8.) Interestingly, he identifies the view that there are both empty and non-empty things with Sautrāntika (since they hold that only present things are ultimately real) and the view that things are neither empty nor non-empty with Yogācāra (since they hold that reality is inexpressible—cf. the *Madhyantavibhāga* 1.3, which Candrakīrti quotes: "Therefore all is said to be neither empty nor non-empty" [LVP 445]).

Bhāviveka considers the following objection: When Mādhyamikas assert that we should not make any of these four possible claims about the ultimate nature of reality, they are guilty of an inconsistency. For they appear to be saying that the ultimate nature of reality cannot be described in any of the four possible ways, and yet this would seem to be a claim about the ultimate nature of reality. Bhāviveka responds that there is no more fault here than there is in the case of someone who, wishing to prevent sound, utters the sound, "Quiet!"* Bhāviveka's reply might be interpreted in either of two different ways.

(1) While no statement about how things ultimately are can express their nature (since all conceptualization falsifies reality), some (strictly

* In *Vigrahavyāvartanī*, Nāgārjuna considers an objection that likens the Mādhyamika to someone who, wishing to prevent all sound, says "Do not make a sound." For his response to this objection, see *Vigrahavyāvartanī* verse 28 (where he quotes 24.10).

negative) statements come closer to adequately representing reality, namely those that reject various false superimpositions.

(2) Statements are to be judged true or false not on the basis of how adequately they express the ultimate nature of reality (there being no such thing) but on the basis of how effective they are at achieving the speaker's aim. The Mādhyamika's aim is to bring an end to our tendency to hypostatize—to suppose that there must be some ultimate reality that our statements are meant to depict. This aim is best achieved by making statements, but different statements will be effective in different contexts.

śāśvatāśāśvatādy atra kutaḥ śānte catuṣṭayam /
antānantādi cāpy atra kutaḥ śānte catuṣṭayam //12//

12. How can "It is eternal," "It is noneternal," and the rest of this tetralemma apply [to the Tathāgata], who is free of intrinsic nature?
And how can "It has an end," "It does not have an end," and the rest of this tetralemma apply [to the Tathāgata], who is free of intrinsic nature?

The Tathāgata being ultimately empty of intrinsic nature, none of the four possibilities in the tetralemmas concerning being eternal and having an end can apply. (On these see the discussion below at 25.17–18.) The Tathāgata could, for instance, be said to be eternal only if there were such an ultimately existing entity as the Tathāgata. And to say that the Tathāgata is empty is to say there is no such thing.

ghanagrāho gṛhītas tu yenāstīti tathāgataḥ /
nāstīti sa vikalpayan nirvṛtasyāpi kalpayet //13//

13. But one who has taken up a mass of beliefs, such as that the Tathāgata exists,

so conceptualizing, that person will also imagine that [the Tathāgata] does not exist when extinguished.

One who throughout countless past lives has employed various useful conceptual distinctions will be inclined to apply them to the case of the Tathāgata. The Tathāgata, having attained final nirvāṇa, is not available as an object to which conceptual distinctions might apply. But due to one's inveterate tendency to use concepts, one is likely to want to know whether, after final nirvāṇa, the Tathāgata continues to exist, does not exist, both exists and does not exist, or neither exists nor does not exist.

svabhāvataś ca śūnye 'smiṃś cintā naivopapadyate |
paraṃ nirodhād bhavati buddho na bhavatīti vā ||14||

14. And the thought does not hold, with reference to this (Tathāgata) who is intrinsically empty,
that the Buddha either exists or does not exist after cessation.

Because the Buddha is extinguished in final nirvāṇa, there is no entity available concerning whose postmortem status we might speculate.

prapañcayanti ye buddhaṃ prapañcātītam avyayam |
te prapañcahatāḥ sarve na paśyanti tathāgatam ||15||

15. Those who hypostatize the Buddha, who is beyond hypostatization and unwavering,
they all, deceived by hypostatization, fail to see the Tathāgata.

Candrakīrti explains that the Buddha is said to be unwavering inasmuch as, being by nature empty and so unarisen, the Buddha is not the sort of thing that could undergo change. Only an ultimately existing Buddha could be the sort of thing for which the question of change could arise (when that question is understood to concern ultimately real things).

tathāgato yatsvabhāvas tatsvabhāvam idaṃ jagat |
tathāgato niḥsvabhāvo niḥsvabhāvam idaṃ jagat ||16||

16. What is the intrinsic nature of the Tathāgata, that is the intrinsic nature of this world.
The Tathāgata is devoid of intrinsic nature; this world is devoid of intrinsic nature.

By "this world" is meant the realm of saṃsāra. (It can also mean the beings who inhabit it.) As Buddhapālita explains, both the Tathāgata and this world are conceptualized in dependence on other things, and hence both are devoid of intrinsic nature. They are alike in being empty.

For many Buddhists, the expression "the Tathāgata" is not just the name of a historical person but stands as well for the supposedly transcendent reality of nirvāṇa. Taken in this way, the equivalence stated here is the same as that asserted in 25.19, which says explicitly that there is no difference between nirvāṇa and saṃsāra.

Buddhapālita's commentary, the *Buddhapālitavṛtti*, seems to end at this point. What is represented in some texts as the comments on chapters 23–27 of *Buddhapālitavṛtti* appears to be a repetition or a paraphrase of the comments of the *Akutobhayā* on those chapters.

23. An Analysis of False Conception

It is a fundamental tenet of the Buddha's teachings that suffering arises because of ignorance concerning such things as our identity, permanence, and the possibility of happiness. We suffer, it is claimed, because we conceptually construct a world that exists nowhere but in our fancy. Out of this imagining there develop those habits of thinking and acting known as the defilements, which in turn are said to fuel the round of rebirth known as saṃsāra. All this could be taken to mean that there must ultimately be such things as false conception and the defilements that occur dependent on it. Indeed it might be thought that there cannot be such a thing as false conception unless there is also such a thing as the ultimate truth concerning how things really are. This chapter claims otherwise. It attempts to refute the ultimate existence of false conception and defilements and thereby undercut the view of truth and falsity that led Ābhidharmikas to their conception of ultimately real entities. The argumentative thread is as follows:

23.1 Presentation of orthodox view that real defilements arise dependent on false conception, etc.
23.2 Reply: Defilements are not real because they are dependent on distinct causes.
23.3–5 Defilements are not real because they lack a locus.

23.6 Defilements are not real because their distinct causes are unreal.

23.7 Objection: The defilements are real because they arise in dependence on six real objects.

23.8–9 Reply: The six objects are themselves merely imagined constructions, so defilements cannot ultimately depend on objects based on them.

23.10–12 Refutation of desire and aversion based on refutation of their cause

23.13–22 Refutation of delusion based on refutation of its cause, false conception

23.13–14: Refutation of false conception based on emptiness

23.15–20: Refutation of the locus of false conception

23.21–22: Refutation of the four kinds of false conception

23.23–25 The defilements can be abandoned through realization of emptiness.

saṃkalpaprabhavo rāgo dveṣo mohaś ca kathyate /
śubhāśubhaviparyāsān saṃbhavanti pratītya hi //1//

1. Desire, aversion, and delusion are said to arise from false discrimination.
These arise in dependence on the good, the bad, and false conception.

This verse presents a view about the roots of suffering that is held in common by most Buddhists. (The commentators disagree as to whether it reports the view of Nāgārjuna or of an opponent, but this is immaterial to the argument of the chapter.) Desire, aversion, and delusion are the three defilements or *kleśa*s (see 14.2). They are said to arise from three sorts of cognitive mistakes: Desire arises in dependence on false discrimination concerning what is good or pleasant in nature (*śubha*), aversion on false discrimination concerning what is bad or unpleasant in nature, and delusion in dependence on false conception. (Throughout this chapter we will use the expression "the good, the bad, and false conception" for these three kinds of error.)

śubhāśubhaviparyāsān saṃbhavanti pratītya ye /
te svabhāvān na vidyante tasmāt kleśā na tattvataḥ //2//

2. What arise in dependence on the good, the bad, and false conception,
those things do not exist intrinsically, therefore the defilements are not ultimately real.

Because the three defilements arise in dependence on the three kinds of false imagining, and intrinsic nature cannot be contingent or dependent on another, it follows that they lack intrinsic nature and are thus not ultimately real.

ātmano 'stitvanāstitve na kathaṃcic ca sidhyataḥ /
taṃ vināstitvanāstitve kleśānāṃ sidhyataḥ katham //3//

3. Neither the existence nor the nonexistence of the self is in any way established.
Without that establishment, how will there be the establishment of the existence or nonexistence of the defilements?

The self is not found under ultimate analysis. It might be thought that this is equivalent to establishing the nonexistence of the self. But Candrakīrti apparently takes "establishing the nonexistence of the self" to mean establishing that it is the many ultimately real, impermanent psychophysical elements such as consciousnesses that together perform the functions we mistakenly attribute to a single enduring self. And these things have likewise been shown not to ultimately exist. Consequently it cannot be said to be ultimately true either that there is a self or that the self does not exist. (Compare 18.6.) The bearing that this has on the existence of the defilements is discussed in the next verse.

kasyacid dhi bhavantīme kleśāḥ sa ca na sidhyati |
kaścid āho vinā kaṃcit santi kleśā na kasyacit ||4||

4. So these defilements belong to something, yet no such thing is established.
Without something [to be their locus], the defilements are defilements of nothing whatsoever.

The defilements must have a locus, just as the color brought about by baking a brick has the brick as its locus. But the locus of the defilements cannot be the self, since it has been established that there is no such thing. Nor is it any of the psychophysical elements, such as consciousness, for they have likewise been shown to not ultimately exist. So the defilements lack a locus and hence cannot be ultimately real.

svakāyadṛṣṭivat kleśāḥ kliṣṭe santi na pañcadhā |
svakāyadṛṣṭivat kliṣṭaṃ kleśeṣv api na pañcadhā ||5|

5. As with the theory that the "I" is one's own body [of skandhas], the defilements are not related to the defiled one in any of the five ways.
As with the theory that the "I" is one's own body [of skandhas], the defiled one is also not related to the defilements in any of the five ways.

Candrakīrti explains that the word *kāya*, which ordinarily means "body," here means the five skandhas taken collectively. (For this usage see AKB ad AK 5.7, Pradhan p. 281.) Thus the view known as *svakāya* is the view that the "I" is just that collection of psychophysical elements that is one's own. Hence the "five ways" are the five different manners in which a subject that is the source of the sense of "I" and "mine" could be related to the five skandhas (see 18.1, 22.1–8). The "defiled one" is the locus of the defilements, the subject that has them. The claim of verse 5ab is then that the defilements are not to be found, since they could not be identical with the subject of the defilements, they could not be distinct from it, it could not be in them, they could not be in it, and it could not be their possessor. In verse 5cd it is claimed in turn that the defiled one is likewise not to be found in any of the five ways it might be related to the defilements.

svabhāvato na vidyante śubhāśubhaviparyayāḥ /
pratītya katamān kleśāḥ śubhāśubhaviparyayān //6//

6. The good, the bad, and false conception do not occur intrinsically;
in dependence on what good, bad, and false conception will there then be defilements?

The defilements of desire, aversion, and delusion, it will be recalled, are said to arise in dependence on false discrimination concerning the pleasant, the unpleasant, and false conceptions respectively. The argument that begins here will be that the defilements are not ultimately real because the factors on which they depend—the pleasant, the unpleasant, and false conception—are themselves not ultimately real.

rūpaśabdarasasparśā gandhā dharmāś ca ṣaḍvidham /
vastu rāgasya doṣasya mohasya ca vikalpyate //7/

7. [Opponent:] Concerning desire, aversion, and delusion, there is constructed six kinds of objects taken as real—color, sound, taste, touch, smell, and the object of inner sense (dharmas).

This is the opponent's answer to the question of 6cd. Our experience of the world is, most fundamentally, the experience of colors, sounds, tastes, touches, smells, and the objects of inner sense. It is on the basis of our experience in these six modalities that we construct objects—things that have color, taste, and so on. And these objects are what we take to be pleasant or unpleasant and about which we have false conceptions. Our taking some object to be pleasant is what gives rise to desire; our taking something to be unpleasant is what gives rise to aversion; our falsely conceiving something as for instance enduring is what gives rise to delusion. So the three defilements arise out of our experience of colors, tastes, etc. The implication is that good, bad, and false conception must after all exist.

rūpaśabdarasasparśā gandhā dharmāś ca kevalāḥ |
gandharvanagarākārā marīcisvapnasaṃnibhāḥ ||8||

8. [Reply:] They are only colors, sounds, tastes, touches, smells, and objects of inner sense,
similar to the city of the gandharvas, like a mirage, a dream.

For the city of the gandharvas, see 7.34. To say that the six sense objects are "only" color and so on is to say they are empty or devoid of intrinsic nature. They are thus things that only appear to be ultimately real, as an illusion only appears to be substantial.

aśubhaṃ vā śubhaṃ vāpi kutas teṣu bhaviṣyati |
māyāpuruṣakalpeṣu pratibimbasameṣu ca ||9||

9. How will their [determination] as either bad or good come to be,
when they [colors, etc.] are like the image of an illusory person and the same as a [mere] reflection?

The object that is taken to be pleasant or unpleasant cannot be constructed if the construction materials—the raw data of sense experience—are themselves not ultimately real.

anapekṣya śubhaṃ nāsty aśubhaṃ prajñapayemahi /
yat pratītya śubhaṃ tasmāc chubhaṃ naivopapadyate //10//

10. Independent of the good there is no bad, the bad being that depending on which we conceive of the good; therefore the good itself cannot be.

The good and the bad are, Candrakīrti says, like the two banks of a river, the long and the short, etc.; the one exists only through relation to the other.

anapekṣyāśubhaṃ nāsti śubhaṃ prajñapayemahi /
yat pratītyāśubhaṃ tasmād aśubhaṃ naiva vidyate //11//

11. Independent of the bad there is no good, the good being that depending on which we conceive of the bad; therefore the bad itself cannot be.

avidyamāne ca śubhe kuto rāgo bhaviṣyati /
aśubhe 'vidyamāne ca kuto dveṣo bhaviṣyati //12//

12. And the good being unreal, how will desire come to be?
The bad also being unreal, how will aversion come to be?

We take things to be good and bad only by virtue of relations of mutual contrast. Hence nothing is intrinsically good or bad, pleasant or unpleasant. From this it follows that false discrimination concerning the good and the bad lack an ultimately real object: Strictly speaking these convictions are about nothing. But desire is said to be the effect of false discrimination concerning the good, while aversion is said to be the effect of false discrimination concerning the bad. So in order for desire and aversion to be ultimately real, these two types of false discrimination must themselves be ultimately real. Given the nature of the good and the bad, neither desire nor aversion can ultimately arise.

anitye nityam ity evaṃ yadi grāho viparyayaḥ |
nānityaṃ vidyate śūnye kuto grāho viparyayaḥ ||13||

13. If it would be a false conception to think that impermanent things are permanent,
then, there being nothing that is impermanent with regard to what is empty, how can there be a false conception?

The false conceptions are those basic ways of thinking that lead to the wholesale delusion that keeps us in saṃsāra. These include, most importantly, the tendency to take what is in fact impermanent as permanent. In order for it to be ultimately true that such a belief is a false conception, it would have to be the case that there are ultimately real things that are impermanent. For it could be ultimately true that it is a false conception only if this way of conceiving of things failed to correspond to their real nature—only if it were ultimately false that things are permanent. But if all things are indeed empty or devoid of intrinsic nature, then there are no ultimately real things that could be impermanent. So the tendency to take things as permanent would not fail to conform to the nature of what is ultimately real. So it could not ultimately be a false conception.

anitye nityam ity evaṃ yadi grāho viparyayaḥ |
anityam ity api grāhaḥ śūnye kiṃ na viparyayaḥ ||14||

14. If it would be a false conception to think that impermanent things are permanent,
then, things being empty, isn't conceiving that things are impermanent also false?

The tendency to take things as permanent is thought to be a false conception because it is thought to be ultimately true that all things are impermanent. But given that all things are empty, the belief that all things are impermanent equally fails to correspond to the nature of things. So it too should count as a false conception. But something can count as a false conception only if there is something that would count as a correct account of how things are. And there is no third possibility here apart from things being permanent or impermanent. So there can ultimately be no false conception.

yena gṛhṇāti yo grāho grahītā yac ca gṛhyate |
upaśantani sarvāṇi tasmād grāho na vidyate ||15||

15. That by means of which one conceives, the conceiving, the conceiver, and what is conceived—
all those things have been extinguished, hence there is no conception.

The instrument, the action, the agent, and the effect of conceiving are all empty or devoid of intrinsic nature. That is, these are revealed to be no more than concepts with no real referents. Once our tendency to think of instrument, action, and so on as ultimately real is extinguished, we come to see that there can likewise not ultimately be any such thing as conception.

avidyamāne grāhe ca mithyā vā samyag eva vā |
bhaved viparyayaḥ kasya bhavet kasyāviparyayaḥ ||16||

16. And there being no conception, whether wrong or correct,
who could have false conception, who could have conception
that is not false?

Since conception is not ultimately real, neither wrong conceiving nor correct conceiving is ultimately real. Moreover, both erroneous and non-erroneous thought are generally believed to require a thinker. Quite apart from the fact that we are unable to find a subject for the defilements (vv. 3–4), there is a new worry with respect to true and false beliefs: Is the subject of, for instance, a false belief someone who has already fallen into error, someone who has not yet fallen into error, or someone presently falling into error? This is the topic of the next two verses.

na cāpi viparītasya saṃbhavanti viparyayāḥ |
na cāpy aviparītasya saṃbhavanti viparyayāḥ ||17||

17. False conceptions are not possible in the case of one who has already falsely conceived.
Nor are false conceptions possible in the case of someone who has not yet falsely conceived.

na viparyasyamānasya saṃbhavanti viparyayāḥ |
vimṛśasva svayaṃ kasya saṃbhavanti viparyayāḥ ||18||

18. False conceptions are not possible in the case of one who is presently falsely conceiving.
Examine it yourself: False conceptions arise for whom?

As the *Akutobhayā* points out, the argument here parallels that of chapter 2 concerning the traversed, the not-yet-traversed, and presently being traversed. For the one who is already in error about impermanence, the error concerning impermanence cannot arise for the simple reason that it already exists. One who is not in error about the impermanent cannot be the one who makes the error, for then error would pertain to those who are enlightened and see things correctly. As for the third possibility, Candrakīrti points out that this asks us to imagine someone who is half wrong and half right. Leaving aside the fact that this could be true only of something with parts (and hence something that is not ultimately real), there is the difficulty that neither part could be the one that is in error, for the reasons just given.

anutpannāḥ kathaṃ nāma bhaviṣyanti viparyayāḥ |
viparyayeṣv ajāteṣu viparyayagataḥ kutaḥ ||19||

19. How will unarisen false conceptions ever come to be?
False conceptions being unproduced, how can there be one
who has arrived at a false conception?

na svato jāyate bhāvaḥ parato naiva jāyate |
na svataḥ parataś ceti viparyayagataḥ kutaḥ ||20||

20. An entity is not born from itself, not born from what is
other,
not born from both itself and the other; hence how can there
be the one who has arrived at a false conception?

Ye (Y 400) omits this verse, following Piṅgala, Bhāviveka, and the *Akutobhayā*. But both Buddhapālita and Candrakīrti attest the verse, and we follow La Vallée Poussin and de Jong in accepting it. Here is yet another difficulty for the hypothesis that there ultimately exists such a thing as false conception. The one who has gone wrong presumably did not always suffer from the particular error that he or she is now committing. This means the error must have been produced. But then the conclusion of chapter 1 applies to this case: Real things cannot be said to arise from themselves, from what is other, and so on. So there can be no arising of error in the one who is thought to have gone wrong, which is absurd.

ātmā ca śuci nityaṃ ca sukhaṃ ca yadi vidyate |
ātmā ca śuci nityaṃ ca sukhaṃ ca na viparyayaḥ ||21||

21. If the self, purity, permanence, and happiness existed,
then [belief in] the self, purity, permanence, and happiness would not be false.

nātmā ca śuci nityaṃ ca sukhaṃ ca yadi vidyate |
anātmā 'śucy anityaṃ ca naiva duḥkhaṃ ca vidyate ||22||

22. If the self, purity, permanence, and happiness do not exist,
then nonself, impurity, impermanence, and suffering do not exist.

What makes the belief that there is a self, for instance, erroneous, a case of false conception, is that it is not the case that there is a self. If there were a self, then this belief would not be erroneous. Its being erroneous, however, is the consequence of the fact that all things are empty. Thus it does not follow that its being erroneous stems from its being ultimately true that there is no self. For if all things are empty, then "There is no self" cannot be ultimately true. If all things are empty, then no statement about reality can be ultimately true.

evaṃ nirudhyate 'vidyā viparyayanirodhanāt |
avidyāyāṃ niruddhāyāṃ saṃskārādyaṃ nirudhyate ||23||

23. Ignorance is thus ceased because of the cessation of false conceptions.
Ignorance having ceased, the volitions/dispositions and so on [that cause rebirth] are ceased.

This is the standard Buddhist account of the cessation of suffering. The twelvefold chain of dependent origination begins with ignorance. For it is out of ignorance that the defilements are said to spring. Once we have dispelled false discrimination concerning the good and the bad and false conceptions, the series of causes leading to old age, death, rebirth, and suffering will be stopped. This much the Mādhyamika must agree to. In this chapter Nāgārjuna has developed a line of reasoning in support of the claim that false conceptions and defilements do not ultimately exist. Presumably this is meant to help us escape our ignorance and so achieve liberation. But now the opponent will object that this means the defilements and the false conceptions that are their cause must exist. The Mādhyamika must agree that defilements and false conceptions can and should be stopped. Otherwise why would they be trying to undermine what they take to be erroneous views? The question is how they can maintain this if they also hold that all things (including false conceptions and defilements) are empty. The next two verses attempt to answer this question.

yadi bhūtāḥ svabhāvena kleśāḥ kecid dhi kasyacit |
kathaṃ nāma prahīyeran kaḥ svabhāvaṃ prahāsyati ||24||

24. If someone had some defilements that were intrinsically real,
how would they be abandoned? Who abandons intrinsic essence?

yady abhūtāḥ svabhāvena kleśāḥ kecid dhi kasyacit |
kathaṃ nāma prahīyeran ko 'sadbhāvaṃ prahāsyati ||25||

25. If someone had some defilements that were intrinsically unreal,
how would they be abandoned? Who abandons the nonexistent?

It is thought that one attains liberation from saṃsāra by uprooting and destroying the defilements. The claim here is that this cannot be ultimately true. For either the defilements are intrinsically real (i.e., have their intrinsic nature), or else they are intrinsically unreal (i.e., are unreal by failing to have their intrinsic nature). But intrinsic nature cannot be destroyed. Candrakīrti gives the example of space, whose nature of nonobstruction can never be lost. But it is likewise impossible to destroy that which is intrinsically unreal. The example here is a cold fire: Since a cold fire does not exist, it is impossible to destroy such a fire by removing the property of cold from it. Hence it cannot be ultimately true that the defilements are destroyed.

Note, however, that this does not mean the defilements cannot be abandoned. The Mādhyamika might draw a distinction between saying "Defilements are ultimately abandoned" and saying "Defilements are abandoned." The distinction would be that the former statement requires that there be ultimately real defilements while the latter does not. To put the point in a slightly different way, the Mādhyamika could claim that while the statement "Defilements are destroyed" cannot be ultimately true (or ultimately false either), it is conventionally true. It is a statement the assertion of which is sometimes useful for bringing about the cessation of suffering.

24. An Analysis of the Noble Truths

THE SUBJECT of this chapter is the Buddha's teaching known as the *four noble truths*. In the first six verses the opponent objects that if, as Nāgārjuna claims, all is indeed empty, then this teaching, as well as all that follows from it, is put in jeopardy. In replying, Nāgārjuna first claims that the opponent has misunderstood the purport of the doctrine of emptiness. He then seeks to turn the tables on the opponent and show that what would actually jeopardize the Buddha's teachings is denying emptiness, or affirming that there are things with intrinsic nature. In outline the argument goes like this:

24.1–6 Objection: Emptiness is incompatible with the core teachings of the Buddha—e.g., the four truths and the three jewels—as well as with ordinary modes of conduct.

24.7 Reply: The opponent misunderstands emptiness.

24.8–10 The opponent does not understand the distinction between the two truths.

24.11–12 The Buddha hesitated to teach emptiness for fear of its being misunderstood.

24.13–15 Assertion: The faults pointed out by the opponent are in fact found in his arguments.

24.16–17 Reason: If things existed with intrinsic nature, they would not originate in dependence on cause and conditions.

24.18–19 To affirm that all things arise in dependence on causes and conditions is to affirm that all things are devoid of intrinsic nature.

24.20–25 If things were not empty, the four noble truths could not hold.

24.26–27c If things were not empty, there could not be the four activities that constitute the path to nirvāṇa.

24.27d–30 If things were not empty, the three jewels—Saṃgha, Dharma, and Buddha—could not exist.

24.31–32 If things were not empty, then these things would all be essentially unrelated: being a buddha, enlightenment, following the Buddha's teaching, and the path of the bodhisattva.

24.33–35 If things were not empty, there would be neither good nor bad actions together with their respective results.

24.36–37 The denial of emptiness means the denial of worldly conduct.

24.38 If things were not empty, the world would be completely static.

24.39 If things were not empty, then conduct aiming at attainment of nirvāṇa would also make no sense.

24.40 Conclusion: One who sees dependent origination sees the four truths.

yadi śūnyam idaṃ sarvam udayo nāsti na vyayaḥ |
caturṇām āryasatyānām abhāvas te prasajyate ||1||

1. [Objection:] If all this is empty, there is neither origination nor cessation.
   It follows for you that there is the nonexistence of the four noble truths.

If all is empty, then there is nothing that is ultimately real. In that case it cannot be ultimately true that things such as suffering undergo origination and destruction. But the second noble truth claims that suffering arises in dependence on causes and conditions, while the third noble truth claims that suffering ceases when these causes and conditions are stopped. So if all things are empty, these claims cannot be ultimately true.

parijñā ca prahāṇaṃ ca bhāvanā sākṣikarma ca /
caturṇām āryasatyānām abhāvān nopapadyate //2//

2. Comprehension, abandonment, practice, and personal realization—
none of these is possible due to nonexistence of the four noble truths.

The four activities mentioned here represent the basic constituents of the Buddha's path or program leading to the cessation of suffering. By "comprehension" is meant the clear understanding of suffering (the first noble truth). "Abandonment" means bringing to an end the attachments that are the chief cause of suffering (the second noble truth being that suffering has a cause). "Practice" refers to practicing the path to the cessation of suffering (the third noble truth being that there is the cessation of suffering). And "personal realization" means completion of the path to nirvana or cessation (the fourth noble truth being that there is such a path). The opponent is here claiming that these four activities could lead to that result only if the four noble truths represent an accurate assessment of the fundamental nature of reality. So the doctrine of emptiness would entail that the Buddha's teachings are not effective.

tadabhāvān na vidyante catvāry āryaphalāni ca /
phalābhāve phalasthā no na santi pratipannakāḥ //3//

3. And due to the nonexistence of those, the four noble fruits [of stream-winner, once-returner, never-returner, and arhat] do not exist.
   If the fruits are nonexistent, then there are neither the strivers for nor the attainers of those fruits.

If the path does not lead to the cessation of suffering, then no one has ever strived for or attained any of the four states of stream-winner and so on. These represent different degrees of proximity to final cessation or exhaustion of rebirth.

saṃgho nāsti na cet santi te 'ṣṭau puruṣapudgalāḥ |
abhāvāc cāryasatyānāṃ saddharmo 'pi na vidyate ||4||

4. The Saṃgha does not exist if the eight kinds of person do not exist.
   And because of the nonexistence of the noble truths, the true Dharma does not exist either.

The eight kinds of person are the four types of strivers for the fruits mentioned in verse 3 and the four kinds of attainers of those fruits. The Saṃgha is the collective body made up of all eight kinds of persons. The Dharma is the teachings of the Buddha.

dharme cāsati saṃghe ca kathaṃ buddho bhaviṣyati |
evaṃ trīṇy api ratnāni bruvāṇaḥ pratibādhase ||5||
śūnyatāṃ phalasadbhāvam adharmaṃ dharmam eva ca |
sarvasaṃvyavahārāṃś ca laukikān pratibādhase ||6||

5. Dharma and Saṃgha being nonexistent, how will the Buddha come to be?
   In this way you deny all three jewels when you proclaim

6. emptiness; you deny the real existence of the karmic fruit,
both good and bad actions,
and all worldly modes of conduct.

The existence of a Buddha is dependent on the existence of Dharma and Saṃgha. A Buddha is someone who, having discovered the Dharma (the causes of and cure for suffering), teaches it to others and thus forms the Saṃgha. So if, as verses 1–4 claim, Dharma and Saṃgha do not exist if all is empty, then the Buddha likewise cannot exist if all things are empty.

Good and bad conduct are actions that lead to pleasant and painful fruits respectively. Worldly modes of conduct include such mundane activities as cooking, eating, coming, and going. All are denied, claims the opponent, if it is held that all dharmas are empty. The reasoning is that since nothing whatsoever could exist if all is empty, there can be no good and bad conduct, etc.

atra brūmaḥ śūnyatāyāṃ na tvaṃ vetsi prayojanam /
śūnyatāṃ śūnyatārthaṃ ca tata evaṃ vihanyase //7//

7. [Reply:] Here we say that you do not understand the point of
[teaching] emptiness,
emptiness itself, and the meaning of emptiness; in this way
you are thus frustrated.

Candrakīrti comments that the opponent's objection is based on the opponent mistakenly imposing on the doctrine of emptiness his own nihilist reading—that to say all things lack intrinsic nature is to say nothing whatsoever exists. Candrakīrti also states that the true purpose of teaching emptiness is that given in 18.5: the extinguishing of hypostatization.

dve satye samupāśritya buddhānāṃ dharmadeśanā |
lokasaṃvṛtisatyaṃ ca satyaṃ ca paramārthataḥ ||8||

8. The Dharma teaching of the Buddha rests on two truths: conventional truth and ultimate truth.

The term we translate as "conventional" is a compound made of the two words *loka* and *saṃvṛti*. Candrakīrti gives three distinct etymologies for *saṃvṛti*. On one etymology, the root meaning is that of "concealing," so conventional truth would be all those ways of thinking and speaking that conceal the real state of affairs from ordinary people (*loka*). The second explains the term to mean "mutual dependency." On the third etymology, the term refers to conventions involved in customary practices of the world, the customs governing the daily conduct of ordinary people (*loka*). He adds that this *saṃvṛti* is of the nature of (the relation between) term and referent, cognition and the cognized, and the like. So on this understanding, conventional truth is a set of beliefs that ordinary people (*loka*) use in their daily conduct, and it is conventional (*saṃvṛti*) because of its reliance on conventions concerning semantic and cognitive relations. It may be worth noting that when Indian commentators give multiple explanations of a term, it is often the last one given that they favor.

The *Akutobhayā* explains that the ultimate truth is the faultless realization of the noble ones (*āryas*), namely that no dharmas whatsoever arise. There are two ways that this might be understood. The first is that according to Madhyamaka, ultimate reality does not contain anything that arises. (And since Buddhists generally agree that there are no eternal entities, this would mean that ultimate reality contains no entities whatsoever.) The realization of emptiness would then be insight into the true character of reality: that it is utterly devoid of existing entities. According to the second possible interpretation, the ultimate truth according to Madhyamaka is just that there is no such thing as the way that reality ultimately is. Or to put this in a somewhat paradoxical way, the ultimate truth is that there is no ultimate truth. On this reading, what the *āryas* realize is that the very idea of how things really are, independently of our (useful) semantic and cognitive conventions, is incoherent.

ye 'nayor na vijānanti vibhāgaṃ satyayor dvayoḥ |
te tattvaṃ na vijānanti gambhīre buddhaśāsane ||9||

9. Who do not know the distinction between the two truths, they do not understand reality in accordance with the profound teachings of the Buddha.

Candrakīrti has the opponent raise an interesting question for the Mādhyamika at this point:

> Suppose that the ultimate truth is indeed without the hypostatization of intrinsic nature. Then what is the point of those other teachings concerning the skandhas, dhātus, āyatanas, noble truths, dependent origination, and the rest, none of them ultimately true? What is not true should be rejected, so why was what should be rejected taught? (LVP p. 494)

Candrakīrti replies that the opponent is right about the status of the Buddha's teachings, that they are not ultimately true. But the next verse answers the question.

vyavahāram anāśritya paramārtho na deśyate |
paramārtham anāgamya nirvāṇaṃ nādhigamyate ||10||

10. The ultimate truth is not taught independently of customary ways of talking and thinking.
Not having acquired the ultimate truth, nirvāṇa is not attained.

The "customary ways of talking and thinking" (*vyavahāra*) referred to here are the everyday practice of ordinary people, what we think of as "common sense." This consists of those ways of getting around in the world that have proven useful in that they generally lead to success in meeting people's goals. As the basis of our commonsense beliefs, it can be equated with conventional truth. So verse 10ab is asserting that ultimate truth cannot be taught without reliance on conventional truth. Candrakīrti likens conventional truth to the cup that a thirsty person must use in order to satisfy a need for water.

The reply to the above objection is thus that ultimate truth cannot be realized without first having mastered the conventional truth that the person is a fiction constructed on the basis of skandhas and so on in relations of dependent origination. The skandhas and so on are themselves conceptual constructions, but they turn out to be useful for purposes of realizing the ultimate truth. And without such realization, nirvāṇa is not attained. In short, what Abhidharma takes to be the ultimate truth turns out, on the Madhyamaka understanding, to be merely conventionally true.

vināśayati durdṛṣṭā śūnyatā mandamedhasam /
sarpo yathā durgṛhīto vidyā vā duṣprasādhitā //11//

11. Emptiness misunderstood destroys the slow-witted,
like a serpent wrongly held or a spell wrongly executed.

As novice snake-handlers and apprentice sorcerers can attest, serpents and magic spells are dangerous instruments in the hands of those who lack the requisite knowledge. (See the *Alagaddūpama Sutta* [M I.130], where the Buddha likens misunderstanding the Dharma to what befalls one who wrongly grasps a snake.) The same is said to be true of emptiness. Candrakīrti discusses two ways in which the "slow-witted" can go astray. The first involves seeing emptiness as the nonexistence of all conditioned things, while the second involves supposing that emptiness is a really existing thing with a real locus. Both errors stem from failing to understand the distinction between the two truths, and both can destroy one's chances of liberation.

ataś ca pratyudāvṛttaṃ cittaṃ deśayituṃ muneḥ |
dharmaṃ matvāsya dharmasya mandair duravagāhatām ||12||

12. Hence the Sage's intention to teach the Dharma was turned back,
considering the difficulty, for the slow, of penetrating this Dharma.

It is said that the Buddha, after attaining enlightenment, hesitated before embarking on the career of a buddha—teaching others the Dharma he had discovered so that they too could attain the cessation of suffering. His hesitation was due to his realization that the Dharma is complex and difficult to grasp. In the end, it is said, it was the intercession of the gods that convinced him to take up his teaching career.

śūnyatāyām adhilayaṃ yaṃ punaḥ kurute bhavān |
doṣaprasaṅgo nāsmākaṃ sa śūnye nopapadyate ||13||

13. Moreover, the objection that you make concerning emptiness
cannot be a faulty consequence for us or for emptiness.

By "the objection" is meant what was stated in verses 1–6. The opponent is apparently among the "slow-witted," for he is said to have failed to grasp emptiness, its meaning and its purpose. For this reason the objection goes wide of the mark.

sarvaṃ ca yujyate tasya śūnyatā yasya yujyate |
sarvaṃ na yujyate tasya śūnyaṃ yasya na yujyate ||14||

14. All is possible when emptiness is possible.
    Nothing is possible when emptiness is impossible.

By "all" is here meant the central teachings of Buddhism, which the opponent claimed the Madhyamaka doctrine of emptiness jeopardized. Candrakīrti explains that when, for instance, it is acknowledged that everything is devoid of intrinsic nature, then dependent origination becomes possible, and this in turn makes it possible for the Buddha's account of the origin and cessation of suffering to be correct. To deny that all things are empty, on the other hand, is tantamount to claiming that there exist things that are not dependently originated, and this undermines Buddhism's core tenets.

sa tvaṃ doṣān ātmanīyān asmāsu paripātayan /
aśvam evābhirūḍhaḥ sann aśvam evāsi vismṛtaḥ //15//

15. You, throwing your own faults on us,
    are like the person mounted on a horse who forgets the horse.

It is the opponent, and not the Mādhyamika, whose view calls into question the Buddha's Dharma. Candrakīrti explains that the opponent is like someone who rebukes another for stealing a horse, forgetting that he is mounted on that very horse.

svabhāvād yadi bhāvānāṃ sadbhāvam anupaśyasi /
ahetupratyayān bhāvāṃs tvam evaṃ sati paśyasi //16//

16. If you look upon existents as real intrinsically,
    in that case you regard existents as being without cause and conditions.

kāryaṃ ca kāraṇaṃ caiva kartāraṃ karaṇaṃ kriyām /
utpādaṃ ca nirodhaṃ ca phalaṃ ca pratibādhase //17//

17. Effect and cause, as well as agent, instrument and act,
arising and ceasing, and fruit—all these you thereby deny.

If things have intrinsic nature, then they cannot originate in dependence on causes and conditions. This in turn means that none of the components of the causal relation—cause, effect, and so forth—can exist. For the arguments meant to show that things with intrinsic nature could not undergo dependent origination see chapters 12, 15, and 20.

yaḥ pratītyasamutpādaḥ śūnyatāṃ tāṃ pracakṣmahe /
sā prajñaptir upādāya pratipat saiva madhyamā //18//

18. Dependent origination we declare to be emptiness.
It [emptiness] is a dependent concept; just that is the middle path.

This is the most celebrated verse of the work, but some care is required in understanding it. Candrakīrti explains that when something like a sprout or a consciousness originates in dependence on causes and conditions (respectively the seed being in warm moist soil, and there being contact between sense faculty and object), its so doing means that it arises without intrinsic nature. And anything that arises without intrinsic nature is empty or devoid of intrinsic nature. On this understanding of 18ab, emptiness is not the same thing as dependent origination; it is rather something that follows from dependent origination. Anything that is dependently originated must be empty, but this leaves it open whether there are empty things that are not dependently originated.

To say of emptiness that it is a dependent concept is to say that it is like the chariot, a mere conceptual fiction. Since the chariot is a mere conceptual fiction because it lacks intrinsic nature (it is only conceived of in dependence on its parts, so its nature is wholly borrowed from its parts), it would then follow that emptiness is likewise without intrinsic nature. That is, emptiness is itself empty. Emptiness is not an ultimately real entity nor a property of ultimately real entities. Emptiness is no more than a useful way of conceptualizing experience. On this point see also 13.7 and 18.11.

For the notion of the Buddha's teachings as a middle path, see 15.7. To call emptiness the middle path is to say that it avoids the two extreme views of being and nonbeing. It avoids the extreme view of being by denying that there are ultimately real existents, things with intrinsic nature. But at the same time it avoids the extreme view of nonbeing by denying that ultimate reality is characterized by the absence of being. It is able to avoid both extremes because it denies that there is such a thing as the ultimate nature of reality.

apratītya samutpanno dharmaḥ kaścin na vidyate /
yasmāt tasmād aśūnyo hi dharmaḥ kaścin na vidyate //19//

19. There being no dharma whatsoever that is not dependently originated,
it follows that there is also no dharma whatsoever that is non-empty.

Candrakīrti quotes Āryadeva to this effect:

> Never is there anywhere the existence of anything that is not dependently originated,
> hence never is there anything anywhere that is eternal. (CŚ 9.2)
> Space and the like are thought to be permanent by ordinary people,
> but the clear-sighted do not see [external] objects in them even by their purified worldly cognition. (CŚ 9.3)

While common sense, as well as many non-Buddhist philosophers, holds that space is a real, eternal entity, most (though not all) Buddhists deny this. (See Candrakīrti's commentary on CŚ 9.5 for a representative argument against the reality of space.) But note that there is no argument given here to establish that all dharmas originate in dependence on causes and conditions. So the present argument for the conclusion that all things are empty seems to rely on our having already accepted the premise that everything ultimately real is dependently originated.

yady aśūnyam idaṃ sarvam udayo nāsti na vyayaḥ /
caturṇām āryasatyānām abhāvas te prasajyate //20//

20. If all this is non-empty, there is neither origination nor cessation.
It follows for you that there is the nonexistence of the four noble truths.

Nāgārjuna here begins to make good on his claim in verses 13–14 that it is the opponent's view and not the Mādhyamika's that undermines the basic teachings of Buddhism. In verse 1 the opponent charged that emptiness falsified the four noble truths. The response here is that if things were non-empty or had intrinsic nature, then they would be eternal. The next five verses spell out how this would falsify each of the four noble truths.

apratītya samutpannaṃ kuto duḥkhaṃ bhaviṣyati /
anityam uktaṃ duḥkhaṃ hi tat svābhāvye na vidyate //21//

21. How will suffering come to be if it is not dependently originated?
Indeed the impermanent was declared to be suffering, and it does not exist if there is intrinsic nature.

The first noble truth is the claim that there is suffering. But the Buddha also said that suffering is due to impermanence. And that which has intrinsic nature, and so is not dependently originated, must be permanent. So if what is real has intrinsic nature, then suffering does not really exist.

svabhāvato vidyamānaṃ kiṃ punaḥ samudeṣyate /
tasmāt samudayo nāsti śūnyatāṃ pratibādhataḥ //22//

22. How will something that exists intrinsically arise again?
 Therefore the arising of suffering does not exist for one who
 denies emptiness.

The second noble truth concerns how it is that suffering arises in dependence on causes and conditions. But if suffering were a real entity with intrinsic nature, then it would have existed from all past eternity. Hence causes and conditions could only bring about a second arising of suffering. And it is agreed by all that existing things do not undergo a second coming into existence. Thus the denial of emptiness entails the rejection of the second noble truth.

na nirodhaḥ svabhāvena sato duḥkhasya vidyate /
svabhāvaparyavasthānān nirodhaṃ pratibādhase //23//

23. There is no cessation of a suffering that exists intrinsically.
 You deny cessation through your maintaining intrinsic
 nature.

The third noble truth claims that there is also such a thing as the cessation of suffering. But things with intrinsic nature do not undergo cessation. So this noble truth must also be rejected if emptiness is denied.

svābhāvye sati mārgasya bhāvanā nopapadyate /
athāsau bhāvyate mārgaḥ svābhāvyaṃ te na vidyate //24//

24. The practice of a path that exists intrinsically is not possible.
But if this path is practiced, then you must say it does not
have intrinsic nature.

The fourth noble truth claims there is a path to the cessation of suffering. This path consists in a variety of practices that are said to result in the attainment of nirvāṇa. But practices involve conduct, and conduct involves change: To practice meditation, for instance, one must begin meditating at a certain time and then cease at another time. If things existed with intrinsic nature, then those things could not change in such ways. So the view that things exist with intrinsic nature entails that there can be no path. If, on the other hand, there is practice of a path, then it cannot have intrinsic nature, since practice requires change, and things with intrinsic nature do not change.

yadā duḥkhaṃ samudayo nirodhaś ca na vidyate |
mārgo duḥkhanirodhaṃ tvāṃ katamaḥ prāpayiṣyati ||25||

25. When there is neither suffering nor the arising and cessation
of suffering,
then what kind of path will lead you to the cessation of
suffering?

Moreover, a path cannot lead to a nonexistent destination. And if suffering has intrinsic nature, it can neither arise nor cease. So no path could lead to the cessation of suffering. Hence the promise of the fourth noble truth is once again called into question by the opponent's thesis.

svabhāvenāparijñānaṃ yadi tasya punaḥ katham |
parijñānaṃ nanu kila svabhāvaḥ samavasthitaḥ ||26||

26. If noncomprehension of suffering is intrinsic, how will there later be its comprehension?
Isn't an intrinsic nature said to be immutable?

The opponent claimed in verse 2 that the four constituent activities of the path would not exist if all things were empty. The first of those is comprehension of suffering and its causes. The present argument is that if the opponent were right that things have intrinsic natures, then the comprehension of suffering could not occur. To say that such comprehension takes place is to say that at one time suffering has the nature of not being comprehended and at a later time it has the nature of being comprehended. But if the natures of things are intrinsic, then their natures cannot undergo change. So either suffering is never comprehended or else it is always comprehended. In either case there cannot be the activity of coming to comprehend its nature and causes.

prahāṇasākṣātkaraṇe bhāvanā caivam eva te |
parijñāvan na yujyante catvāry api phalāni ca ||27||

27. In the same manner, abandonment, personal realization, and practice,
like comprehension, are impossible for you, and so too the four fruits.

Abandonment, personal realization, and contemplative practice were the other three of the four activities mentioned by the opponent in verse 2. The same considerations that ruled out an activity of comprehension also apply to these three, and so all four components of the path turn out to be impossible under the opponent's supposition that real things have intrinsic nature.

The four fruits are the results of these activities. In verse 3 the opponent argued that in the absence of the four activities, there cannot be the four fruits. Nāgārjuna agrees but uses this as a reason to reject not emptiness but the view that there is intrinsic nature.

svabhāvenānadhigataṃ yat phalaṃ tat punaḥ katham /
śakyaṃ samadhigantuṃ syāt svabhāvaṃ parigṛhṇataḥ //28//

28. For those holding that there is intrinsic nature, if the lack of acquisition of the fruit is intrinsic, how would it be possible to acquire it later?

A fruit is something that one obtains at some particular time, not having had it at an earlier time. If there are intrinsic natures, then the nature of not having a certain fruit (such as arhatship) would be intrinsic. But then whatever had that nature could not come to have the quite different nature of acquiring the fruit. So once again there could not be the four fruits.

phalābhāve phalasthā no na santi pratipannakāḥ /
saṃgho nāsti na cet santi te 'ṣṭau puruṣapudgalāḥ //29//

29. If the fruits are nonexistent, then there are neither the strivers after nor the attainers of those fruits.
The Saṃgha does not exist if the eight kinds of person do not exist.

abhāvāc cāryasatyānāṃ saddharmo 'pi na vidyate /
dharme cāsati saṃghe ca kathaṃ buddho bhaviṣyati //30//

30. And because of the nonexistence of the noble truths, the true Dharma does not exist either.
Dharma and Saṃgha being nonexistent, how will a Buddha come to be?

Nāgārjuna here simply repeats the charges of the opponent in verses 3cd–5ab. Only now of course the charges are directed not at the proponent of emptiness but at those who hold there are things with intrinsic nature.

apratītyāpi bodhiṃ ca tava buddhaḥ prasajyate /
apratītyāpi buddhaṃ ca tava bodhiḥ prasajyate //31//

31. And it follows for you that there can even be a buddha not dependent on enlightenment.
It follows for you as well that there can even be enlightenment not dependent on a buddha.

If the state of being a buddha is intrinsic, then having that state cannot be dependent on other factors, such as attaining enlightenment. Likewise if being enlightened is an intrinsic nature, then its occurrence cannot depend on the existence of anything else, such as an enlightened being. Hence it should be possible for enlightenment to exist all by itself, without any locus.

yaś cābuddhaḥ svabhāvena sa bodhāya ghaṭann api /
na bodhisattvacaryāyāṃ bodhiṃ te 'dhigamiṣyati //32//

32. One who is unenlightened by intrinsic nature, though that one strives for enlightenment,
will not, according to you, attain enlightenment in the course of the bodhisattva's practice.

The bodhisattva is someone who, while unenlightened, aspires to become a buddha and seeks to attain that status by engaging in the practices necessary to accumulate the requisite skills. Such conduct would be pointless if such natures as being unenlightened were intrinsic. Hence no one could ever become a buddha.

na ca dharmam adharmaṃ vā kaścij jātu kariṣyati /
kim aśūnyasya kartavyaṃ svabhāvaḥ kriyate na hi //33//

33. Moreover, no one will ever perform either good or bad actions.
What is there that is to be done with regard to the non-empty? For what has intrinsic nature is not done.

In verse 6 the opponent accused the Mādhyamika of removing all reason to engage in any sort of conduct, whether good or bad. Here the response is that if there is intrinsic nature, then there can be no reason to perform any action. To perform an action—to do something—is to bring about a state of affairs that did not obtain earlier. If things have intrinsic nature, then any state of affairs that does not obtain at one time must retain that nature through all time. So our conduct could not result in something being done (whether good or bad).

vinā dharmam adharmaṃ ca phalaṃ hi tava vidyate /
dharmādharmanimittaṃ ca phalaṃ tava na vidyate //34//

34. For you, indeed, there is fruit even without good or bad actions;
for you there is no fruit conditioned by good or bad actions.

If things exist with intrinsic nature, then such karmic fruits as rebirth into pleasant and painful states cannot depend for their occurrence on performance of good and bad deeds. For anything that exists with intrinsic nature has its nature independently of other things. So although we may want to obtain pleasant fruits and avoid painful fruits, doing the right and shunning the evil will be utterly pointless in this regard.

dharmādharmanimittaṃ vā yadi te vidyate phalam /
dharmādharmasamutpannam aśūnyaṃ te kathaṃ phalam //35//

35. Or if, for you, the fruit is conditioned by good or bad actions,
how is it that for you the fruit, being originated from good or
bad actions, is non-empty?

To say that fruit is determined by good or bad actions is to say that fruit originates in dependence on such conduct. And if everything dependently originated is devoid of intrinsic nature (as was claimed in verse 18), it follows that fruit cannot be non-empty, cannot be something that has intrinsic nature. So the opponent cannot maintain both that fruit is determined by good and bad actions and that fruit is non-empty.

sarvasaṃvyvahārāṃś ca laukikān pratibādhase /
yat pratītyasamutpādaṃ śūnyatāṃ pratibādhase //36//

36. You also deny all worldly modes of conduct
when you deny emptiness as dependent origination.

By "worldly modes of conduct" is meant just those basic activities that go to make up the behavior of our everyday lives. Candrakīrti lists coming, going, cooking, reading, and standing as examples. Since these are also dependently originated, their occurrence is incompatible with the claim that things are non-empty or have intrinsic nature.

na kartavyaṃ bhavet kiṃcid anārabdhā bhavet kriyā /
kārakaḥ syād akurvāṇaḥ śūnyatāṃ pratibādhataḥ //37//

37. There would be nothing whatsoever that was to be done,
action would be uncommenced,
and the agent would not act, should emptiness be denied.

To say of an action that it should be done is to say that it should be caused to occur. This can be true only if actions can originate in dependence on causes and conditions. If real things have intrinsic nature, then they do not originate in dependence on cause and conditions. Hence if real things are non-empty, there can be nothing that is to be done. Similar reasoning leads to the conclusions that no action can commence or begin and that nothing can be an agent of an action.

ajātam aniruddhaṃ ca kūṭasthaṃ ca bhaviṣyati /
vicitrābhir avasthābhiḥ svabhāve rahitaṃ jagat //38//

38. The world would be unproduced, unceased, and
 unchangeable,
 it would be devoid of its manifold appearances, if there were
 intrinsic nature.

It is a fundamental fact about our experience that the world presents itself in a variety of different ways. The claim here is that this fact would be inexplicable if there were intrinsic nature. For then new states of the world could not come into existence, and old states could not go out of existence. The world could not undergo any change in how it appears to us.

asaṃprāptasya ca prāptir duḥkhaparyantakarma ca /
sarvakleśaprahāṇaṃ ca yady aśūnyaṃ na vidyate //39//

39. The obtaining of what is not yet obtained, activity to end
 suffering,
 the abandonment of all the defilements—none of these exists
 if all this is non-empty.

It is not only worldly conduct that is undermined by the view that things have intrinsic nature. Conduct meant to bring about the end of suffering is likewise threatened. The reasoning is the same as in verses 36–38. If, for instance, the defilements (see 17.26) are not abandoned at an earlier time, nothing one can do can bring it about that they are abandoned later.

yaḥ pratītyasamutpādaṃ paśyatīdaṃ sa paśyati /
duḥkhaṃ samudayaṃ caiva nirodhaṃ mārgam eva ca //40//

40. He who sees dependent origination sees this:
suffering, arising, cessation, and the path.

The four noble truths are referred to as the truths of (1) suffering, (2) arising (of suffering), (3) cessation (of suffering), and (4) the path (to the cessation of suffering). So the claim here is that one cannot understand the four noble truths without understanding dependent origination. Of course most Buddhists would agree with this claim. But in the present context, it means that one cannot grasp the four noble truths without recognizing that all things are empty.

25. An Analysis of Nirvāṇa

NĀGĀRJUNA'S EXAMINATION of nirvāṇa comes in response to the objection that his doctrine of emptiness would rule out the existence of the state that is supposedly the aim of the Buddha's teachings. He responds first by arguing that the same consequence follows from the thesis that there are non-empty things and then by attempting to show that no statement concerning nirvāṇa could be ultimately true. In doing the latter he follows the precedent of the Buddha's teachings on the so-called indeterminate questions, and the chapter concludes by showing how the doctrine of emptiness can be viewed as an elaboration of the Buddha's treatment of those disputed points. In outline it runs as follows:

25.1 Objection: If everything were empty there could be no such thing as nirvāṇa.
25.2 Reply: Nonexistence of nirvāṇa also follows from existence of non-empty things.
25.3 Assertion: Nothing can be asserted concerning nirvāṇa.
25.4–6 Refutation of possibility that nirvāṇa is an existent
25.7–8 Refutation of possibility that nirvāṇa is an absence
25.9–10 Tentative solution: Nirvāṇa is neither an existent nor an absence.
25.11–14 Refutation of possibility that nirvāṇa is both an existent and an absence

25.15–16 Refutation of possibility that nirvāṇa is neither an existent nor an absence

25.17 Rejection of four possible views concerning the existence of the Buddha in nirvāṇa

25.18 Application of the same analysis to saṃsāra, which likewise is not existent, an absence, etc.

25.19–20 There is not the slightest gap between nirvāṇa and saṃsāra.

25.21–23 This analysis likewise disposes of the other indeterminate questions.

25.24 Soteriological consequence: the halting of hypostatization. No dharma was taught by the Buddha.

yadi śūnyam idaṃ sarvam udayo nāsti na vyayaḥ |
prahāṇād vā nirodhād vā kasya nirvāṇam iṣyate ||1||

1. [Objection:] If all this is empty, there is neither origination nor cessation.
Due to abandonment or cessation of what is nirvāṇa then acknowledged?

The opponent raises another objection to the claim that everything is empty. If this were true, then there could ultimately be neither the arising nor the disappearance of phenomena. This much Nāgārjuna has already asserted in 1.1. But in that case, it seems there could be no such thing as nirvāṇa. For nirvāṇa is said to be of two types, with and without remainder. The former involves abandonment of the defilements, so that cessation of rebirth is assured but still involves psychophysical elements resulting from past karma, so one is still embodied. The latter comes about when one's karma is exhausted, so that the causal series of psychophysical elements is destroyed. Both involve cessation. The former involves the cessation of false views of an existing "I," while the latter involves cessation of the psychophysical elements. If neither arising nor cessation ultimately occurs, then it seems one cannot attain either form of nirvāṇa, since both require the arising and cessation of really existing things. Consequently the claim that all is empty is incompatible with the teachings of the Buddha.

yady aśūnyam idaṃ sarvam udayo nāsti na vyayaḥ /
prahāṇād vā nirodhād vā kasya nirvāṇam iṣyate //2//

2. [Reply:] If all this is non-empty, there is neither origination nor cessation.
Due to abandonment or cessation of what is nirvāṇa then acknowledged?

To this Nāgārjuna replies that if we instead believe there are things that are non-empty, then we shall be unable to explain how nirvāṇa is possible. For then arising and cessation are impossible. Bhāviveka and Candrakīrti both explain that this is because something that has intrinsic nature (and hence is non-empty) cannot undergo origination or destruction. This reply might appear to be a *tu quoque*. But Candrakīrti states that those who hold the doctrine of emptiness do not have this difficulty. And Bhāviveka says all sides agree to the conventional truth of the claim that nirvāṇa is attained. Since he thinks the only truths Mādhyamikas may assert (apart from the doctrine of emptiness) are conventional truths, this means he also believes they can escape the objection of the opponent. The reason for this will emerge in the remainder of the chapter.

aprahīṇam asaṃprāptam anucchinnam aśāśvatam /
aniruddham anutpannam etan nirvāṇam ucyate //3//

3. Not abandoned, not acquired, not annihilated, not eternal,
not ceased, not arisen, thus is nirvāṇa said to be.

In his comments, Candrakīrti quotes a verse attributed to the Buddha to the effect that when all phenomena have ceased, then the notions of "exists" and "does not exist" are impediments to the cessation of suffering. Related ideas are to be found in the Nikāyas. In the *Aggi-Vacchagotta Sutta* (M I.483), the Buddha says that since enlightened ones have cut off all roots of rebirth, one cannot say of the postmortem enlightened ones that they will be reborn, that they will not be reborn, and so on. (There being no such person, the question simply does not arise.) And in the *Kaccāyanagotta Sutta* (S II.17, III.134–35) the Buddha says that "exists" and "does not exist" are equally inappropriate extreme views. (Nāgārjuna referred to this sūtra in 15.7.) Putting together the thoughts expressed in these two passages, one can perhaps say the following about "final" nirvāṇa (cessation without remainder). Since the causes of further rebirth have ceased, the liberated one will not be reborn; the causal series of psychophysical elements that constitutes one's life-series will come to an end at death. So one cannot say that the liberated one exists after death. This is often taken to mean that "final" nirvāṇa amounts to utter annihilation, that the liberated one does not exist after death. And of course this makes nirvāṇa sound distinctly unappealing to many. But on the view being presented in these sūtra passages, that response would be mistaken. Since there is no owner of the elements making up the causal series, it would be inappropriate to describe the ceasing of the causal series as "I will not exist." Hence neither "exists" nor "does not exist" can be said.

This much virtually all Buddhist schools would probably agree on. But Nāgārjuna has something deeper in mind. What that might be will emerge in the remainder of the chapter. Nāgārjuna conducts his examination by considering whether nirvāṇa might be an existent (i.e., a positive being, *bhāva*), an absence (a negative being, *abhāva*), both, or neither. In this he is following the standard logical format of the *catuṣkoṭi* or tetralemma.

bhāvas tāvan na nirvāṇaṃ jarāmaraṇalakṣaṇam /
prasajyetāsti bhāvo hi na jarāmaraṇaṃ vinā //4//

4. Nirvāṇa is not, on the one hand, an existent; if it were, its
having the characteristics of old age and death
would follow, for there is no existent devoid of old age and
death.

It is an orthodoxy for Buddhists that all existents are characterized by suffering, impermanence, and nonself. These are said to be the three universal characteristics of existing things. Being subject to old age and death is the standard specification of what it means for something to be impermanent. This specification is also meant to bring out a connection between impermanence and suffering, since it is universally acknowledged that old age and death are unwelcome phenomena. Because nirvāṇa is supposed to be the cessation of suffering, it follows that it could not be characterized by old age and death.

bhāvaś ca yadi nirvāṇaṃ nirvāṇaṃ saṃskṛtaṃ bhavet /
nāsaṃskṛto vidyate hi bhāvaḥ kva cana kaś cana //5//

5. And if nirvāṇa were an existent, nirvāṇa would be
conditioned,
for never is there found any existent that is not conditioned.

The argument here is that all existents are subject to origination, duration, and cessation. So if nirvāṇa were an existent, it would likewise be subject to origination, duration, and cessation. This is obviously incompatible with the claim that nirvāṇa represents the permanent cessation of suffering. There were Abhidharma schools that included in their list of dharmas or ultimate reals certain unconditioned dharmas. The Vaibhāṣikas, for instance, held that space and the two types of cessation were ultimately real unconditioned entities. It can, however, be claimed that these are not to be thought of as existents but rather as absences, so their inclusion does not conflict with the claim that all existents are conditioned. Space, for instance, is defined as what lacks resistance. But see verse 5.2 above, where the example of space is brought under a general rule that is said to hold for all existents (*bhāva*).

bhāvaś ca yadi nirvāṇam anupādāya tat katham /
nirvāṇaṃ nānupādāya kaścid bhāvo hi vidyate //6//

6. And if nirvāṇa were an existent, how could one say that nirvāṇa is nondependent?
   For never is there found any existent that is nondependent.

The motivation behind calling nirvāṇa nondependent is presumably that this is the only way of insuring that it represents a permanent cessation of suffering. If it were said to depend on conditions, then its continuation would be contingent on those conditions continuing to obtain. The difficulty with calling nirvāṇa nondependent, though, is that this conflicts with the Buddhist orthodoxy that every existing thing originates in dependence on causes and conditions.

bhāvo yadi na nirvāṇam abhāvaḥ kiṃ bhaviṣyati /
nirvāṇaṃ yatra bhāvo na nābhāvas tatra vidyate //7//

7. If nirvāṇa is not a [positive] existent, how will nirvāṇa be an absence?
   Where there is no existent, there is no absence.

According to Bhāviveka, the argument here is directed at the Sautrāntikas, who held that nirvāṇa is a mere absence. (The term we translate here as "absence," *abhāva*, we elsewhere render "nonexistent"; we make this change because to do otherwise would wrongly suggest the idea that there is no such thing as the state of nirvāṇa.) Candrakīrti identifies the target as the view that nirvāṇa is the absence of the defilements and birth. The argument against this is, according to Candrakīrti, that then nirvāṇa would be just as impermanent as defilements and birth are. To this it might be objected that nirvāṇa would still have the sort of permanence that is desired; while it would have a beginning in time, it would not have an end. But Candrakīrti claims the view leads to the absurd consequence that nirvāṇa could be attained effortlessly: Since each occurrence of a defilement or of birth is impermanent (like everything else), it ceases regardless of effort. Thus the absence of each defilement and birth will occur regardless of whether or not one strives to attain nirvāṇa.

yady abhāvaś ca nirvāṇam anupādāya tat katham /
nirvāṇaṃ na hy abhāvo 'sti yo 'nupādāya vidyate //8//

8. And if nirvāṇa is an absence, how can nirvāṇa be nondependent? There is no absence that exists without dependence.

If we suppose there to be such a thing as an absence, then we must say that its occurrence is dependent on other things, namely those things of which it is the absence. The Nyāya school puts this in terms of its rule: no absence without an existing counterpositive. By this rule there cannot be such a thing as the absence of the horns of a hare, since the horns of a hare do not exist. (There can, though, be the absence of horns from the head of a hare.) But this makes the occurrence of an absence contingent on its counterpositive existing at some place or time. So if the opponent calls nirvāṇa an absence, this once again contradicts the claim that nirvāṇa is nondependent.

So far we have been told that nirvāṇa is not an existent and that it is also not an absence. One seemingly logical response might be to combine these two claims and say that nirvāṇa is neither existent nor an absence. This is just what is proposed, and defended on the basis of the authority of the Buddha, in the next two verses. But we will see that this does not represent Nāgārjuna's own view, since it is one that he will reject later, in verses 15–16.

ya ājavaṃjavībhāva upādāya pratītya vā |
so 'pratītyānupādāya nirvāṇam upadiśyate ||9||

9. That which when dependent or conditioned comes into and goes out of existence,
that, when not conditioned or dependent, is called nirvāṇa.

prahāṇaṃ cābravīc chāstā bhavasya vibhavasya ca |
tasmān na bhāvo nābhāvo nirvāṇam iti yujyate ||10||

10. And the teacher taught the abandonment of coming into and going out of existence.
Thus it is correct to call nirvāṇa neither existent nor an absence.

The reference of 10ab appears to be to Sn verse 514. Candrakīrti explains that by "coming into and going out of existence" is meant the state of coming and going through a succession of births and deaths. Such a state arises on the basis of the conditions of ignorance and so on as light arises in dependence on the lamp, and it is conceptualized in dependence on the psychophysical elements, as the long is conceived in dependence on the short. Nirvāṇa is said not to be conditioned by ignorance, etc., or not to be conceptualized in dependence on the psychophysical elements. In that case it, being the mere nonoccurrence of conditioning through ignorance, or the mere nonoccurrence of conceptual dependence on the psychophysical elements, cannot be said to be either an existent or an absence. The reasoning here seems to be that of the Personalism (Pudgalavāda) school. This school held that the person, while ultimately real, is neither identical with nor distinct from the psychophysical elements on the basis of which it is named and conceptualized. Given that nirvāṇa is the state of the person when no longer conditioned by or dependent on the psychophysical elements, it stands to reason that nirvāṇa should be thought of as a state that likewise defies classification in terms of the dichotomous concepts of existent and absence.

At this point the text appears to be endorsing the view that nirvāṇa is neither an existent nor an absence. In the next four verses it takes up and rejects the view that nirvāṇa is both an existent and an absence. This might look like support for the view that it is neither. But in verses 15–16 the "neither" option is rejected. This makes it clear that the endorsement of "neither" in the present verse represents the position of an opponent, not Nāgārjuna.

bhaved abhāvo bhāvaś ca nirvāṇam ubhayaṃ yadi /
bhaved abhāvo bhāvaś ca mokṣas tac ca na yujyate //11//

11\. If nirvāṇa were both an existent and an absence,
then liberation would be an absence and an existent, and that is not correct.

The *Akutobhayā* points out that there is mutual incompatibility between the existence of something and its absence occurring at the same time. Candrakīrti adds that liberation would then be both the arising of composite things and their ending. The same thing cannot arise and end at the same time. So one cannot say that nirvāṇa is both an existent and an absence.

bhaved abhāvo bhāvaś ca nirvāṇam ubhayaṃ yadi /
nānupādāya nirvāṇam upādāyobhayaṃ hi tat //12//

12. If nirvāṇa were both an existent and an absence,
then nirvāṇa would not be nondependent, for it would depend on both.

If nirvāṇa is to be ultimately real, then it must be nondependent—that is, something that is not named and conceptualized in dependence on other things. But a nirvāṇa that was both an existent and an absence would be named and conceptualized in dependence on existent composite things and on their absence. And that is clearly impossible.

bhaved abhāvo bhāvaś ca nirvāṇam ubhayaṃ katham /
asaṃskṛtaṃ hi nirvāṇaṃ bhāvābhāvau ca saṃskṛtau //13//

13. How can nirvāṇa be both an existent and an absence?
For nirvāṇa is noncomposite, and existents and absences are both composite.

For the meaning of "composite" (*saṃskṛta*) see chapter 13.

bhaved abhāvo bhāvaś ca nirvāṇa ubhayaṃ katham /
tayor abhāvo hy ekatra prakāśatamasor iva //14//

14. How could nirvāṇa be both an existent and an absence?
For they do not occur in the same place, just as with light and darkness.

Since darkness is the absence of light, to say that nirvāṇa is both a positive existent and an absence is like saying that there can occur both light and darkness in the same place at the same time. The commentators have already said in commenting on verse 11 and verse 12 that existence and absence are mutually incompatible. Nāgārjuna explicitly makes that point here with the example of light and darkness.

naivābhāvo naiva bhāvo nirvāṇam iti yāñjanā |
abhāve caiva bhāve ca sā siddhe sati sidhyati ||15||

15\. The assertion "Nirvāṇa is neither existent nor an absence"
is established only if there were established both absence and
existent.

Nāgārjuna here returns to the view that was apparently endorsed in verse 10, that nirvāṇa is neither an existent nor an absence. The claim now is that it also must be rejected. The argument is that this "neither" thesis could be ultimately true only if sense could be made both of the thesis that nirvāṇa is an existent and the thesis that nirvāṇa is an absence. Since those two theses have already been rejected, it follows that "neither" must be as well. The reasoning is that since the "neither" thesis is purported by its proponent to be ultimately true, it must be understood as a negatively phrased positive characterization of nirvāṇa, one that describes it by saying what it is not. But if there is no such thing as the way it is not, then the thesis cannot hold.

If we think of this situation in terms of classical logic, we might suspect that Nāgārjuna is committing a logical error here. He has just rejected the thesis that nirvāṇa is neither an existent nor an absence. The negation of "neither *p* nor *not p*" is "either *p* or *not p*." And for the latter to be true, at least one of the two statements *p* and *not p* must be true. But in verses 4–8 we were told that both "nirvāṇa is an existent" and "nirvāṇa is an absence" are to be rejected. Has Nāgārjuna become confused by the logic involved in negating the negation of a disjunction?

According to Candrakīrti's explanation of the argument, Nāgārjuna did not commit a logical error here. The reason is that there are two ways in which a statement can fail to be ultimately true. One way is for it to be ultimately false. If *p* fails to be ultimately true by being ultimately false, then *not p* is ultimately true. But the other way is for *p* to be about something that simply does not really exist. If *p* is actually not about anything at all, then it can be neither ultimately true nor ultimately false, because it really has no meaning at all (at least not from the perspective of ultimate truth). In other words, in order to say that *not p* is ultimately true, we have to be able to imagine how it would be possible for *p* to be ultimately true. The statement *p* must really be about something in order to be true or to be false. And what was presumably shown in verses 4–8 is that "nirvāṇa is an existent" and "nirvāṇa is an absence" cannot be ultimately true; it was not shown there that these statements are ultimately false. If "nirvāṇa is an existent" and "nirvāṇa is an absence" cannot be ultimately true, then the negation of their disjunction, "nirvāṇa is neither existent nor an absence," likewise cannot be ultimately true.

naivābhāvo naiva bhāvo nirvāṇaṃ yadi vidyate |
naivābhāvo naiva bhāva iti kena tad ajyate ||16||

16. If nirvāṇa were found to be neither an existent nor an absence,
then by what is it revealed that it is neither existent nor an absence?

To claim that ultimately nirvāṇa is neither an existent nor an absence is to claim that it has this character. The question here is how this could possibly be known. If the psychophysical elements on the basis of which the person is conceptualized have been abandoned, then it cannot be an object of consciousness. Were it thought that it can be cognized by means of the cognition of emptiness, then insofar as the latter involves the absence of all hypostatization, it likewise cannot be grasped as corresponding to the concept "neither an existent nor an absence," since this is itself an instance of conceptual proliferation. Thus there could be no reason to hold this thesis.

We have now seen reason to reject all four possible views concerning the ontological status of nirvāṇa. The next two verses show that there is a Buddhist precedent for this way of rejecting all four of the lemmas under consideration in verses 4–16.

paraṃ nirodhād bhagavān bhavatīty eva nājyate |
na bhavaty ubhayaṃ ceti nobhayaṃ ceti nājyate ||17||

17. It is not to be asserted that the Buddha exists beyond cessation,
nor "does not exist" nor "both exists and does not exist," nor "neither exists nor does not exist"—none of these is to be asserted.

tiṣṭhamāno 'pi bhagavān bhavatīty eva nājyate |
na bhavaty ubhayaṃ ceti nobhayaṃ ceti nājyate ||18||

18. Indeed it is not to be asserted that "The Buddha exists while remaining [in this world],"
nor "does not exist" nor "both exists and does not exist," nor "neither exists nor does not exist"—none of these is to be asserted.

As Bhāviveka makes explicit, the reference here is to the indeterminate questions (*avyākṛta*) discussed at S III.112, M I.483–88, and S IV.374–402. These are questions to which it was commonly assumed an enlightened person would know the answer. They include such questions as whether the liberated person continues to exist postmortem, whether the world is eternal, whether the life-force is identical with the body, and so on. Their consideration is usually put in the form of a tetralemma: Is it that *p*, *not p*, both *p* and *not p*, or neither *p* nor *not p*? The questions are called "indeterminate" because for each such possibility, the Buddha rejects that thesis without embracing any other. This has led some modern scholars to suppose that the Buddha does not always obey the laws of classical logic. To reject *p*, for instance, would seem to commit one to *not p*, yet the Buddha rejects this as well. But the example of the fire that has gone out (M I.487–88) shows that the Buddha takes each of the four possibilities to involve a false presupposition, for example, that there ultimately is such a thing as the Buddha who might be said to exist, not exist, etc., after cessation. Since this presupposition is false, one can reject the claim that the Buddha exists postmortem as well as the claim that the Buddha does not exist postmortem without violating any law of classical logic. A similar treatment would allow Nāgārjuna to avoid the charge that he contradicts himself when he says (10cd) that nirvāṇa is not to be called either an existent or an absence and also (15–16) that nirvāṇa is not to be said to be neither an existent nor an absence.

na saṃsārasya nirvāṇāt kiṃcid asti viśeṣaṇam |
na nirvāṇasya saṃsārāt kiṃcid asti viśeṣaṇam ||19||

19. There is no distinction whatsoever between saṃsāra and nirvāṇa.
There is no distinction whatsoever between nirvāṇa and saṃsāra.

nirvāṇasya ca yā koṭiḥ koṭiḥ saṃsaraṇasya ca |
na tayor antaraṃ kiṃcit susūkṣmam api vidyate ||20||

20. What is the limit of nirvāṇa, that is the limit of saṃsāra.
There is not even the finest gap to be found between the two.

The same reasoning that leads to the rejection of the four lemmas with respect to nirvāṇa applies as well to saṃsāra. Since all things are, according to Nāgārjuna, empty of intrinsic nature, it follows that ultimately there is no such state as saṃsāra. For in order for saṃsāra to be something about which ultimately true claims could be made, there would have to be ultimately real mental forces that could produce it. And if all things are empty, then there are no mental forces that are ultimately real. Consequently one cannot say that ultimately saṃsāra exists, does not exist, and so forth. Note, however, that this says nothing about the conventional status of nirvāṇa and saṃsāra. A Mādhyamika can still hold it to be conventionally true that nirvāṇa and saṃsāra are very different states, that the former should be sought while the latter should be stopped, and so on.

paraṃ nirodhād antādyāḥ śāśvatādyāś ca dṛṣṭayaḥ /
nirvāṇam aparāntaṃ ca pūrvāntaṃ ca samāśritāḥ //21//

21. The views concerning what is beyond cessation, the end of the world, and the eternality of the world
are dependent [respectively] on nirvāṇa, the future life, and the past life.

Among the indeterminate questions the Buddha refused to answer are questions concerning whether there is a state of being following the cessation of such composite things as persons, whether the world is limited in space, and whether the world has limits in time. These questions all presuppose one or another answer to the question whether nirvāṇa has a beginning and an end. The argument of chapter 11 was to the effect that there can be no prior and posterior parts of saṃsāra. And in that chapter it was claimed that the same analysis applies to all supposed existents. (See 11.8.) Here its application to the case of nirvāṇa is being utilized.

śūnyeṣu sarvadharmeṣu kim anantaṃ kim antavat /
kim anantaṃ cāntavac ca nānantaṃ nāntavac ca kim //22//

22. All dharmas being empty, what is without end, what has an end?
What is both with and without end, and what is neither without end nor having an end?

kiṃ tad eva kim anyat kiṃ śāśvataṃ kim aśāśvatam /
aśāśvataṃ śāśvataṃ ca kiṃ vā nobhayam apy atha //23//

23. What is identical with this, what is distinct? What is eternal, what noneternal?
What is both eternal and noneternal, and what is then neither?

To say of all dharmas that they are devoid of intrinsic nature is to say that there are no ultimately real entities. And since a statement can be ultimately true only by virtue of correctly describing an ultimately real entity, it follows that no possible view concerning nirvāṇa and the person who attains it can be ultimately true. Notice the inclusion here of a question that was not mentioned earlier—the question of identity and distinctness. One might, for instance, wonder whether the enlightened person is identical with the person who sought enlightenment or is instead some distinct person. Given the present understanding of nirvāṇa, such a question cannot arise.

sarvopalambhopaśamaḥ prapañcopaśamaḥ śivaḥ /
na kvacit kasyacit kaścid dharmo buddhena deśitaḥ //24//

24. This halting of cognizing everything, the halting of hypostatizing, is blissful.
No Dharma whatsoever was ever taught by the Buddha to anyone.

Since it follows from the universal emptiness of all dharmas that there is ultimately nothing to be cognized, and suffering is said to result from hypostatization (see 11.6), it follows that the realization of emptiness is "blessed" or the cessation of suffering. Of course it also follows from this that the Dharma, the teachings of the Buddha, contains no single statement that is ultimately true. But this, says Candrakīrti, presents no difficulty for the Mādhyamika. For to the extent that the Buddha's teachings are useful in helping us overcome suffering, they are conventionally true.

Some modern scholars take the text to end here; they claim that the remaining two chapters are later additions and not the work of Nāgārjuna. In support of this claim they point out that the earliest of the existing commentaries, the *Akutobhayā*, might seem to have ended at this point. What are presented, in currently available editions of this commentary, as its last two chapters (i.e., commentary on chapters 26–27) are for the most part just the verses themselves, with no elucidatory comments. It might also be said in particular that chapter 26 presents no distinctively Madhyamaka views. Still, both Bhāviveka and Candrakīrti took the last two chapters as authentically Nāgārjuna's work. We take no stand on this controversy.

26. An Analysis of the Twelvefold Chain

BHĀVIVEKA frames this chapter as Nāgārjuna's response to the opponent who objects to what was just said in the immediately preceding verse (25.24)—that the Buddha taught no Dharma. The opponent says that if this were so then the Buddha must not have taught the doctrine of *pratītyasamutpāda*, or dependent origination. More specifically, he must not have taught the application of the idea of dependent origination to the case of the person, the doctrine of the twlevefold chain of dependent origination. This doctrine is accepted as orthodox by all schools of Buddhism. It is generally understood as explaining the mechanisms whereby one who has been born into this life due to factors present in the last life generates factors that will bring about a future rebirth and thus perpetuate saṃsāra. It is thus taken to lay out the details underpinning the second of the four noble truths, that suffering originates in dependence on causes and conditions. This makes it a core Buddhist teaching. So if Nāgārjuna's doctrine of emptiness has as a consequence that the Buddha taught no such thing, Nāgārjuna can be no Buddhist.

If Nāgārjuna's intention in the present chapter is to reply to this objection, then his response is the perfect model of orthodoxy. Verses 1–10 give the standard account of the twelvefold chain and how it leads to suffering. Verses 11–12 then give the gist of the third noble truth that the cessation of suffering is also possible. What is not immediately apparent is how all this is compatible with what Nāgārjuna said in 25.24 or, more generally, with the doctrine of emptiness. A possible answer, one suggested by the commentaries of Candrakīrti and Bhāviveka, is that while the doctrine of emptiness concerns ultimate truth, the doctrine of *pratītyasamutpāda* is only conventionally true.

The twelve factors making up the links in the twelvefold chain are as follows:

1. ignorance
2. volitions
3. consciousness
4. *nāmarūpa* (the five *skandha*s or groups of psychophysical elements)
5. the six sense organs
6. contact
7. feeling
8. desire
9. appropriation
10. being
11. birth
12. suffering (old age, death, etc.)

The arising of these factors, as well as their cessation, are explained in the following order:

26.1–10 Successive origination of twelve factors of the twelvefold chain

26.1: Explication of factors 1 and 2
26.2: Explication of factors 3 and 4
26.3: Explication of factors 5 and 6
26.4: Explication of factors 4 and 3
26.5: Explication of factors 6 and 7
26.6: Explication of factors 8 and 9
26.7: Explication of factor 10
26.8–9: Explication of factors 11 and 12
26.10: Conclusion: The ignorant and not the wise form volitions responsible for suffering.

26.11–12 Successive cessation of twelve factors of the twelvefold chain

punarbhavāya saṃskārān avidyānivṛtas tridhā /
abhisaṃskurute yāṃs tair gatiṃ gacchati karmabhiḥ //1//

1. One who is enveloped in ignorance forms three kinds of volitions that lead to rebirth;
and by means of these actions one goes to one's next mode of existence.

This verse explains what it was in the past life that led to the present life. Ignorance—namely ignorance concerning the facts of suffering, impermanence, and nonself—led one to form volitions (*saṃskāra*s), the mental forces that bring about actions. The "three kinds" may refer to volitions that cause physical, verbal, and mental actions. But Candrakīrti explains the three kinds as wholesome, unwholesome, and neutral. These then served as proximate cause of rebirth into the present life.

vijñānaṃ saṃniviśate saṃskārapratyayaṃ gatau /
saṃniviṣṭe 'tha vijñāne nāmarūpaṃ niṣicyate //2//

2. Having volitions as its conditions, consciousness enters into the new mode of existence.
Consciousness having entered into the new mode of existence, *nāmarūpa* [i.e., the five skandhas] becomes infused [with life].

The first line of this verse gives the standard account of the first moment of the present life. At conception the volitions of the prior life cause a moment of consciousness that comes to be associated with a particular embryo. This embryo will be in a particular state—divine, human, etc. If the volitions of the past life were predominantly wholesome, then the embryo in question might be in a divine mode (i.e., be the product of parents who are both gods) or in an especially fortunate human mode; if they were unwholesome, then the embryo might be in the mode of one of the hells; and so on. Candrakīrti adds that the relation between volitions and consciousness is like that between the moon and its reflection, or between a seal and a wax impression made from it. In both these cases the second item (the reflection, the impression) is numerically distinct from the first (the moon, the seal), and yet the nature of the second item is determined by the nature of the first. The point here is to guard against interpreting rebirth as a case of some entity traveling from the past life to the present life. On this see also Vism 554, where Buddhaghosa quotes a verse giving the example of an echo (*patighosa*), a new sound that arises in dependence on an earlier noise.

The term *nāmarūpa* is sometimes (and somewhat misleadingly) translated as "name and form." The term is a collective name for the five skandhas (on which see chapter 4). The claim here is that once a moment of consciousness has become associated with an embryo, this brings about the development of those physical (*rūpa*) and psychological (*nāma*) elements that make up the psychophysical complex, a sentient living organism.

> *niṣikte nāmarūpe tu ṣaḍāyatanasaṃbhavaḥ |*
> *ṣaḍāyatanam āgamya saṃsparśaḥ saṃpravartate ||3||*

3. But *nāmarūpa* having become infused [with life], the six sense organs occur.
The infused *nāmarūpa* having attained the six sense organs, contact takes place.

The development of the full psychophysical complex yields a living organism with six sense organs, each having a distinctive sensory capacity: seeing, hearing, taste, smell, touch, and the inner sense. Once they have arisen, they come into contact with objects in the environment: The eye touches color-and-shape and so on. The term we here translate as "sense organ" is āyatana. (See chapter 3.) The āyatanas are usually numbered twelve, including both the six sense organs and their respective object-spheres.

cakṣuḥ pratītya rūpaṃ ca samanvāhāram eva ca /
nāmarūpaṃ pratītyaivaṃ vijñānaṃ saṃpravartate //4//

4. Dependent on the eye, color-and-shape, and attention,
dependent thus on *nāmarūpa*, (eye-)consciousness occurs.

Consciousness is said to arise in dependence on a sense organ and its object given the mental force of attentiveness. In the case of visual consciousness, the sense organ is the eye, and the eye's domain is occurrences of color-and-shape. It is noteworthy that in this account, visual consciousness is distinct from hearing consciousness and so on. There is no single consciousness that is directly produced by and apprehends something external through two different sense modalities.

Candrakīrti explains that since eye and color-and-shape are classified as *rūpa* skandha while attention is classified as among the *nāma* skandhas, visual consciousness arises in dependence on both *rūpa* and *nāma*. In 2ab we were told that *nāmarūpa* originates in dependence on consciousness. Here we are told that consciousness originates in dependence on *nāmarūpa*. This makes it seem as if there is a reciprocal causal relation between *nāmarūpa* and consciousness. Some Abhidharma thinkers took this to mean that there can be reciprocal causal relations between simultaneously existing things, each being both cause and effect of the other. But there is no indication here that Nāgārjuna and his commentators subscribe to that view. The *nāmarūpa* mentioned in 2ab seems to be that of the developing embryo, while the *nāmarūpa* mentioned here appears to be that of a developed organism interacting with its environment. Likewise the consciousnesses mentioned in the two verses would seem to be distinct occurrences in the continuum of mental events.

saṃnipātas trayāṇāṃ yo rūpavijñānacakṣuṣām |
sparśaḥ sa tasmāt sparśāc ca vedanā saṃpravartate ||5||

5. The conjunction of three things—color-and-shape, consciousness, and the eye—
that is contact; and from that contact there occurs feeling.

Candrakīrti explains that contact is just the functioning through mutual interaction of the sense faculty, sense object, and resulting consciousness. This in turn produces feeling—that is, a sensation of pleasure, pain, or indifference.

vedanāpratyayā tṛṣṇā vedanārthaṃ hi tṛṣyate |
tṛṣyamāṇa upādānam upādatte caturvidham ||6||

6. Dependent on feeling is desire, for one desires the object of feeling.
Desiring, one takes up the four kinds of appropriation.

Desire is produced as a result of feeling: Desire for something results from pleasurable feeling; aversion—desire to rid oneself of something—results from unpleasant feeling; and so on. Appropriation is the process of identification—regarding some factor as "I" or "mine." Insofar as one cannot wish for more or less of some stimulus without regarding it as in some way affecting something that is thought of as an "I," desire leads to appropriation. The four kinds of appropriation are said to be that connected with pleasure, that pertaining to (false) views, that pertaining to moral conduct and religious vows, and that pertaining to belief in a self.

upādāne sati bhava upādātuḥ pravartate |
syād dhi yady anupādāno mucyeta na bhaved bhavaḥ ||7||

7. There being appropriation, there is the coming into existence of the appropriator,
for if one were without appropriation, one would be liberated; there would be no further existence.

Instances of appropriating have as their precondition the being of the agent who appropriates. That is, there cannot be the thought of some state as "I" or "mine" without the belief that there is that for which the state is an object of appropriation. On the Buddhist analysis, the mechanisms of karma operate through actions fueled by this belief. Thus in the absence of the belief in an appropriator, one would be liberated from saṃsāra.

pañca skandhāḥ sa ca bhavo bhavāj jātiḥ pravartate |
jarāmaraṇaduḥkhādi śokāḥ saparidevanāḥ ||8||
daurmanasyam upāyāsā jāter etat pravartate |
kevalasyaivam etasya duḥkhaskandhasya saṃbhavaḥ ||9||

8. And this existence is the five skandhas; from existence results birth.
The suffering of old age, death, and so on—grief accompanied by lamentations,
9. frustration, and despair—these result from birth.
Thus arises this entire mass of suffering.

The existence that sets the stage for the next life is actually just the five skandhas that arose due to the karma generated by past actions based on belief in an "I." All five are involved, according to Candrakīrti, because bodily and verbal actions involve *rūpa*, while mental actions involve the four *nāma* skandhas.

The result of all this is birth into the future life. So far we have seen how a sequence of two factors in the past life—ignorance and volition (verse 1)—brought about a sequence of eight factors in the present life—consciousness followed by *nāmarūpa* (verse 2), six sense organs and contact (verse 3), feeling (verse 5), desire and appropriation (verse 6), and being (verse 7). Now, in verses 8–9, we have entry into the future life, with birth inevitably leading to old age and death and thus existential suffering. This completes the twelvefold chain of dependent origination, which is the detailed explanation for the origination of suffering spoken of in the second noble truth.

saṃsāramūlaṃ saṃskārān avidvān saṃskaroty ataḥ |
avidvān kārakas tasmān na vidvāṃs tattvadarśanāt ||*10*||

10. Thus does the ignorant one form the volitions that are the roots of saṃsāra.
The ignorant one is therefore the agent; the wise one, having seen reality, is not.

By "the agent" is here meant the person who, out of desire for pleasant feelings and aversion toward painful feelings, performs actions and thus accumulates karmic seeds. Candrakīrti explains that the wise one, who does not perceive anything whatsoever and thus does not see anything to be done, is not an agent. This opens up the possibility that knowledge of emptiness plays a role here: It might be that the wise one fails to perceive anything due to seeing that all things (and not just the person) are empty.

avidyāyāṃ niruddhāyāṃ saṃskārāṇām asaṃbhavaḥ |
avidyāyā nirodhas tu jñānasyāsyaiva bhāvanāt ||*11*||

11. Upon the cessation of ignorance there is the nonarising of volitions.

> But the cessation of ignorance is due to meditation on just
> the knowledge of this.

Once one knows how saṃsāra is perpetuated, meditation on the twelvefold chain of dependent origination leads to the cessation of those desires that fuel the cycle. This is the fourth of the noble truths, that of the path to the cessation of suffering. It is worth noting that nothing in the verses of this chapter is incompatible with the Abhidharma understanding of the teaching of the twelvefold chain. According to Abhidharma it is just knowledge of the essencelessness of persons (that the person is empty of intrinsic nature) that is the relevant knowledge. And the *Akutobhayā* (or, more cautiously, the commentary on this chapter that is represented as the *Akutobhayā*—see our comments at the end of the previous chapter) says that all this may be studied more extensively in the sūtras and in Abhidharma texts. But Candrakīrti explicitly invokes knowledge of emptiness in his comments on this verse. According to him it is knowledge of the emptiness of intrinsic nature of all things that is the effective knowledge mentioned in the verse:

> Ignorance is destroyed by correct and nondeceptive meditation on this dependent origination. One who correctly sees dependent origination perceives no own-form [i.e., intrinsic nature] of even the most subtle entity. One enters into meditation on the emptiness of intrinsic nature of all entities, like a reflection, a dream, a fire circle [see 11.2], an impression of a seal. One who has realized the emptiness of intrinsic nature of all entities perceives nothing whatsoever, be it external or internal. One who does not perceive is not confused about any dharma, and one who is not confused does not perform action. One perceives that this is so through meditation on dependent origination. The yogin who sees the truth has assuredly abandoned ignorance. Volitions of the one who has abandoned ignorance are suppressed. (LVP 559)

The mention of meditation, in the verse and in Candrakīrti's comments, is also significant. It is widely accepted that the path to the cessation of suffering discussed in the fourth of the noble truths involves not only the understanding or insight developed through philosophical practice (such as that of Mādhyamika philosophers like Nāgārjuna) but also the practice of meditation. Candrakīrti here hints at why that might be important: The yogin or meditator comes to directly see the emptiness of each thing presented in experience. This might be different from the sort of theoretical knowledge acquired through philosophical activity. If so, then this would explain why the karma-generating volitions of the yogin are all suppressed.

tasya tasya nirodhena tat tan nābhipravartate /
duḥkhaskandhaḥ kevalo 'yam evaṃ samyag nirudhyate //12//

12. By reason of the cessation of one factor in the twelvefold chain, another successor factor fails to arise.
Thus does this entire mass of suffering completely cease.

Since the arising of each factor in the chain is dependent on the occurrence of its predecessor, with the cessation of ignorance the production of suffering must come to an end. Bhāviveka feels compelled to add that all this is only true conventionally, not ultimately. Since according to Madhyamaka no elements in the twelvefold chain are ultimately real, it cannot be ultimately true that upon the cessation of ignorance there is the cessation of volition and the rest.

27. An Analysis of Views

THE "VIEWS" discussed in this chapter are the ones the Buddha was asked about concerning the past and future existence of the person, the world, and so on (see S II.25–27). The orthodox Buddhist view concerning these questions is that they are ill formed in that they all involve false presuppositions. And because they are ill formed, none of the four possible answers to a question should be affirmed. (See the discussion of the "indeterminate questions" above at 25.17–18.) In this chapter Nāgārjuna gives his own account of their rejection. Most of what is said here would be perfectly acceptable to at least many Ābhidharmikas. It is only at the end of the chapter that the doctrine of emptiness is explicitly mentioned. This might be taken to suggest that the real purpose is to show that Madhyamaka thought represents a legitimate extension of the Buddha's teachings. The thread of the chapter's argument is as follows:

27.1–2 Views about relation between present person and past and future persons depend on real existence in the past life and the future life.

27.3–13 Examination of views concerning relation between present person and past person

27.3–8: Refutation of the possibility that the present person existed in the past

27.9–12: Refutation of the possibility that the present person did not exist in the past

27.13: Summary: The present person cannot be said to have existed in past, not existed, etc.

27.14–18 Examination of views concerning relation between present person and future person

27.15: Refutation of possibility that present person is identical with future person

27.16: Refutation of possibility that present person is distinct from future person

27.17: Refutation of possibility that present person is both identical with and distinct from future person

27.18: Refutation of possibility that present person is neither identical with nor distinct from future person

27.19–28 Examination of views concerning the extent of saṃsāra

27.19–20: Refutation of possibility that saṃsāra has a beginning and that it has no beginning

27.21–24: Refutation of possibility that saṃsāra has an end and that it has no end

27.25–27: Refutation of possibility that saṃsāra both has and does not have an end

27.28: Refutation of possibility that saṃsāra neither has nor does not have an end

27.29 Emptiness of all things means the rejection of all views.

27.30 Salutation to the Buddha Gautama

abhūm atītam adhvānaṃ nābhūvam iti dṛṣṭayaḥ /
yās tāḥ śāśvatalokādyāḥ pūrvāntaṃ samupāśritāḥ //1//

1. The views, "I existed in the past" and "I did not exist,"
that the world is eternal, etc., are dependent on the past life.

In the present verse it is questions about the past that are under scrutiny. Here the "etc." indicates the third and fourth members of the tetralemma, for example, "I both existed and did not exist" and "I neither existed nor did not exist." Such views concerning the "I" all presuppose the existence of some past thing that might be: identical with the present "I," distinct from the present "I," both identical and distinct, or neither identical nor distinct.

dṛṣṭayo na bhaviṣyāmi kim anyo 'nāgate 'dhvani /
bhaviṣyāmīti cāntādyā aparāntaṃ samāśritāḥ //2//

2. The views "Shall I not exist as someone else in the future?"
"Shall I exist?" and that the world has an end, etc., are dependent on the future life.

In this verse it is views about the future that are under examination. These are likewise all based on an assumption, namely that there will exist some future entity (an "I") that might be identical with, distinct from, both identical with and distinct from, or neither identical with nor distinct from the presently existing entity. Having thus classified the full range of views, Nāgārjuna now proceeds to examine first those that concern the past life (verses 3–13) and then, in verses 14–18, those that concern the future life.

abhūm atītam adhvānam ity etan nopapadyate /
yo hi janmasu pūrveṣu sa eva na bhavaty ayam //3//

3. It is not the case that the statement "I existed in the past" holds,
for whoever existed in prior births is not this present person.

To entertain the first of the four possible views with respect to the "I" and the past, the view that I existed in past lives, is to hold that the presently existing "I" had prior existence in other lives. So for instance what is now a human being might have been an inhabitant of one of the hells in an earlier life. And this, we are told, cannot be. The reason is given in the following verses.

sa evātmeti tu bhaved upādānaṃ viśiṣyate /
upādānavinirmukta ātmā te katamaḥ punaḥ //4//

4. If it were that "That is just myself," [then appropriation would not be distinct from the appropriator "I"]; however, appropriation is distinct.
How, on the other hand, can your self be utterly distinct from appropriation?

Concerning appropriation, see 3.7, 10.15, and 26.6–7. According to Candrakīrti, the argument of the first half of the verse is that if the present "I" were identical with the being in the past life, then the act of appropriation would be identical with the appropriator, which is absurd, since agent and action are distinct. Here appropriation is understood, in accordance with the formula of the twelvefold chain, as those factors in the past life that brought about the present, while the appropriator is the being in the present life that resulted from them and in turn brings about future birth, old age, and death. The argument, in short, is that to think that I existed in the past life is to suppose that this present "I" is at once a product and the producer of that very product.

The difficulty that results from this is that the self that is the appropriator cannot be found apart from acts of appropriation. It is the nature of the self, *qua* appropriator, to engage in acts of appropriation. While such acts can be discerned, the agent that performs them cannot. And what is wanted here is the agent, not its acts. The argument that is unfolding here is an instance of the "neither identical nor distinct" variety that Nāgārjuna has used elsewhere.

upādānavinirmukto nāsty ātmeti kṛte sati |
syād upādānam evātmā nāsti cātmeti vaḥ punaḥ ||5||

5. It being agreed that there is no self utterly distinct from appropriation,
then the self would be nothing but the appropriation; in that case there is no such thing as this self of yours.

If the opponent were to concede that the self that is distinct from the psychophysical elements is not to be found and maintain instead that the self that appropriates is just the elements themselves, then there is a new difficulty, stated in the next verse.

na copādānam evātmā vyeti tat samudeti ca |
kathaṃ hi nāmopādānam upādātā bhaviṣyati ||6||

6. It is not the case that the self is identical with the appropriation, for that appropriation ceases and arises.
How indeed will the appropriation become the appropriator?

The difficulty with attempting to reduce the self *qua* appropriator to the appropriation (the psychophysical elements) is that the latter are radically impermanent while the former would have to endure. Hence appropriator and appropriation have incompatible properties and thus cannot be identical. Moreover, there then results the identity of agent and object of action, which is absurd, as can be seen from the examples of fire and fuel, knife and object to be cut, potter and pot, and so on.

anyaḥ punar upādānād ātmā naivopapadyate |
gṛhyeta hy anupādāno yady anyo na ca gṛhyate ||7||

7. Further, a self that is distinct from appropriation is not at all possible.

If it were distinct then it would be perceived without appropriation, but it is not perceived.

Distinctness of appropriator and appropriation would also mean that the appropriator self can exist in complete independence from the elements, just as a pot, which is distinct from a cloth, can exist in the absence of any cloth. But something cannot be an appropriator apart from all acts of appropriation, and there can be no acts of appropriation without the appropriated elements. So a distinct appropriator cannot be grasped.

evaṃ nānya upādānān na copādānam eva saḥ |
ātmā nāsty anupādāno nāpi nāsty eṣa niścayaḥ ||8||

8. Thus it is not distinct from appropriation, nor is it identical with appropriation.
There is no self without appropriation, but neither is it ascertained that this does not exist.

This summarizes the argument of the preceding five verses against the view that "I" existed in the past. The one new note is at the end of the verse: One should also not conclude that there is no "I" that exists in both the past and the present. Candrakīrti explains that this "I" is said to be conceptualized in dependence on the psychophysical elements. This makes it quite different from the case of the son of a barren woman, which is both utterly nonexistent and also not conceptualized in dependence on any psychophysical elements. One can say of the son of a barren woman that he does not exist, but one cannot say this of the "I." Candrakīrti adds that since he has treated this topic of the self extensively in his *Madhyamkāvatāra*, he will not repeat that discussion here. (See MA 6.120–65.)

It should be noted that this is a denial of nonself and not the affirmation of an existent self. Moreover, there is precedent in the Buddha's teachings for the denial of nonself. On at least one occasion the

Buddha expressed concern that those who did not fully understand his teachings would take the statement "There is no self" to mean that one's death entails one's annihilation (and thus the end of one's liability to karmic reward and punishment; see S IV.400–401). This annihilationist view is not considered wrong on the grounds that there actually is a self; it is wrong because it does presuppose a self, one that is not eternal. It was to avoid aligning himself with that view, we are told, that the Buddha refrained on that occasion from accepting the statement "There is no self." It is this consideration that also led the Abhidharma schools to maintain that the person is conventionally real: Appropriating and thus identifying with past and future parts of the causal series of psychophysical elements can be useful (up to a point).

nābhūm atītam adhvānam ity etan nopapadyate /
yo hi janmasu pūrveṣu tato 'nyo na bhavaty ayam //9//

9. It is not the case that the statement "I did not exist in the past" holds;
for this present person is not distinct from whoever existed in prior births.

yadi hy ayaṃ bhaved anyaḥ pratyākhyāyāpi taṃ bhavet /
tathaiva ca sa saṃtiṣṭhet tatra jāyeta cāmṛtaḥ //10//

10. For if this present self were indeed distinct from the past, then it would exist even if the past were denied.
And the past person would abide just as it was, or it would be born here without having died.

If the present being is not the same person as the past being, then the present being cannot be caused by the past being. In particular it cannot be due to the cessation of the past being. Candrakīrti gives the example of the production of a pot and the destruction of cloth. Since pot and cloth are utterly distinct, the arising of the former cannot have the cessation of the latter as a causal condition. But this in turn suggests that the past self should endure. Alternatively it would mean that one is born without having died earlier. And for those who accept beginningless rebirth, this is absurd.

ucchedaḥ karmaṇāṃ nāśaḥ kṛtam anyena karma ca |
pratisaṃvedayed anya evamādi prasajyate ||11||

11. There would be annihilation [of the past self] and then destruction of [fruits of] actions; then [the fruits] of an action done by one person
would be reaped by another. This and the like consequences would follow.

The absurdity of supposing that one who is born is not someone who died earlier stems from the fact that, in accordance with karmic causal laws, the situation of one's birth is the result of actions performed at some earlier time. If one's birth were not a rebirth, then the good or bad station of one's birth could not be explained as the fruits of one's own earlier actions. And in that case one's situation could not be deserved; inequality of birth would become a blatant injustice. Then those who accept the theory of karma would no longer see in it a reason to perform good actions and avoid evil actions, for it would not be me who will reap the pleasant and painful fruits of actions I perform in this life.

nāpy abhūtvā samudbhūto doṣo hy atra prasajyate |
kṛtako vā bhaved ātmā saṃbhūto vāpy ahetukaḥ ||12||

12. Neither is it the case that it, having not existed, comes into existence, for this has an unwanted consequence:
The self would then either be produced or else it would be arisen uncaused.

To say that the self comes into existence from prior nonexistence is to say that it is a product. But a product requires an effective producer. And if there is no prior existence of this self, then it is difficult to see what might have produced it. If on the other hand one were to deny that it was produced while still maintaining its prior nonexistence, this would be tantamount to saying it came into existence completely spontaneously, with no cause whatsoever. And this sort of utter randomness we know never obtains.

evaṃ dṛṣtir atīte yā nābhūm aham abhūm aham |
ubhayaṃ nobhayaṃ ceti naiṣā samupapadyate ||13||

13. Thus the views that in the past I did not exist, I did exist,
both, and neither—none of these holds.

This completes the examination of views concerning the relation of the present person to the past. Only the first and second lemmas—that I did exist in the past and that I did not—have been discussed and not the third and fourth. But Candrakīrti comments that since the first and second have been ruled out, the third must likewise be rejected, since it is the conjunction of two rejected theses. And given that the third lemma is to be rejected, so must the fourth, which is just the negation of the third (see the comments on 25.14).

Next comes the examination of views concerning the relation of the present person to the future.

adhvany anāgate kiṃ nu bhaviṣyāmīti darśanam |
na bhaviṣyāmi cety etad atītenādhvanā samam ||14||

14. The view "Will I exist in the future?"
and the view "Will I not exist?"—these are just like [the case of] the past.

The four lemmas concerning the relation of the present person to one in the future are subject to the same logic of identity and difference as are those regarding the past. Hence they are to be rejected just as the first four were.

sa devaḥ sa manuṣyaś ced evaṃ bhavati śāśvatam /
anutpannaś ca devaḥ syāj jāyate na hi śāśvatam //15//

15. "This god is the same person as that human": if this were so
then there would be eternalism;
and the god would be unarisen, for what is eternal is not born.

For this use of the term *eternalism*, see the comments on 17.10. The example concerns a human who, having done exceptionally good deeds in this life, will be reborn as a god. On the hypothesis that that future god will be me, there must be a self that endures from one life to the next and hence is eternal. Since eternalism was said by the Buddha to be fundamentally mistaken, it follows that identity of present and future persons must be rejected. Moreover, the eternality of the person leads to the absurd result that the god will exist without having been born. (This is absurd because, since gods are subject to rebirth, they must be born; they are said to live exceptionally long and happy lives, but they are born and they eventually die.) To be born is to come into existence, and an eternal entity never comes into existence.

The basic difficulty here is that if the present human and the future god are both to count as "me," then it would seem they must be identical, and yet a human and a god seem to be utterly distinct beings. Each, for instance, comes into existence at a particular time, namely the time of its birth; and for the human and the god in this example those are distinct times. The only solution is to say that the present human and the future god share a single self, something that, being eternal, can go from one life to another. But then either that future god is identical with the eternal self or else it is distinct. If it is identical, then we must say, absurdly, that a god is not born. If it is distinct, then I shall not be that god, so it is false that my good deeds will lead to my being reborn as a god.

devād anyo manuṣyaś ced aśāśvatam ato bhavet |
devād anyo manuṣyaś cet saṃtatir nopapadyate ||16||

16. If it is held that the present human is distinct from the future god, then noneternalism would follow.
If it is held that the present human is distinct from the future god, then there can be no continuum.

If we grant that the present human being and the future god are distinct entities, then the person is not eternal—is not the sort of thing that can go from one life to the next. It might be thought that these can still represent distinct stages in one continuous series. But distinctness of human and god makes it difficult to explain how they can make up such a series. For the presently existing lump of clay and the future cloth are equally distinct, yet they are not thought to make up a continuous series. One might try to explain the difference between the human-god case and the clay-cloth example by appealing to the causal connections that supposedly obtain in the case of the present human and the future god. But the results of chapters 1 and 20, which showed that causal connections cannot be said to obtain between allegedly ultimately real entities, rule out all such appeals.

divyo yady ekadeśaḥ syād ekadeśaś ca mānuṣaḥ |
aśāśvataṃ śāśvataṃ ca bhavet tac ca na yujyate ||17||

17. If it were one part divine and one part human,
it would be both noneternal and eternal, and that is not correct.

The thesis that human and god are identical leads to eternalism. The thesis that they are distinct leads to annihilationism (noneternalism). Both having been rejected, we now turn to the consideration of the thesis that they are both identical and distinct. This is one of the rare cases where Nāgārjuna explicitly examines the third of the four lemmas possible with respect to some question. Here the claim is that there is one entity, the person, with distinct temporal parts—the present human and the future god. In that case human and god can be said to be identical (*qua* person) and yet also distinct (*qua* kinds of living things). And thus I would be both eternal and noneternal. Since that future god will be me, I am eternal. But since the present human who is now me will then no longer exist, I am subject to annihilation.

aśāśvataṃ śāśvataṃ ca prasiddham ubhayaṃ yadi /
sidhyen na śāśvataṃ kāmaṃ naivāśāśvatam ity api //18//

18. If it were acknowledged both that it is eternal and that it is noneternal,
then it would accordingly be established that it is neither eternal nor noneternal.

The fourth lemma—neither eternalism nor noneternalism—relies on the intelligibility of the first and second. And since these must be rejected, the fourth must likewise. Candrakīrti reasons that since both the thesis of eternalism and that of noneternalism are unestablished, and the thesis of neither is the denial of the disjunction of both, there being no object to be negated, the fourth thesis cannot hold. (See the comments on 25.14.)

kutaścid āgataḥ kaścit kiṃcid gacchet punaḥ kvacit /
yadi tasmād anādis tu saṃsāraḥ syān na cāsti saḥ //19//

19. If it were the case that someone were to exist, having come here from somewhere and subsequently be going somewhere else,
then saṃsāra would be beginningless; but that [person] does not exist.

It is commonly said by Buddhists that saṃsāra is beginningless. This thesis requires that there be a being who, for any given life in some determinate station (e.g., as a human or as a god), can have been born into that life from some prior life, and who will at the end of that life be reborn into yet another station (until such time as that person attains liberation). But there is no such being, so it cannot be asserted that saṃsāra is beginningless. Candrakīrti explains that this holds whether the being is thought of as permanent or as impermanent. If it were permanent then it could not be subject to the change that occurs in going from one life to another. If it were impermanent then it could not be said to move from one life to the next, since its impermanence would mean that it ceases at the end of a life. But this can also be seen as a straightforward result of the prior arguments against the person (*pudgala*) discussed in chapters 9, 10, and 11.

nāsti cec chāśvataḥ kaścit ko bhaviṣyaty aśāśvataḥ /
śāśvato 'śāśvataś cāpi dvābhyām ābhyāṃ tiraskṛtaḥ //20//

20. If it is held that nothing whatsoever is eternal, then what will be noneternal?
What will be both eternal and noneternal, and also what will be distinct from these two?

If there is no eternal being, then there does not exist the right sort of thing for the thesis of noneternality to hold. The subject of rebirth (the entity that undergoes the process of rebirth) would have to be permanent, and if rebirth lacks a subject, then we cannot entertain the hypothesis that its subject is transitory. The same holds for the third and fourth lemmas of the tetralemma concerning saṃsāra.

antavān yadi lokaḥ syāt paralokaḥ kathaṃ bhavet |
athāpy anantavāṃl lokaḥ paralokaḥ kathaṃ bhavet ||21||

21. If this world had an end, how could there be the other world?
But if this world were without an end, how could there be the other world?

One set of questions the Buddha was asked and refused to answer concerned whether the *loka* has an end or limit (see 22.12). The Sanskrit term *loka* can be translated as "world," and this is how it is often translated when it occurs in the passages concerning that set of questions. But it also means "inhabitant of the world," and that is how it is actually being used in that context. The question concerns whether the existence of the being who is currently living a particular life has an end or not. Both possibilities are to be rejected. The reason, according to the commentators, is that there in fact is another world—that is, there is rebirth. The reasoning is spelled out in the next seven verses.

skandhānām eṣa saṃtāno yasmād dīpārciṣām iva |
tasmān nānantavattvaṃ ca nāntavattvaṃ ca yujyate ||22||

22. The series of skandhas proceeds like that of the flames of a lamp,
so it is not correct that it is endless nor that it has an end.

The analogy of the lamp flame is commonly used to explain personal continuity in the absence of a self. (See, e.g., Mil 40.) The idea is that an individual flame only lasts a moment, yet a lamp may stay lit for a whole night. (A flame is momentary because it is just a collection of incandescent gas particles, and the individual particles making up that collection rapidly cool and dissipate.) It is possible for the lamp to stay lit for the night because each flame, as it goes out of existence, serves as the cause of a successor flame. So what we think of as one continuously existing light is actually a series of momentary lamp flames.

pūrve yadi ca bhajyerann utpadyeran na cāpy amī /
skandhāḥ skandhān pratītyemān atha loko 'ntavān bhavet //23//

23. If, the past ones having been broken up, these skandhas were not to arise
that are dependent on those past skandhas, then it would be the case that this world has an end.

Rebirth, like the light of the lamp, involves one set of psychophysical elements ceasing but causing another set of psychophysical elements to arise. To say that the world (i.e., the person) has an end is to say that this causal series is interrupted. Just as when one flame is extinguished due to exhaustion of fuel oil, no successor flame can arise, so if the earlier set of elements were to be dissipated without being able to generate the subsequent set, then it would be the case that the person has an end. But this would be a case in which no rebirth takes place. For rebirth is precisely the continuation of the causal series.

pūrve yadi na bhajyerann utpadyeran na cāpy amī /
skandhāḥ skandhān pratītyemān loko 'nanto bhaved atha //24//

24. If, the past ones not having been broken up, these skandhas were not to arise
that are dependent on those past skandhas, then it would be the case that this world has no end.

To say the world (i.e., the person) has no end would be to say that the elements making up the present person do not go out of existence. In that case they could not give rise to successor elements in the series, and so once again there would be no rebirth. So for instance the elements making up a human could not give rise to the elements making up a god in the subsequent life.

antavān ekadeśaś ced ekadeśas tv anantavān /
syād antavān anantaś ca lokas tac ca na yujyate //25//

25. If it were that it is one part with an end and one part without end,
then this world would have an end and be without end, and that is not correct.

The third lemma, that the world (i.e., the person) both has an end and is without end, might be thought to hold if there were one part of the person that did end while another part continued to exist unceasingly. This is the view of those, for instance, who think that rebirth involves the transmigration of a self and the destruction of the other elements of the psychophysical complex. The difficulty for this view is spelled out in the next three verses. But the *Akutobhayā* anticipates by pointing out that in this case the being would have two intrinsic natures.

kathaṃ tāvad upādātur ekadeśo vinaṅkṣyate /
na naṅkṣyate caikadeśa evaṃ caitan na yujyate //26//

26. How will it be that on the one hand, one part of the appropriator is destroyed
and yet one part is not destroyed? This is not correct.

Here the "appropriator" is that set of elements in the present life that gives rise to the elements in the subsequent life. On the present hypothesis, some of these elements are destroyed while others carry over into the future life. In the case of rebirth of a human as a god, this might mean that the human part of the appropriator is destroyed while the divine part is not. But this would also mean that the human was already divine, which is absurd. To call the present being human is precisely to say that it has a human nature, which is quite different from a divine nature.

upādānaikadeśaś ca katham nāma vinaṅkṣyate /
na naṅkṣyate caikadeśo naitad apy upapadyate //27//

27. How will it be that one part of appropriation is destroyed
and one part is not destroyed? This also cannot be.

Here the "appropriation" is that set of elements in the subsequent life that originates in dependence on the earlier set called the "appropriator." Reasoning similar to that of the preceding verse demonstrates the absurdity here.

antavac cāpy anantaṃ ca prasiddham ubhayaṃ yadi /
sidhyen naivāntavat kāmaṃ naivānantavad ity api //28//

28. If both "with an end" as well as "without an end" were
acknowledged,
then it would accordingly be established that it is neither with
an end nor without an end.

The fourth lemma relies for its intelligibility on the intelligibility of the first and second, since it is said to be the negation of their disjunction. Thus the fourth must be rejected if the third is. This verse parallels verse 18.

atha vā sarvabhāvānāṃ śūnyatvāc chāśvatādayaḥ /
kva kasya katamāḥ kasmāt saṃbhaviṣyanti dṛṣṭayaḥ //29//

29. So since all existents are empty, views such as eternalism and the like—where will they occur, to whom will they occur, which of them will occur, and for what reason will they occur?

Since all things are empty, there can ultimately be neither a place nor a time where views like eternalism arise; there is no being who can entertain and hold such views; such views not themselves existing, there are none that could be held; and nothing could serve as the reason for holding such views.

sarvadṛṣṭiprahāṇāya yaḥ saddharmam adeśayat /
anukampām upādāya taṃ namasyāmi gautamam //30//

30. I salute Gautama, who, based on compassion, taught the true Dharma for the abandonment of all views.

This final verse echoes the thought of the dedicatory verse at the beginning of the work. In that verse we were told that the Buddha's central teaching of dependent origination must be understood through the lens of eight negations: Existing things neither cease to exist nor do they arise, they are neither eternal nor are they annihilated, they are neither one nor many, and they do not move or undergo any other sort of alteration. These negations were said to free us from the sorts of hypostatizations that had grown up around the teaching of dependent origination. Now Candrakīrti identifies what is here called "the true Dharma" with the Buddha's teaching of dependent origination. But in the dedicatory verse it was hypostatizations concerning dependent origination that were said to be an obstacle to liberation, whereas here "all views" include any theory concerning how things ultimately are. So apparently the range of the eight negations has expanded considerably beyond what an Ābhidharmika would accept.

We have learned several things in the interim, however. First, we have encountered a wide range of arguments meant to refute a wide variety of theories about the ultimate nature of reality. In each case a key assumption of the theory under attack was that there are things with intrinsic nature. Second, we learned (18.5) that the purpose of the doctrine of emptiness is to end hypostatization concerning anything whatever that might be thought to be ultimately real. And finally we were told (24.18) that dependent origination entails emptiness. So it now seems appropriate to take the Buddha's treatment of the indeterminate questions as the model for understanding the doctrine of emptiness.

There is a second way in which doing so might be appropriate. We have also been told on several occasions (e.g., at 13.8) that emptiness is itself empty, that emptiness is not to be thought of as the correct account of the ultimate truth. Viewing verse 29 in that light, we can see that its argument applies as much to the doctrine of emptiness itself as to any other metaphysical theory. Still when we are told that the rival views on some topic are all false, there is a strong temptation to take whatever concepts were used in their refutation as providing the correct replacement to those erroneous theories. What Nāgārjuna has been at pains to show in the present chapter is just how the Buddha succeeded in rejecting all the rival views concerning the self, living beings, and happiness without installing his own view on those subjects. The Buddha's strategy of invoking dependent origination as a middle path is just a procedure of rejecting all the logically possible views by rejecting their common presupposition. The suggestion is that this strategy may help us avoid turning emptiness into yet another metaphysical theory. In that case Madhyamaka would deserve its name of Middle Path School.

Bibliography

Primary Sources

A Aṅguttara Nikāya. In R. Morris and E. Hardy, eds. 1885–1900. *The Aṅguttara Nikāya.* 5 vols. London: Pali Text Society. Reprint 1976–79. English trans. by Bhikkhu Bodhi. 2012. *The Numerical Discourses of the Buddha.* Boston: Wisdom Publications.

AKB *Abhidharmakośabhāṣyam of Vasubandhu.* Prahlad Pradhan, ed. 1975. Patna: Jayaswal Research Institute.

As Atthasālinī. In E. Müller, ed., 1897. *Atthasālinī: Buddhaghosa's Commentary on the Dhammasaṅgaṇi.* London: Pali Text Society.

CŚ *Catuḥśataka* of Āryadeva. In K. Lang, ed. and trans. 1986. *Āryadeva's Catuḥśataka: On the Bodhisattva's Cultivation of Merit and Knowledge.* Indiske Studier 7. Copenhagen: Akademisk Forlag.

D Dīgha Nikāya. In T. W. Rhys Davids and J. E. Carpenter, eds. 1889–1910. *The Dīgha Nikāya.* 3 vols. London: Pali Text Society. Reprint 1983–92. English trans. by Maurice Walshe. 1987. *The Long Discourses of the Buddha.* Boston: Wisdom Publications.

M Majjhima Nikāya. In Trenckner and Chalmers, eds. 1888–99. *The Majjhima Nikāya.* 3 vols. London: Pali Text Society. Reprint 1977–79. English trans. by Bhikkhu Ñānamoli and Bhikkhu Bodhi. 1995. *The Middle Length Discourses of the Buddha.* Boston: Wisdom Publications.

MA *Madhyamakāvatāra* of Candrakīrti. In L. de la Vallée Poussin, ed., 1912. *Madhyamakāvatāra par Candrakīrti.* St. Petersburg: l'Académie imperial des sciences. English trans. by C. W. Huntington Jr. 1989. *The Emptiness of Emptiness.* Honolulu: University of Hawai'i Press.

Mil *Milindapanho.* In V. Trenckner, ed. 1928. *The Milindapanho.* London:

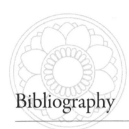

Pali Text Society. Reprint 1962. English trans. by T. W. Rhys Davids. 1890–94. *The Questions of King Milinda*. Oxford: Oxford University Press. Reprint 1965.

MMK *Mūlamadhyamakakārikā* of Nāgārjuna. Editions of MMK consulted:

Y Ye Shaoyong. 2011. *Zhunglunsong: Fanzanghan Hejiao, Daodu, Yizhu* (《中论颂》：梵藏汉合校 · 导读 · 译注) [*Mūlamadhyamakakārikā: New Editions of the Sanskrit, Tibetan and Chinese Versions, with Commentary and a Modern Chinese Translation*]. Shanghai: Zhongxi Book Company (中西书局).

LVP La Vallée Poussin, Louis de. 1913. *Mūlamadhyamakakārikās (Mādhyamikasūtras) de Nāgārjuna, avec la Prasannapadā Commentaire de Candrakīrti*. Bibliotheca Buddhica 4, 1st ed. St. Petersburg: Academie Impériale des Sciences. Reprint Osnabrück: Biblio Verlag, 1970.

P Pandeya, Raghunath, ed. 1988. *The Madhyamakaśāstram of Nāgārjuna*, with the Commentaries *Akutobhayā* by Nāgārjuna, *Madhyamakavṛtti* by Buddhapālita, *Prajñāpradīpavṛtti* by Bhāvaviveka, and *Prasannapadā* by Candrakīrti. Delhi: Motilal Banarsidass.

de Jong, J. W. 1977. *Nāgārjuna Mūlamadhyamakakārikāḥ*. The Adyar Library Series Vol. 109. Chennai: The Theosophical Society. Reprint revised by Chr. Lindtner, 2004.

PP *Prasannapadā* of Candrakīrti, in LVP.

S Saṃyutta Nikāya. In L. Feer, ed. 1884–98. *The Saṃyutta Nikāya*. 5 vols. London: Pali Text Society. Reprint 1975–2006. English trans. by Bhikkhu Bodhi. 2000. *The Connected Discourses of the Buddha*. Boston: Wisdom Publications.

Sn Suttanipāta. In D. Anderson and H. Smith, eds. 1913. *The Suttanipāta*. London: Pali Text Society. Reprint 1990.

SNS *Sāmmitīya Nikāya Śāstra*. In R. Venkataraman, trans. 1953. "*Sāmmitīya Nikāya Śāstra*," *Viśvabhārati Annals* V: 165–242.

Vism *Visuddhimagga*. In C. A. F. Rhys Davids, ed. 1920–21. *Visuddhimagga of Buddhaghosa*. London: Pali Text Society.

VV *Vigrahavyāvartanī* of Nāgārjuna. In P. L. Vaidya, ed. 1960. *Madhyamakaśāstra of Nāgārjuna (Mūlamadhyamakakārikās) with the Commentary: Prasannapadā by Candrakīrti*. Dharbanga: Mithila Institute.

Further Readings

Arnold, Dan. 2005. *Buddhists, Brahmins, and Belief: Epistemology in South Asian Philosophy of Religion.* New York: Columbia University Press.

Burton, David. 1999. *Emptiness Appraised: A Critical Study of Nāgārjuna's Philosophy.* Richmond: Curzon.

Garfield, Jay L. 1990. "Epoche and Śūnyatā: Skepticism East and West." *Philosophy East and West* 40 (3): 285–307.

Hayes, Richard. 1994. "Nāgārjuna's Appeal." *Journal of Indian Philosophy* 22: 299–378.

Katsura, Shōryū. 2000a. "Nāgārjuna and the Tetralemma (*catuśkoṭi*)." In *Wisdom, Compassion, and the Search for Understanding, The Buddhist Studies Legacy of Gadjin M. Nagao*, edited by Jonathan Silk, pp. 201–20. Honolulu: University of Hawai'i Press.

———. 2000b. "Nāgārjuna and the Trilemma or *traikālyāsiddhi*." In *Studia Indologiczne*, vol. 7, *On the Understanding of Other Cultures: Proceedings of the International Conference on Sanskrit and Related Studies to Commemorate the Centenary of the Birth of Stanislaw Schayer (1899–1941)*, edited by P. Balcerowicz and M. Mejor, pp. 373–98. Warsaw: Oriental Institute of the University of Warsaw.

Lindtner, Chr. 1982. *Nāgārjuniana: Studies in the Writings and Philosophy of Nāgārjuna.* Copenhagen: Akademisk Forlag.

Nagao, G.M. 1991. *Mādhyamika and Yogācāra: A Study of Mahāyāna Philosophies.* Translated by L. S. Kawamura in collaboration with G.M. Nagao. Albany: State University of New York Press.

Oetke, Claus. 2003. "Some Remarks on Theses and Philosophical Positions in Early Madhyamaka." *Journal of Indian Philosophy* 31 (4): 449–78.

Robinson, Richard H. 1967. *Early Madhyamaka in India and China.* Madison: The University of Wisconsin Press.

Ruegg, David Seyfort. 1977. "The Uses of the Four Positions of the *Catuṣkoṭi* and the Problem of the Description of Reality in Mahāyāna Buddhism." *Journal of Indian Philosophy* 5: 1–71. Reprinted in David Seyfort Ruegg. 2010. *The Buddhist Philosophy of the Middle: Essays on Indian and Tibetan Madhyamaka*, pp. 37–112. Boston: Wisdom Publications.

———. 1981. *The Literature of the Madhyamaka School of Philosophy in India* (History of Indian Literature, vol. 7, fasc. 1). Wiesbaden: Harassowitz.

Saitō, Akira. 2007. "Is Nāgārjuna a Mādhyamika?" *Hokekyō to Daijōkyōten no Kenkyū* (Studies in the *Saddharmapuṇḍarīka Sūtra* and Mahāyāna Scriptures): 153–64.

———. 2010. "Nāgārjuna's Influence on the Formation of the Early Yogācāra Thought: from the *Mūlamadhyamakakārikā* to the *Bodhisattvabhūmi*." *Journal of Indian and Buddhist Studies* 58 (3): 1212–18.

Salvini, Mattia. 2011a. "The *Nidānasamyukta* and the *Mūlamadhyamakakārikā*: Understanding the Middle Way through Comparison and Exegesis." *The Thai International Journal of Buddhism* 2: 57–101.

———. 2011b. "*Upādāyaprajñaptiḥ* and the Meaning of Absolutives: Grammar and Syntax in the Interpretation of Madhyamaka." *Journal of Indian Philosophy* 39: 229–44.

Siderits, Mark. 1980. "The Madhyamaka Critique of Epistemology I." *Journal of Indian Philosophy* 8: 307–35.

———. 2000. "Nyāya Realism, Buddhist Critique." In *The Empirical and the Transcendental*, edited by Bina Gupta, pp. 219–31. Boulder, CO: Rowman and Littlefield.

———. 2004. "Causation in Early Madhyamaka." *Journal of Indian Philosophy* 32: 393–419.

Taber, John. 1998. "On Nāgārjuna's So-Called Fallacies: A Comparative Approach." *Indo-Iranian Journal* 41: 213–44.

Tillemans, Tom J. F. 2003. "Metaphysics for Mādhyamikas." In *The Svātantrika-Prāsaṅgika Distinction: What Difference Does a Difference Make?*, edited by Georges Dreyfus and Sara McClintock, pp. 93–123. Boston: Wisdom Publications.

———. 2001. "Trying to Be Fair to Madhyamaka Buddhism." In *Expanding and Merging Horizons. Contributions to South Asian and Cross-Cultural Studies in Commemoration of Wilhelm Halbfass*, edited by Karin Preisendanz, pp. 507–24. Vienna: Österreichische Akademie der Wissenschaften.

———. 2009. "How Do Mādhyamikas Think? Remarks on Jay Garfield, Graham Priest, and Paraconsistent Logic." In *Pointing at the Moon: Buddhism, Logic, Analytic Philosophy,* edited by J. Garfield, M. D'Amato, and T. Tillemans, pp. 83–103. New York: Oxford University Press.

Westerhoff, Jan. 2009. *Nāgārjuna's Madhyamaka. A Philosophical Introduction*. Oxford: Oxford University Press.

———. 2010. "Nāgārjuna." *The Stanford Encyclopedia of Philosophy* (Fall 2010 Edition). Edited by Edward N. Zalta. http://plato.stanford.edu/archives/fall2010/entries/nagarjuna/.

Williams, Paul. 1980. "Some Aspects of Language and Construction in the Madhyamaka." *Journal of Indian Philosophy* 8: 1–45.

———. 1991. "On the Interpretation of Madhyamaka Thought." *Journal of Indian Philosophy* 19: 191–218.

Wood, Thomas E. 1994. *Nagarjunian Disputations: A Philosophical Journey through an Indian Looking-Glass*. Monographs of the Society for Asian and Comparative Philosophy 11. Honolulu: University of Hawai'i Press.

Index

M

N

O

About the Translators

SHŌRYŪ KATSURA is Emeritus Professor of Hiroshima University. He taught Indian philsophy and Buddhism for a long time at Hiroshima University and Ryukoku University, Kyoto. His major publications include *The Role of the Example (Dṛṣṭānta) in Classical Indian Logic* (ed. with E. Steinkellner, 2004); *Indojin no Ronrigaku* (*Indian Logic*) (1998); and *Inmyoshorimonron Kenkyu* (*A Study of the* Nyayamukha) (1977–87). His major research interests include Buddhist logic and epistemology, Abhidharma philosophy, Madhyamaka and Yogācāra philosophy, and Mahāyana sūtras.

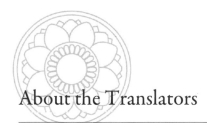

MARK SIDERITS is Emeritus Professor of Philosophy of Seoul National University. He taught philosophy for many years at Illinois State University before moving to Seoul National University in 2008. He is the author of *Indian Philosophy of Language* (Kluwer, 1991), *Personal Identity and Buddhist Philosophy: Empty Persons* (Ashgate, 2003), and *Buddhism as Philosophy* (Ashgate and Hackett, 2007), and the editor of several other books. His principal area of research interest is analytic metaphysics as it plays out in the intersection between contemporary analytic philosophy and classical Indian and Buddhist philosophy.

About Wisdom Publications

WISDOM PUBLICATIONS, a nonprofit publisher, is dedicated to making available books about Buddhism for the benefit of all. We publish works by ancient and modern masters across Buddhist traditions, translations of important texts, and original scholarship. We also offer books that explore East-West themes, which continue to emerge as traditional Buddhism encounters modern culture in all its complexity. Our titles are published with an appreciation of Buddhism as a living philosophy, and with a commitment to preserve and transmit important works from Buddhism's many traditions.

You can contact us, request a catalog, or browse our books online at our website. You can also write to us at the address below.

Wisdom Publications
199 Elm Street
Somerville, Massachusetts 02144 USA
Telephone: (617) 776-7416
Fax: (617) 776-7841
Email: info@wisdompubs.org
www.wisdompubs.org

Supporting the *Classics of Indian Buddhism* Series

The volumes in the *Classics of Indian Buddhism* series adhere to the highest standards of accuracy and readability, making them works that will stand the test of time both as scholarship and as literature. The care and attention necessary to bring such works to press demand a level of investment beyond the normal costs associated with publishing. If you would like to partner with Wisdom to help make the series a success, either by supporting the meticulous work of translators and editors or by sponsoring the publication costs of a forthcoming volume, please send us an email at cib@wisdompubs.org or write to us at the address above. We appreciate your support.

Wisdom is a nonprofit, charitable 501(c)(3) organization affiliated with the Foundation for the Preservation of the Mahayana Tradition (FPMT).